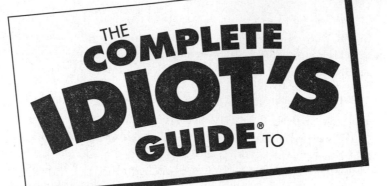

THE
COMPLETE
IDIOT'S
GUIDE® TO

Preserving Food

Ph.D.

5/13

ALPHA

A member of Penguin Group (USA) Inc.

To my mother-in-law, the late Frances Briggs Brees, who showed me how to begin.

ALPHA BOOKS

Published by the Penguin Group

Penguin Group (USA) Inc., 375 Hudson Street, New York, New York 10014, USA

Penguin Group (Canada), 90 Eglinton Avenue East, Suite 700, Toronto, Ontario M4P 2Y3, Canada (a division of Pearson Penguin Canada Inc.)

Penguin Books Ltd., 80 Strand, London WC2R 0RL, England

Penguin Ireland, 25 St. Stephen's Green, Dublin 2, Ireland (a division of Penguin Books Ltd.)

Penguin Group (Australia), 250 Camberwell Road, Camberwell, Victoria 3124, Australia (a division of Pearson Australia Group Pty. Ltd.)

Penguin Books India Pvt. Ltd., 11 Community Centre, Panchsheel Park, New Delhi—110 017, India

Penguin Group (NZ), 67 Apollo Drive, Rosedale, North Shore, Auckland 1311, New Zealand (a division of Pearson New Zealand Ltd.)

Penguin Books (South Africa) (Pty.) Ltd., 24 Sturdee Avenue, Rosebank, Johannesburg 2196, South Africa

Penguin Books Ltd., Registered Offices: 80 Strand, London WC2R 0RL, England

Note: This publication contains the opinions and ideas of its author. It is intended to provide helpful and informative material on the subject matter covered. It is sold with the understanding that the author and publisher are not engaged in rendering professional services in the book. If the reader requires personal assistance or advice, a competent professional should be consulted.

The author and publisher specifically disclaim any responsibility for any liability, loss, or risk, personal or otherwise, which is incurred as a consequence, directly or indirectly, of the use and application of any of the contents of this book.

Most Alpha books are available at special quantity discounts for bulk purchases for sales promotions, premiums, fund-raising, or educational use. Special books, or book excerpts, can also be created to fit specific needs.

For details, write: Special Markets, Alpha Books, 375 Hudson Street, New York, NY 10014.

Publisher: *Marie Butler-Knight*
Editorial Director: *Mike Sanders*
Senior Managing Editor: *Billy Fields*
Senior Acquisitions Editor: *Paul Dinas*
Development Editor: *Lynn Northrup*
Production Editor: *Kayla Dugger*
Copy Editor: *Amy Lepore*

Cartoonist: *Steve Barr*
Cover Designer: *Bill Thomas*
Book Designer: *Trina Wurst*
Indexer: *Celia McCoy*
Layout: *Brian Massey*
Proofreader: *Laura Caddell*

Contents at a Glance

Contents

6 Freezing Meat, Poultry, Seafood, and Game   77

Introduction

Home food preservation is enjoying a remarkable surge in interest as people look for ways to cut costs, eat healthier foods, and eliminate unnecessary additives and preservatives from their diets. Combined with the increased interest in home gardening, the expansion of bulk foods warehouses, and the burgeoning growth of farmers' markets, the timing couldn't be better to begin preserving food at home.

Some of us learned to preserve foods by watching our mothers and grandmothers, asking questions, and peeling countless apples and pears while we apprenticed in this art. Others of us didn't have that early experience and came to home food preservation via books or classes taught by experts in the field. However it happened, we got hooked.

The saying, "Life is hard by the yard; it's a cinch by the inch," applies nicely to learning how to preserve foods. Take it one step at a time, follow the directions, use tested and approved recipes, and you'll be a pro before you know it.

It's fun. Sometimes that part of putting up food gets overlooked. It's a hobby that pays you back instead of costing you bucks. It lets you get creative with gift possibilities. And not to put too fine a point on it, it lets you play with food.

Whatever your reasons for perusing this book, you've come to the right place if you want to get started "putting food by," as the old phrase used to say. If you have any questions about preserving and you don't find them answered here, drop me a line and I'll do my best to answer them. That's what a food safety advisor and master food preserver for the Cooperative Extension Service does. You can reach me at karenbrees@yahoo.com. I look forward to hearing from you. Happy preserving!

How to Use This Book

The chapters in this book are organized into six main parts, with each one representing one aspect of food preservation:

Part 1, "To Your Health," discusses the many reasons for preserving food at home. You'll discover the many methods available for putting up food, plus important safety procedures for protecting your preserved foods.

Part 2, "Freezing," provides a great starting place for the novice home food preserver. You'll learn essential procedures, get experience, and gain confidence. Pick your own produce or patronize the farmers' market, and you'll start with the freshest ingredients—the key to great-quality frozen foods.

Part 3, "Canning," raises the ante. With the basics under your belt, you're ready to move to the next level. You'll learn how to fill your pantry with nutritious foods at a fraction of their grocery store prices.

Part 4, "Pickles, Relishes, and Fermented Foods," shares the secrets of pickling and fermenting and gives you choices of traditional or quick recipes to add just the right touch to complete your main courses.

Part 5, "Fruit Spreads," celebrates the wonderful world of jams and jellies, conserves and chutneys. Get the whole family involved and start a new family tradition.

Part 6, "Drying, Salting, Smoking, and Root Cellaring," takes you on a quick trip through time. You'll explore ancient methods of preserving foods, although with a decidedly modern twist. Complete your food preserving repertoire with one or more of these methods.

Following the chapters, you'll find some helpful information in the appendixes:

Appendix A is the glossary. If you're stumped by an unfamiliar term, here's where you'll find the answer.

Appendix B lists abbreviations for cooking terms and also gives you a handy list of equivalencies.

Appendix C is the syrup chart, which gives you exact amounts of sugar and water to create different syrup strengths.

Appendix D gives you the recommended processing times for different foods. It includes recommendations for when to use boiling water or the pressure canner.

Appendix E is a handy reference for recommended freezer storage times for different foods.

Appendix F gives you the best methods for preserving different types of foods.

Appendix G provides additional resources to help you expand your food preserving knowledge.

Extras

Throughout the book, you'll find important tidbits of knowledge to make the job of preserving food easier. These include the following:

def•i•ni•tion

Food science has its own special terms and phrases. Here you'll find out just what they mean.

Preserving Pointers

These are helpful tips and suggestions to make food preserving fast, fun, and easy.

In Other Words

Gain time-honored wisdom and fresh advice from experienced food preservers.

Safety Check

Heed these cautions and concerns to keep you on the right track.

Acknowledgments

I'd like to thank Jane Marrs for reading and critiquing; Ardis Boll and Pam McGarry for help with the pictures; Joey Peutz, Extension Educator-Food and Consumer Science, for answering all my questions; Bob Hill and Rita Peders, from May Hardware, McCall, Idaho, for the loan of the modern pressure canner; L & L Custom Meats, New Meadows, Idaho, for the meat-wrapping lesson; C & M Lumber, New Meadows, Idaho, my local source for canning supplies; John W. Brees, my husband, for his patience in formatting photos; Andrea Hurst, my literary agent; Paul Dinas, Senior Acquisitions Editor for Alpha Books; Lynn Northrup, Development Editor; Kayla Dugger, Production Editor for Alpha Books; and Amy Lepore, Copy Editor.

Trademarks

Part 1

To Your Health

Food nourishes our bodies, provides comfort, and binds us together in shared traditions. Of all the reasons to preserve food, the most important is health. In Part 1, we'll take a look at what food preservation is. We'll also review some of the basic principles of food safety.

What Is Food Preservation?

In This Chapter

- The many definitions of food preservation
- You really are what you eat
- Getting your money's worth
- Partnering with the Cooperative Extension Service
- Living richly

The practice of preserving food extends back to the beginnings of civilization, and the earliest methods used the heat of the sun to dry food. New technologies have made preserving food much simpler and more fun, and they also retain more of the food's nutrients. If you're interested in preserving food, there are many ways you can go about it.

Why Practice Food Preservation?

What is food preservation? It seems like a simple enough question, but the answer is complex. The easy answer is that food preservation is saving surplus food for a time when you'll need it. It's probably the earliest domestic art and one closely tied to the survival of our species.

There's a basic law of economics that says, "All goods are scarce." This means there is a limited supply of everything. Some items occur in more abundance than others, it's true, but there isn't an infinite amount of anything, and this "scarcity" is how we come to place a value on what the world has to offer—from diamonds to rutabagas.

We've become used to a safe and reliable food supply. We've come to expect it and take it for granted. Recent developments, however, have called this safety and reliability into question, and we can no longer be so sure.

There are several reasons why safety issues regarding food have taken center stage. Our federal health and safety standards do not extend beyond our borders, and we import food from countries that may not have the same standards of safety that we do.

A case in point is China, which has been documented as the source of contaminated pet food products in 2007 and contaminated infant formula in 2008. China also uses human waste for fertilizing fruits and vegetables, a serious potential source of disease.

Foodborne illness can have its source much closer to home, however. Peppers shipped from Mexico recently resulted in a salmonella outbreak in the United States that caused close to 1,500 people to fall ill.

As devastating as these and other international incidents can be, they are not intentional. They're caused by ignorance and carelessness. It's truly a worldwide phenomenon, however, and the United States isn't immune. The most stringent standards are only effective if they're followed 100 percent of the time. There's just not enough oversight available in the country to run herd on every food worker and on every step of food processing.

Safety Check

Many kinds of foodborne illness can have serious and lifelong effects. Kidney failure is a long-term consequence of *E. coli* in infants. The Centers for Disease Control and Prevention (CDC) report that food poisoning results in 76 million illnesses, 325,000 hospitalizations, and up to 5,000 deaths annually.

The February 18, 2008, edition of the *International Herald Tribune* (The Global Edition of *The New York Times*) reported on the largest recall of beef ever in the United States. The recall consisted of 143 million pounds of beef from a slaughterhouse that supplied school lunch programs. It was a precautionary measure, but one that raised concern among consumers nationwide.

The United States Department of Agriculture (USDA) Food Safety and Inspection Service keeps a webpage of active food recall cases (www.fsis.usda.gov/fsis_recalls/ Open_Federal_Cases/). It's worth consulting both for the types of foods involved and also as a resource for information on public health alerts.

In addition to the unintentional threats to our food supply, there is a potential intentional threat that needs to be taken seriously, and the Department of Homeland Security has done just that.

"Farm to Fork: Partnerships to Protect the Food You Eat" was the topic of a subcommittee hearing on July 9, 2007. The gist of the hearing was to devise strategies to keep our food supply safe from terrorist attacks. The greater the distance the food must travel, the more vulnerable to attack it is.

Tufts University notes that what shows up on your dinner plate may have traveled anywhere from 1,500 to 2,500 miles to reach you. Stop to consider the number of hands that have touched your food during this process, and it gives a whole new dimension to the consumer advice to "buy locally."

What is home food preservation? It's the informed consumer's response to issues of food safety. If you reduce the number of hands that touch your food, you reduce the number of opportunities that foodborne illness has to reach you.

The ideal situation, of course, is to grow your own food, and many people do just that. You don't need 40 acres and a plow to grow a considerable amount of produce. A window sill, the back deck, or a portion of the backyard can yield an astounding harvest. If this isn't your cup of tea, however, seek out the many farmers' markets that have sprouted in cities and rural areas alike. Buy farm direct and you eliminate many hands from touching what you eat.

What You're Really Eating

The next aspect of home food preservation follows naturally from the previous section, with emphasis on the word *natural*. In addition to what's *on* your food, what's *in* the food you eat? Or to phrase it a bit differently, "When isn't a can of beans a can of beans?"

Read the labels on the canned foods you generally buy, and you'll get an education on what's included along with the principal ingredient. Ingredients on labels are listed in order from most to least. For example, here's the list of ingredients on a can of a national brand of beef stew:

◆ Beef broth

◆ Beef

◆ Potatoes

- Carrots
- Tomatoes (water, tomato paste)
- Peas
- Beef fat
- Wheat flour
- Potato starch
- Salt
- Modified food starch
- Flavoring
- Caramel color
- Monosodium glutamate
- Spices

Here's the list of ingredients on a can of home-preserved beef stew:

- Beef
- Carrots
- Onions
- Potatoes
- Beef stock
- Spices

You can draw your own conclusions. If you or someone in your family has special dietary considerations—whether a food allergy or a need to reduce salt or sugar intake—or if you simply want to eliminate additives, which can of stew will you choose? There's no magic or mystery to canning stews and other foods at home, and it's a great way to create foods using the recipes your family enjoys.

Produce has its own concerns. We've become conditioned to demand perfect-looking fruit. We don't want bruises or blemishes of any kind, and bigger is always better. But is it really? Here's the journey one apple has taken from the tree to your fruit basket:

1. Sprayed with pesticide approved for use on foods.

2. Picked too early to ensure it doesn't get overripe before it's bought and boxed.

3. Removed from the box and washed and waxed (to replace the wax lost during washing, sort of like your car).

4. Boxed.

5. Shipped to the store where it's handled (again), unboxed, and set up in a display.

6. Handled by consumers while it's waiting to be bought.

By a conservative count, at least six people have handled your apple and potentially a great many more. Now take a look at what transpires with an apple that's organically grown and offered for sale at a farmers' market:

1. The apple is picked and boxed.

2. You purchase the apple.

By any count, the number of handlings is markedly decreased, there's no pesticide residue or chance of residue, and the apple hasn't traveled any greater distance than from the tree to the roadside stand, to the nearest farmers' market.

Is the fruit perfect? It all depends on how you define perfect. Is the fruit guaranteed to be mega sized, blemish free, and picture perfect? No. And as the organic farmer says, "No, and proud of it."

You won't get the image of perfection; you'll get the real deal. This apple will have crunch, flavor you haven't tasted in years, and a guarantee that it's not older than your Great Aunt Tillie. And when you make applesauce, apple butter, apple jelly, or spiced apples, you'll have something truly special. (See Part 5 for some tasty fruit recipes.)

Preserving Pointers

Farmers' markets go back to the foundations of colonial America. In 1643, Hartford, Connecticut, was ordered by the General Court of the colony to provide a public market.

What is food preservation? It's using fresh, healthy ingredients when putting up fruits and vegetables, fruit spreads, pickles, and relishes.

Waste Not, Want Not

Thrift is a charter member of the virtues. To paraphrase Shakespeare, "Some are born thrifty, some achieve thrift, and some have thrift thrust upon them." Whether we're thrifty because it's a personal characteristic or because economic circumstances have required us to become thrifty, the end result is the same. The home food preserver practices thrift.

We waste a great deal. We live in a throwaway society that seems to have a foundation of built-in obsolescence. Technology is proof of that. Today's must-have component is tomorrow's landfill nightmare. Home food preservation can reconnect us to what has stood the test of time. It can reconnect us to our roots and our traditions and teach us respect for the bounty of Mother Earth.

In Other Words

If you don't economize, prepare to agonize.

—Confucius, ancient Chinese philosopher

Food preservation was born out of necessity: how to keep foods from spoiling while maintaining their nutritional value. The heat of the sun provided one answer. In hot climates, the heat was sufficient to dry all the moisture out of food before the spoilage microorganisms could spring into action and cause the food to rot.

Salting, which you'll read about in Chapter 21, was another early method. Especially in seafaring regions, salt was readily available and could be used to dry fish. This worked best in dry climates where the humidity didn't conspire to reconstitute the dried foods and cause them to spoil. Later, salt mines were developed inland, and this spurred the use of salt for drying meats and vegetables.

Smoking, covered in Chapter 22, was the final form of early food preserving, reserved primarily for fish, meats, and the occasional cheese. The smokehouse doubled as a processing plant and storage facility—the earliest form of multitasking.

This remained the state of food preservation for many centuries until canning entered the picture in the early nineteenth century. Again, it was an invention of necessity, spurred on by the need to feed armies on the move.

Freezing (see Part 2) was dependent on the discovery of refrigeration principles. Early on, this was the exclusive province of the commercial sector. Most urban residents had electricity, but it took the creation of the Rural Electric Administration (REA) in 1935 to bring electricity to the 90 percent of rural Americans without it.

The state of the art today would astound someone for whom salting was modern technology. Portable food dehydrators, freezer bags, two-piece adjustable canning lids, and pressure canners have revolutionized this ancient practice into a modern-day art.

What is food preservation? It's a commitment to keep faith with the past and to invest in the future.

Partnership with Experts

The home food preserver's best friend is the Cooperative Extension Service, which has been offering expert advice and tested recipes to the home food preserver for many, many years. In fact, the origins of the service go back to the time of Abraham Lincoln and an important piece of legislation he signed in 1862, the Morrill Act, which established the land-grant universities that became part of the West.

Half a century later, in 1914, the Smith-Lever Act created a link between these land-grant colleges and the USDA, and the Cooperative Extension Service was created as a result. Its mission was to provide education and practical demonstrations in state-of-the-art technology in agriculture.

During both world wars, extension agents helped people deal with food shortages by helping with gardens and preserving foods grown in these gardens. The famous "victory gardens" of World War II were a result of these efforts.

Preserving Pointers

There are 2,900 extension offices around the country, and you can reach the one closest to you by simply looking up its number in your phone book. Check out Appendix G for resources available from the Extension Service. Or go online to find the Cooperative Extension Service office nearest you. The USDA hosts the Cooperative State Research, Education, and Extension Service webpage. Go to www.csrees.usda.gov/Extension/ and click on your state. When this page opens, click on your county. Holding your cursor over a county reveals its name, if your geography is a bit rusty. You'll then access a page that contains all you'd ever need to know about your county office, including e-mail, phone, fax, physical address, and web address.

What is food preservation? It's partnering with experts to learn the latest techniques and safest methods for safeguarding your food supply.

Personal Satisfaction

Food has many qualities—texture, flavor, color, and aroma—but it's the last quality that is the most powerful. Catching a whiff of bread baking, lasagna in the oven, or an apple pie cooling on the counter can bring back memories that span a lifetime.

Food is so much more than sustenance. Think of any ceremony, tradition, or family custom, and food is there. We mark milestones, celebrate achievements, and offer comfort with gifts of food. Each family has its own traditional dishes and each culture its traditional fare. Re-creating those recipes and preserving those foods to enjoy at a time of your choosing is just one more benefit to home food preserving.

When people are asked why they are home food preservers, a sense of achievement is one of the most commonly given answers. It's a sense of control over what you eat. You don't need to accept a commercial product that has less of what you want or too much of what you don't want. You decide what goes into what you serve your family.

"I made it myself." There are few sentences that better sum up the pride and sense of accomplishment involved in creating something. What would you like to make? The possibilities are endless when you're a home food preserver.

What is home food preservation? It's passing down traditions. It's celebrating food and all that food can do.

Giving Food as Gifts

Home food preservation is an almost endless source of gift-giving possibilities. As you expand your skill set, you'll undoubtedly discover your particular penchant. Will you be the jam or jelly expert? The pickle person? Will it be your clam chowder that becomes your signature dish? If you cook it, you can preserve it.

In Other Words

I received a spice bag, several jars of different spices, cinnamon sticks, some designer half-pint jelly jars, and a recipe for making canned spiced peaches for my birthday 10 years ago. I've been making spiced peaches ever since.

—Joyce, nurse

The beauty of putting up foods as they come into season is you've got a wide variety to choose from when it comes time for giving gifts. There are other benefits to giving gifts of home-preserved foods:

- It gets eaten.

- Nobody has to dust it.

- No last-minute frantic shopping is involved.

- There are no returns or exchanges.

There are more benefits, but you get the idea. All you need to do is gather a supply of small or large baskets, some bows, and some decorative wrap, and you're set for the year. Always include the recipe. Punch a hole in the card and attach it to the jar rim with a ribbon.

The Least You Need to Know

- Purchasing fresh foods locally can help reduce the potential for foodborne illness.

- Preserving foods at home puts you in control of what you eat. You can choose what goes into your foods when you can your own.

- You can make the most of your food dollars by putting up your own foods as they come into season.

- The Cooperative Extension Service is your source for all answers on preserving foods.

- Preserving food is fun! And you'll never run out of unique gifts as you share your art.

Basic Food Safety Procedures

In This Chapter

- Clean and sanitary
- Emergency preparedness
- Safe to keep or better to toss?
- All about temperatures

Product safety recalls and foods contaminated by unclean handling practices are important concerns for all consumers. Dealing with these issues after the fact is small comfort if you've contracted a foodborne illness or been sickened as the result of improper processing procedures.

Many of our food products are imported from foreign countries, and in some cases these countries do not have the same types of controls that our government places on food handling. Even at home, however, it takes just one careless or uncaring individual to cause harm to many others.

Safe food handling and processing are essential to producing high-quality preserved foods, whether in the commercial arena or at home. Being prepared to handle emergency situations is also important. Fortunately, there's no mystery to proper food management techniques, and as a home food preserver, you can take steps to provide your family with nutritious foods that have been prepared with their health in mind.

Safety and Food Preparation

Cleanliness may be next to godliness, but in the kitchen it stands alone. There's nothing more important and essential than cleanliness. So what does "clean" mean? It first means that you wash your hands in warm, soapy water for at least 20 seconds (or as long as it takes to recite the alphabet) before you pick up a kitchen utensil; before you handle food; and after you've handled raw poultry, meat, or seafood.

Next, take a critical look at your work area. You're going to be preparing food here, so everything should sparkle—but sparkle isn't enough.

Scrub the countertops with a commercial cleaning product designed for the particular surface you have—granite, tile, formica—or sanitize with a solution of 1 teaspoon chlorine bleach in a quart of water. Then scrub the sink. While you're at it, what does your kitchen sink drain look like? Be sure it's free of residual food particles and then sanitize it. You can also run the removable kitchen plug or drainer through your dishwasher to give it an extra good cleaning.

Safety Check

Toss the kitchen sponges. They're a petri dish of bacteria and other organisms that can make you sick. As for popping them in the microwave to disinfect them, there are some safety hazards involved—fire primarily. Use kitchen dishcloths and wash them at the end of the day.

With the counters and sink ready for work, it's time to take a cleanliness inventory of your kitchen equipment. The cutting board will get a great deal of use while you're preparing food for processing, so be sure it's not a source of contamination for that food.

Cutting boards made from hard woods, plastic, and marble are easy to clean and sanitize. Check to be sure there are no cracks or splits in them, as these places harbor bacteria. Clean and sanitize them thoroughly after they've been used for cutting meats, poultry, and seafood. Having two cutting boards will cut down on the work. You can use one for meats, poultry, and seafood, and the other for other foods. You can purchase sets of cutting boards with four labeled colors per set: one each for meat, poultry, seafood, and other foods. That way there's less chance of cross-contamination. You'll come across these at kitchen supply stores or the big chains.

Safety and Food Storage

Food safety means keeping foods at safe temperatures. It's counterproductive to keep everything clean and sanitary while you're preparing foods only to have them spoil on the counter or in the fridge afterward.

Think two! Two hours is the recommended maximum time perishable foods should be left out of the refrigerator, and it's less in warm weather. Cold foods should be kept cold (below 40°F) and hot foods hot (above 140°F). If you're going to be traveling with perishable foods that need to be kept cold, take along a cooler and fill it with ice or frozen gel packs. Hot foods should be stored in insulated carrying containers and used as soon as possible.

Safety Check

Keep a thermometer in your refrigerator and consult it periodically. It should register no higher than 40°F.

Frozen foods should be kept frozen, dried foods dry, and canned foods stored away from light and heat. These are the basics, but a great part of safe food storage is keeping it available in case of an emergency.

Food Safety in Emergencies

The difference between an emergency and a disaster is often preparation. The best time to prepare is now, since an emergency can quickly become a disaster if you haven't made preparations to deal with it. A three-day emergency supply of food and water is the bare minimum, and ideally, you should plan for a week of total self-sufficiency. As a home food preserver, you're already ahead of the curve.

Emergency supplies need to be stored in watertight containers in a place you'll be able to access. This means having an emergency preparedness plan in place. In addition to food and water, you'll need some other essentials. The Department of Homeland Security has a website devoted to helping families prepare for emergency situations. Go to www.ready.gov to learn more.

As a home food preserver, you're prepared, resilient, and forward thinking. You understand the importance of planning, and you pride yourself on being self-sufficient. All these qualities will serve you well if you're faced with an emergency.

Often people wait for others to help them. Sometimes, however, that help doesn't come right away. If you're prepared to help yourself, you'll be able to deal with the curveballs until help does arrive.

Preserved Foods and Floods

Flood waters are doubly deadly. First they destroy life and property, and then they cause havoc with your food supply. What can you do to protect your home-preserved foods? Think higher. That's the operative word when the weather forecast warns that flooding is possible in your area. Do everything you can to raise your food supply above the level of flood waters. Refrigerators and freezers can be elevated by placing blocks (preferably of cement, which won't move that easily) under the four corners.

In Other Words

I keep an emergency supply of food (crackers and granola bars) and water in my car. Disaster situations don't always happen at home, and if I'm on the road, I may not be able to get home right away.

—Linnea, rancher

Move your preserved foods to higher shelves. If they're in the basement, move them to the main floor or a second floor, if necessary. Think closet shelves and even table tops. If your home-canned foods come into contact with flood water, the Cooperative Extension Service (www.csrees.usda.gov) considers them not safe to eat. In fact, most foods that come in contact with flood waters should be discarded. The reason is that flood waters may be contaminated with sewage, chemicals, and other substances that may be poisonous or harbor disease.

So what is safe? Only undamaged, commercially canned foods can be considered safe after coming into contact with flood waters—and then only if the outsides of the cans are sanitized. To do this, the Cooperative Extension Service recommends these steps:

1. Fill one bucket with a strong detergent solution.

2. Fill another bucket with a solution made of 1 teaspoon chlorine bleach for each quart of water.

3. Put on rubber gloves.

4. Using an indelible marker, write the contents of the can on the lid.

5. Take the label off the can and dispose of it in the trash. Paper can be contaminated with bacteria and other harmful agents.

6. Place the can in the detergent solution and scrub it thoroughly with a scrub brush.

7. Take the can from the detergent solution and place it in the bucket containing the bleach solution. Leave it there for 15 minutes.

8. Remove the can from the bleach solution and allow it to air dry before opening the can.

What else should you discard if it comes in contact with flood waters? Again, the Cooperative Extension Service comes to the rescue:

♦ Meat, poultry, fish, and eggs. The eggshells do not protect bacteria from entering the egg.

♦ Any fresh fruits or vegetables.

♦ Any fruit spreads preserved with paraffin. Paraffin can crack or separate from the glass and allow harmful bacteria to enter.

♦ Commercially produced glass products with a waxed cardboard seal inside the lid, corks, pop tops, or peel-off tops. These include most mayonnaise jars and salad dressings. Even if you haven't opened them before, contaminants can work their way inside.

♦ Anything in a cardboard box (like cookies, crackers, and cereals), foil, cellophane, paper, or any combination of these.

♦ Spices, extracts, and seasonings.

♦ Any opened containers or packages.

♦ Anything you have put in a canister, such as coffee, flour, sugar, etc.

♦ Cans that are dented, bulging (which you shouldn't even think about using under any conditions, let alone a flood), or rusted.

Safety Check

It may hurt to discard food you believe may be safe to eat, but it's a lot cheaper to toss a can of food than to have to deal with a foodborne illness that has the potential to be fatal.

Unfortunately, what you have left may not be much. That's why preparing ahead of time is important. In addition to food, you'll need water. There are a few ways to ensure that your water supply is safe. If you've used up the water you've set aside, you'll need to purify the water that's available to you.

Purifying Your Water Supply

Water filters and water purification tablets contain iodine, halazone, or chlorine. The United States Department of Agriculture (USDA) recommends that since these tablets will kill most waterborne bacteria, viruses, and some parasites—but not all—a water filter must also be used.

A water filter works on a very simple premise: the barrier's micropores allow water molecules to pass through, but are so small that they keep bacteria—which are bigger—from passing to the other side. Some filters are so small they can even keep viruses from passing through.

Read the labels carefully before you purchase a water filter. The recommendation is that these devices must be 1 micron absolute or smaller. This information will be on the label. A micron is $1/125,000$ of an inch. That's small!

Water purification tablets can lose potency over time, so you should replenish your supply regularly. Water sanitizing tablets are not the same as water purification tablets. The former are used for washing dishes, not for purifying drinking water. You can find these supplies at camping and outdoor supply centers.

You can add liquid bleach, such as Clorox or Purex, to your water supply to purify it for drinking purposes. This procedure calls for 16 drops of bleach (about ¼ teaspoon) to each gallon of water. Mix the water and bleach together thoroughly and then let it sit for 30 minutes before using. If the water is cloudy or cold, increase the time before using to 60 minutes. The water should have a slight chlorine odor. If it does not, repeat the entire process and let stand an additional 15 minutes.

def•i•ni•tion

Cryptosporidium is a waterborne protozoa—a parasite that can take up residence in the human intestine and cause illness. In the case of individuals with suppressed immune systems, that illness can be fatal. It is found in waters contaminated with sewage and animal waste.

Chlorine bleach will not kill *cryptosporidium* cysts that may be present in flood waters. Boiling is the best means of dealing with these.

If you suspect your water is harboring harmful bacteria, boiling provides the best means of purifying. Pour water into a clean cooking pot and bring it to a full, rolling boil. Continue to boil for 1 to 3 minutes. This is the recommended procedure at sea level. You will need to adjust for altitude by increasing the boiling time several minutes at higher elevations. Keep the cooking pot covered while the water cools. When cool, pour the water into clean containers.

Preserved Foods and Fires

Both fire and the chemicals used to fight it can damage your preserved foods and make them unsafe to eat. Heat can activate bacteria inside jars and commercially canned foods and can also cause jars to crack and split, allowing air and harmful bacteria to enter.

Burning materials release toxic fumes. These fumes can penetrate many types of food packaging, including cardboard, plastic wrap, and screw-top containers. These foods are not safe to eat and should be discarded. Additionally, these fumes can penetrate refrigerator and freezer seals and contaminate the food stored inside. If the food has an off odor or off taste, dispose of it.

Any raw foods that have come in contact with fumes from the fire should be discarded. This includes potatoes, onions, or fruits.

The chemicals used in fighting fires also contain toxic materials that cannot be washed off food. Any foods that have come into contact with these chemicals should be discarded. These include foods with screw-top lids as well as foods stored in plastic, paper, or cardboard containers.

To decontaminate canned goods and cooking utensils that have come in contact with chemicals, first wash them in a strong detergent solution. Then immerse them in a solution of 1 teaspoon chlorine bleach per 1 quart of water for 15 minutes. Remove items from the solution and allow to air dry before using.

Preserved Foods and Earthquakes

If floods mean higher in terms of salvaging home-preserved foods, earthquakes definitely mean lower but not basement level. Store your canning jars on low, sturdy shelves at ground-floor level, preferably in a sturdy cabinet with doors that close securely. If they lock, so much the better. This added protection can help keep the doors closed if the ground action gets violent. Have the key secured to the outside of the door so it stays put and is accessible.

Not being able to get to your food is one problem; having all that hard work destroyed just compounds the problem. Earthquakes strike without warning, so preparation is essential. After an earthquake, broken glass is everywhere, and this may include your canning jars.

You'll need to check the jars if they have ended up on the floor or have fallen over on the shelf. Use sturdy gloves when handling jars. Pick up each jar and check the seal. If the seal is intact and the glass doesn't appear cracked, dip the jar in a bucket of water and scrub to remove any residue that may be sticking to it from other jars that have broken. Then reexamine the jar carefully to be sure it is intact. Dry the jar and store it in a safe location, as aftershocks are common and are capable of causing as much damage as the original earthquake.

Preserved Foods and Power Outages

There are two types of power outages: scheduled and unscheduled.

You'll receive a notice from the utility company for a scheduled power interruption. They are generally scheduled during the workday to allow utility workers to make repairs or upgrade the system. While inconvenient, they shouldn't pose any hazard to your refrigerated or frozen foods.

Common sense applies here. Limit the number of times you open and close the refrigerator and freezer. If possible, remove items from the freezer that you'll need that day and keep them in the refrigerator. Then think before you open the refrigerator door. "Is this trip really necessary?" should be your mantra for the day.

Preserving Pointers

A small, gasoline-powered generator can supply power to keep your freezer operating and safeguard the food inside. It's a useful item to have on hand. They're relatively inexpensive and available at hardware stores.

It's the unscheduled power outages that can threaten your food supply. Again, preparation is key to handling them successfully. That means knowing how to determine what is safe to eat and what is not and stocking up on supplies you'll need during the outage.

Your refrigerator and freezer(s) should have thermometers inside them. If they don't, it's time to get one for each of these appliances and put it in a place where you'll be able to read it easily and without keeping the door open too long.

Keep the refrigerator door closed. That's the first rule. If you absolutely must open the door, take out everything you'll need for the next 2 hours. Then close the door quickly and leave it closed. Warmth is the enemy here, as harmful bacteria grow in the danger zone, which begins above 40°F.

If you can keep the inside temperature of the refrigerator between 34°F and 40°F, properly stored food should be safe to eat. Generally, if the power is out for no longer than 4 hours, your refrigerated items should be safe; however, never taste food you think may have spoiled. If the food has an off odor or color or if the texture seems different than it should, discard it without tasting it.

It may be prudent to gather up your insulated food coolers and put in a good amount of ice or frozen gel packs if you're getting close to the 4-hour mark and the power still hasn't come back on. Put the food in the ice, along with a thermometer, and close the lid securely. Add more ice as needed to keep the temperature at 40°F or below.

Getting ice when the power's out can be difficult, and if the outage is widespread, for all practical purposes it can be impossible. Having a supply of gel packs in your freezer is one way to prepare for this emergency situation. Your local grocery store may also have a supply of ice, but it will probably go quickly.

Dry ice is also an option if you can find a resource for it. A good time to find that resource is now, before you need it. The USDA advises that a 50-pound block of dry ice will keep a full 18-cubic-foot freezer at a safe temperature for 2 days. Wear gloves or use tongs when handling dry ice, as it will give you a severe burn. Dry ice has a temperature of –216°F.

If the outage occurs during the winter and outside temperatures are below freezing, you can put containers filled with water outdoors to freeze. When they're frozen, you can use them to keep your cooler cold. Don't store food outdoors, though, as sunlight and temperature fluctuations may cause it to spoil. Also, nocturnal animals can settle in for a feast and you'll awaken to the remains of their picnic.

Safety Check

It's human nature to want to check on things to see what's happening, but every time you open the refrigerator or freezer door or the cooler lid, cold air escapes and warm air enters. Resist this impulse.

Your freezer is designed to keep foods at 0°F. It functions most efficiently when full. A full freezer will hold food safely for about 2 days, provided you do not open the door.

When the power comes back on, it's time to check the freezer. If food still contains ice crystals, it can be safely refrozen. Also, if the temperature is 40°F or below, the food can be safely refrozen. The quality may not be as good, but it is safe.

If the temperature is 40°F or below but there are no ice crystals, you can cook the food and then freeze the cooked food or can it.

The Cooperative Extension Service recommends that the following foods be discarded if they have been exposed to temperatures above 40°F for 2 or more hours:

- Raw or cooked meats, including lunchmeats, hot dogs, poultry, and fish
- Dairy products, including milk, creams, soft cheeses, yogurt, and custards
- Eggs (including egg substitutes)
- Any products with cream or custard fillings
- Creamy salad dressings
- Soups and stews
- Casseroles
- Refrigerated cookie dough
- Custard, cheese, or chiffon pies

Opened jars of mayonnaise, tartar sauce, or horseradish should be discarded if they have been held at temperatures above 50°F for more than 8 hours.

Food products that should be safe at room temperature for a few days include:

- Butter, margarine, and hard and processed cheeses
- Fruit pies
- Opened jars of vinegar-based salad dressings
- Jellies
- Relishes, barbecue and taco sauces, mustard, ketchup, olives, and peanut butter

If anything develops mold or an off odor, it should be discarded.

Power outages that occur during the winter in colder climates can create other problems with your food supply. Your house will become cold. In extreme climates, your canned foods may actually freeze. Canned foods that have frozen may still be safe to eat. Metal cans that have frozen are safe if they have not split and allowed their contents to become exposed to air. If the seam has split and the contents have thawed, the food should be discarded.

Broken or cracked glass canning jars should be discarded. If both the jars and their seals are intact, the food is safe. Allow them to thaw gradually at room temperature. As with all home-canned foods, check to be sure the seal is intact before using the food. If the seal has failed and contents have thawed, the product should be discarded.

The Least You Need to Know

- ◆ Cleanliness is the most important factor in keeping your food safe.

- ◆ Preparing for emergencies before they occur will help protect your food preservation investment.

- ◆ The danger zone for growth of harmful bacteria is from 40°F to 140°F.

- ◆ Perishable foods should not be left out of the refrigerator for more than 2 hours to keep them safe to eat.

Part 2

Freezing

Here's your opportunity to make the most of your food dollar. Buy in bulk, buy in season, and preserve nature's bounty for your use all year long. Freezing is a relative newcomer to the home food preservation scene, and it's one area in which the technology has made some incredible advances in both ease and practicality.

Chapter 3

Introduction to Freezing

In This Chapter

- Freezing comes of age
- Why freeze foods?
- The big-ticket item: the freezer
- What you need to get started
- Having a plan and working the plan
- Safely thawing frozen foods

There's some interesting science behind how freezing works to preserve food, and this chapter will take a look at how to put that science to work for you. I'll discuss the equipment and supplies you need to begin freezing foods and will cover the basic procedures involved.

The Science Behind Freezing

In 1924, Clarence Birdseye invented a method of quick-freezing foods and ended up revolutionizing the food preservation industry. He got the idea while fishing in Canada, and as with most ingenious discoveries, he just simply became aware of what was happening around him. It was so cold that the fish froze about as soon as he hauled them out of the water. When thawed months later, he noted that the quality was good. Quick-freezing, he decided, was the way to go.

Up until this time, freezing foods wasn't an especially quick process, and because of this, large ice crystals formed in the foods. This caused rupturing of the cell membranes of the foods being frozen. This was not good. When the foods were thawed, all the ice melted, water drained from the food, and the flavor and texture suffered.

Preserving Pointers

Freeze-drying is a different process from freezing. While home freezing works to remove as much air as possible from foods, freeze-drying (also known as lyophilization) is a commercial process that first freezes food and then vaporizes the frozen water contained in it. Without the water content, the food has much less bulk and then can be vacuum sealed.

Birdseye got busy and developed a couple of ways to quick-freeze foods. One method used calcium chloride, and the other used ammonia. Ammonia—or more specifically, evaporating the ammonia to get a temperature of −25°F—allowed fruits and vegetables to be frozen in about 30 minutes and a 2-inch-thick package of meat to be frozen in about 90 minutes. The rest, as they say, was history, and the frozen food industry that we take for granted today owes its existence to an observant fisherman. The Birdseye brand of frozen foods became a supermarket staple and is still a staple today.

How Freezing Works

When you freeze foods, you're freezing the water content of that food. Water expands as it freezes and creates ice crystals inside the food. These ice crystals can rupture the cell walls of the food being frozen, but freezing the food quickly will result in smaller ice crystals and less damage to the cell walls.

Maintaining a temperature of 0°F or below also keeps ice crystal formation in check, but constant temperature fluctuations will result in larger ice crystal formation and more damage to the texture of the food. Keep opening and closing the freezer door to a minimum to prevent this from happening!

The Spoilers

Air, microorganisms, chemical changes, and enzymes are the enemies of frozen foods. Proper processing, packaging, and storage are necessary for dealing with these potential food spoilers.

Freezing stops microorganisms from growing, but it's just temporary. It doesn't destroy them, so when foods begin the thawing process, those microorganisms start to multiply again and can cause food to spoil.

The presence of air can result in oxidation as well as freezer burn. Both adversely affect the texture and flavor of frozen foods. The oxidation process causes fats in frozen meats to go rancid in the presence of air. In freezer burn, air causes moisture loss from the frozen foods—ice crystals evaporate from the product, and when you unwrap it, you'll see frost on top of whatever you've frozen. The surface will look dry and brown or sometimes white. The food is safe to eat, but it will definitely be less than good.

Enzymes control the ripening process in fruits and can cause light-colored fruits to turn brown when their cut surfaces are exposed to air. Freezing slows down the enzyme process but doesn't stop it. Ascorbic acid or commercial antidiscoloration products can keep these fruits from turning brown (see Chapter 4), and blanching will protect the quality of vegetables. (Blanching is discussed later in this chapter. Specific blanching times for vegetables are covered in Chapter 5.)

Benefits of Freezing Foods

All methods of preserving foods have their benefits, but freezing definitely has quite a bit going for it as far as the home food preserver is concerned:

- Freezing temporarily stops the growth of organisms (such as bacteria, yeast, and molds) that cause spoilage in foods. It doesn't kill them but essentially puts them in a state of suspended animation.

- Freezing inactivates enzymes, which are responsible for controlling the ripening process.

- Properly frozen foods generally keep more of their nutrients, flavor, and texture than foods preserved by other methods.

- Freezing foods saves space. Frozen foods can be stacked in the freezer, whereas glass canning jars cannot be stacked.

The Freezer

When it comes to freezing foods, the biggest and most expensive item to consider, of course, is a freezer, but it's an investment you'll amortize over time. The other supplies and equipment you'll need are relatively inexpensive, and like the freezer, most will last for years with proper care.

Freezer capacity is measured in cubic feet, ranging from 5 to 25 cubic feet. You may be tempted to buy the biggest freezer you can find, but before you plunge ahead and purchase a mega-freezer, stop to consider how you will use this appliance.

Keeping a smaller freezer full will be more energy efficient than running a larger freezer that's less than half full. Modern, smaller freezers have more storage capacity than older, bigger freezers. This is due to improvements in insulation technology that have reduced the need for thicker walls.

Smaller units generally use less electricity than larger ones, but the difference isn't huge. What is huge is keeping your freezer as full as possible to get the most return on your food-preserving dollar. Freezers are designed to run more efficiently when full, so keeping your freezer at least half (and preferably three quarters or more) filled is the way to go.

If you have a large or growing family, the larger freezer may make sense. Also, if you're planning on stocking up for the year, a larger freezer will store that much for you. However, if your family is small or if you're planning on preserving foods by other means as well, such as canning or drying, a smaller unit may make more sense.

Many families have two freezers and put them to different uses—for example, one for meats, and the other for bulk food purchases.

Important Features

There are certain features you'll want to look for in a freezer. Most of them are standard in newer models. These include the following:

- **A power on light.** This light tells you that the freezer is working.

- **A locking mechanism with a key.** This is an essential item, especially in homes with children.

- **An adjustable temperature control dial with a "fast freeze" setting.** This quickly gets your foods to the optimum temperature. Once the food has frozen, you can then return the freezer to 0°F.

- **A light.** Especially with chest freezers, peering into the dark abyss can be frustrating. Holding a flashlight in one hand while you're rummaging with the other is annoying.

- **ENERGY STAR designation.** The Environmental Protection Agency developed the ENERGY STAR program to identify and promote energy-efficient products.

- **A defrost drain.** This is found in the bottom for manual defrost units.

Safety Check _____

It only takes a few minutes for a child to open a freezer door and get locked inside. If you're disposing of an older freezer, always remove the freezer door. Once trapped inside, smaller children may not have the strength to open the door, even if you inactivate the locking mechanism.

Automatic or Manual Defrost?

Of the two, automatic defrost is definitely the easier way to go. You don't have to devote a morning or afternoon to scraping, wiping, draining, and especially moving all your frozen foods into boxes while you clean out their home.

On the other hand, manual defrost units are generally less expensive than automatic defrost units. Also, if you have a tendency to drop items haphazardly into the freezer instead of carefully entering them on an inventory sheet and putting them in their proper place, a semiannual investigation of your freezer's contents can yield some interesting discoveries. Additionally, it will prompt you to use those items that are nearing the end of their recommended storage times (see Appendix E). It can be quite refreshing to perform this chore on an especially hot summer day—just remember to keep those cardboard boxes stacked and covered and return them to the freezer as quickly as possible.

Making the Decision

When purchasing a freezer, consider the initial capital outlay along with the cost to operate. Making an informed choice about which kind of freezer to purchase will require some research and careful study. You have a choice of two types of freezers: upright and chest. Each has advantages and drawbacks.

An upright freezer has a smaller footprint than a chest type. It's vertical with shelves. The chest type is horizontal with a vast amount of open interior space. It also has baskets that fit across the opening to hold smaller items.

Here are some upright plusses:

- Adjustable shelving
- Suitable for smaller quantities of food
- Door storage for easy access to frequently used foods
- Pullout drawer at the bottom
- Same footprint as a refrigerator

Here are some upright minuses:

- Less energy efficient (large air loss each time door is opened)
- Larger items may be difficult to store
- 10 to 15 percent less usable space than a chest
- Costs more than a chest

Here are some chest plusses:

- Uses less energy because less air escapes each time you open the door
- Tends to last longer than other model types (especially if you buy a manual defrost chest model)
- Best for bigger items and bulk purchases
- Entire unit is usable space

Here are some chest minuses:

- Requires reaching, bending, and lifting to retrieve items
- Requires careful organization (can use cardboard boxes to help with organizing)
- No shelves, although does have baskets
- Bigger footprint

Ultimately, you'll make the decision based on your own needs and available space. Prices vary widely. You can expect to find a small unit for about $150, or you can spend 10 times that amount on a huge freezer with all the bells and whistles. Do some comparison shopping before you buy.

Situating the Freezer

The main requirements are a dry, level space that's not subject to extremes in temperature. If your garage is heated or if winter temperatures in your area are mild, this may be the best place. The basement is another option, but only if you live in areas where earthquakes do not occur.

In Other Words

Once I realized we didn't have to put the freezer in the kitchen, and that the garage was a better choice, we went with a larger model.

—Bobbie, clinician

Other Equipment and Supplies

There are several options when it comes to deciding which type of containers you will use for freezing foods, and new technology has expanded your choices. Whether you choose to be traditional or modern, you'll easily find just what you want.

Glass Canning and Freezing Jars

You've probably heard these jars referred to as mason jars. They're named for John Mason, who back in 1858 invented a machine that was able to cut threads into zinc lids. After that, it was just one more step to make jars with threads in their necks that would receive the threaded lids for a tight fit. The third piece that completed the seal was a rubber ring that fit between the lid and the jar. Since that time, the technology has vastly improved and simplified the process.

You may not have thought about mason jars as candidates for holding foods you'll be freezing, but modern glass canning and freezing jars work just fine. The glass is designed to withstand extremes of both temperature and pressure, so they're truly double-duty items.

Safety Check

If you have any antique canning jars, enjoy them as additions to your home décor but don't try to freeze or can in them. They're not up to the job and are likely to shatter and crack.

Keep your eyes open when you're shopping at the grocery store. Several items, including spaghetti sauce and fruits, now are packaged in mason jars. Look for the distinctive design and labeling.

Mason jar.

Glass canning and freezing jars come in sizes ranging from half-pint to half-gallon, with pints and quarts being the ones you'll use most often. They also come in regular or wide mouth.

Range of sizes.

There is no difference in the carrying capacity of wide-mouth and regular-mouth jars. If your hands are small and fit inside a regular-mouth jar, you may find that you prefer them. If your hands are larger, coping with narrow-mouth jars can get tiresome.

Diameter of a regular-mouth jar (left) and a wide-mouth jar (right).

The first box of canning jars you buy will also come equipped with rings and lids. If you need additional rings and lids, they're sold together in a tall box.

Rings and lids.

After that, you'll buy new lids in boxes of 12. It's recommended that you buy new lids at the start of each canning season, although there's no guarantee that you're getting a fresh supply. Stores can warehouse them until the following season.

Today's lids are self-sealing, in contrast to the olden days when the home food preserver had to perform several steps to ensure that the lids would seal. Today the lid is a round metal piece with a slightly raised "dome" in the center. You may hear them referred to as "dome lids." There is sealing compound around the edge of the lid, which is designed for one-time use only. Used lids cannot be reused and must be discarded.

> **Preserving Pointers**
>
> The two most commonly available brands of jars are Ball and Kerr, and it's the same with lids and rings. Prices differ between these two brands, but there seems to be little reason for it. Both are manufactured by the same company, Jarden, which also makes Bernardin and Golden Harvest jars!

Rings, also known as screw bands, last a long time but may eventually rust if they are in constant contact with moisture. If they rust, toss them and buy new ones. They'll make a cleaner contact with the threads on the neck of the canning jar, ensuring a good fit, and you can avoid the frustration of trying to force them on if rust is interfering. Rusty rings can prevent your lids from sealing.

Freezer Containers and Freezer Bags

Freezer containers are made of rigid plastic with tight-fitting lids and are moisture and vapor resistant to prevent freezer burn. Some are designed to allow you to raise one corner of the lid after packing and burp out the extra air. You won't get rid of all of it, of course, but every little bit helps. Pint and quart sizes are the most versatile. These containers stack nicely and take up less space in your freezer than glass jars. Like glass jars, they're reusable and are reasonably priced.

There are different types of freezer bags: envelopes with slides that help lock the bag, envelopes without slides but with tracks that fit together to create a tight seal, and soft bags that can be secured with a twisty tie.

You may find it easier to expel air from the softer bags since they conform more easily to the shape of the food in them. With the stiffer bags, you may be able to fold them over, starting at the bottom and pushing out the air as you go up to the seal. These have a greater tendency to cause freezer burn since it can be difficult to expel enough air.

Two types of freezer bags.

Vacuum Packaging Machines

Vacuum packaging machines or vacuum sealers are designed to remove air from packages of food and thereby increase their storage life. Different kinds of systems are available, and prices vary widely. They work well when used for their specified purpose, but there are serious safety issues to consider before you decide to purchase one.

Most bacteria that cause food spoilage thrive in the presence of oxygen. When food is going bad because of these microorganisms, there's a better than good chance you'll find out about it. The food will smell bad, it may get slimy, and the color will look definitely "off." You will notice all this and should dispose of the food so that no one gets sick.

It would seem logical, then, that removing this oxygen from the food's environment would solve the problem, and it does—for those bacteria that love oxygen. The problem is that there is another genus of bacteria that thrives in the absence of oxygen, and this *anaerobic* bacteria is potentially lethal. It's responsible for tetanus, gas gangrene, and botulism. The bacteria is *Clostridium*. Food that's contaminated with *Clostridium* may not smell bad, look bad, or taste bad, but it can kill you.

def•i•ni•tion

Anaerobic means "without oxygen." Specifically, it refers to something that can live in the absence of oxygen and to which oxygen can be toxic.

If you are using a vacuum sealing system, you must be aware of proper food storage for low-acid, perishable foods such as vegetables, meats, poultry, and seafood. Vacuum packaging is not a replacement for proper pressure canning of low-acid foods, nor is it a replacement for proper refrigeration and freezing of foods that would otherwise require refrigeration and freezing.

You must also be aware that perishable food always carries the potential for contamination with pathogens such as bacteria. Previously frozen foods, when thawed, will spoil more quickly than their fresh counterparts. After thawing, keep them refrigerated until ready for use.

Bottom line: if the food will not keep at room temperature without spoiling, it must be refrigerated or frozen after being vacuum sealed. Nonperishable food items (such as dried nuts, crackers, lentils, or other dried foods) are good candidates for vacuum sealing since they have very little moisture content. However, these items store very well in regular storage containers with tight-fitting lids, and you can remove the product as needed and replace the lid. Once you open the vacuum seal package, you must go through the resealing process again.

Freeze and Cook Bags

These are nifty for doing just what the name says. You can freeze foods in them and then transfer them directly from the freezer to a cooking pot. They're designed to handle from below 0°F to above boiling. They're pricey but convenient, plus you save on cleanup.

You can buy these bags in 1½ pint or quart size, and they also come in a roll so you can cut whatever size you need. This is handy for odd-shaped items that won't fit in standard freezer containers. You'll need a heat sealer if you go the roll route. These are sold separately and are available at most larger department or chain stores.

General Supplies

You've decided which freezer will serve your needs, you've stocked up on glass canning and freezing jars and/or plastic freezer containers, and you're ready to preserve food. You'll need some other supplies as well:

- Pots and pans
- A colander
- Utensils (knives, spoons, vegetable peeler)

- Clean dish cloths and towels

- Sugar (if you're freezing fruits in sugar or liquid pack)

- A timer

- A cutting board

- Plastic wrap, freezer wrap, and aluminum foil

- Freezer tape

General Procedures for Freezing

First examine all your containers and jars. Discard any plastic containers with cracks or chips. Examine your glass freezing and canning jars and discard any with chips or cracks. Run your finger around the rim to detect any small nicks and dispose of any jars that don't pass muster into the recycling bin.

Cleanliness is the order of the day. Wash all containers and jars in hot soapy water, rinse, and invert them on a clean towel.

Once you've gotten your containers washed, you can turn your attention to the items you'll be freezing. Wash fruits and vegetables in cool water. Next cut the items according to how you plan to use them (cubes, slices, etc.). Packaging instructions for various types of foods are discussed in the following chapters.

Safety Check

Be aware of the possibility of cross-contamination and always sanitize your cutting board and utensils before and after working with meat, poultry, or seafood. (See Chapter 2 for more on basic safety procedures.)

Blanching

Most vegetables will need to be blanched in order to stop enzyme action from causing the food to deteriorate during storage. Blanching doesn't destroy these enzymes, but it does inactivate them.

Blanching means to put the veggies in boiling water or to steam them for a specified period of time and then plunge them into ice cold water for rapid cooling. Different vegetables require different blanching times (see Chapter 5).

Microwave blanching is possible if you're working with small quantities of vegetables. It doesn't save any time, and it does require electricity, so you're not saving energy. Also, most charts only give blanching times for boiling water, so unless you've kept the instructions for your microwave, you'll end up guessing and may produce less than satisfactory results.

After blanching and cooling, vegetables need to be drained to remove as much water as possible before being packed for the freezer.

Headspace

Water expands when it freezes, so you must allow enough room for that expansion when you're packing foods for the freezer. The room between the food and the lid is called *headspace*.

Headspace requirements vary according to the type of food being frozen and whether or not it contains syrup or liquid. Proper amounts of headspace for freezing fruits and vegetables are discussed in the following chapters.

Preventing Discoloration

Light-colored fruit oxidizes in the presence of oxygen. This means that it turns brown. Apples and peaches are especially vulnerable. This discoloration can be prevented by using ascorbic acid or a commercial antidiscoloration product. Directions for using these products are discussed in Chapter 4.

Storing Frozen Foods

During the initial freezing process, packages or jars should come in direct contact with the surface of the freezing unit. This will hasten the freezing of the foods.

Don't crowd the packages. Leave some air space between packages or jars of food being frozen. This keeps the cold air on the move and more able to do its job. Once everything is frozen, you can stack, cram, and arrange to your heart's content.

Thawing Procedures

For every safe way of doing something, it's almost a given that someone will come up with a creative but totally unsafe way of accomplishing the same task. The United

States Department of Agriculture (USDA) takes these maverick methods seriously and warns against defrosting foods in any of the following ways:

- In the basement

- In your car

- In plastic garbage bags

- In the dishwasher

- Outdoors

- On the porch

- In a pan of hot water

- On the kitchen counter

You probably wouldn't dream of trying any of these methods, except perhaps for the last one. So what's wrong with setting a package of meat out on the counter to defrost? Could be plenty.

As food thaws, the bacteria that are present (and that were inactive while the food was frozen) begin to get frisky. They multiply when any part of the meat gets to 40°F or above. So while the interior section of the meat is still frozen, the outer layers have passed into the danger zone, which begins at 40°F and extends to 140°F.

Thawing in the Refrigerator

Planning ahead is best. If you know what you'll want for dinner, take the package out of the freezer the night before and put it in the refrigerator to thaw. Temperatures vary throughout the refrigerator, so take advantage of the warmer portions when you want something to thaw. Generally, the lower shelves are best for thawing if your freezer unit is on top.

Put the package of frozen food on a plate or inside a bowl to contain any liquid that leaches through the wrappings. This is especially important for meat or poultry juices that shouldn't come in contact with other foods stored in the refrigerator.

Plan on using thawed ground meats within a day or two—the same goes for poultry. Solid cuts of beef, such as roasts or steaks, should keep up to five days. If your plans change, you can refreeze foods that have thawed, although the quality will not be as good.

Thawing in Cold Water

This works more quickly than the refrigerator method, but it does require that you be on hand to keep changing the water to be sure it stays cold. It can also be messy, especially if the freezer bag is leaking. Not only can bacteria enter through the opening, but water can turn your food product into a soggy mess. If in doubt, put the package in another freezer bag (double-bag it) just to be sure.

Change the water about every half hour. You can expect a 1-pound package to thaw in about an hour. Once the food has thawed, it must be cooked right away. If you change your mind about using the product right away, it should still be cooked before refreezing.

Thawing in the Microwave

Microwaves are probably used more for reheating coffee and defrosting foods than for any other purpose. You'll need to keep a close eye on the defrosting process when you use the microwave, however, as outer portions of the food can begin cooking while the interior is still hard as a rock.

Once food has thawed by this means, it should be cooked right away to prevent bacteria from growing. If you decide to refreeze the food, it should still be cooked before you return it to the freezer. Again, there will be some loss of quality in a refrozen product.

The Least You Need to Know

- Freezing preserves more nutrients than any other method of home food preserving.

- Freezing deactivates bacteria and other microorganisms that can cause food to spoil.

- Enzyme action is slowed by freezing but isn't stopped, so proper preparation, processing, and packaging is essential to have a good-quality product.

- Selecting the right freezer for your family's needs will help you maximize your food dollar.

- Freezer containers and glass freezing and canning jars are essential equipment for freezing foods properly.

- Proper thawing is as important as proper freezing.

Chapter 4

Freezing Fruits

In This Chapter

- ◆ Freezing fruits without fuss
- ◆ When to sweeten
- ◆ Keeping fruit bright and colorful
- ◆ The skinny on skins

If you're brand new to preserving food, freezing fruits is the place to start. It's fast and it's easy! It's almost impossible to make a mistake, you need very little in the way of equipment and supplies, plus you get an instant return on your efforts. You have a great deal of latitude regarding whether to use sugar or not, and you can learn some tricks of the trade to make peeling a breeze and to ensure your fruit doesn't darken during storage.

Berries

Berries are versatile (they make great jams, jellies, cobblers, and pies), they're healthy (high in antioxidants and other good things), and they're fun to eat. Berries come in a variety of sizes and shapes and in a rainbow of colors. Berries are generally broken down into two categories: hard and soft.

Hard Berries

Hard berries include blueberries, cranberries, huckleberries, and youngberries. These berries are firm and round, and a cranberry in prime condition will actually bounce. In fact, cranberries were originally called *bounceberries.*

Blueberries are generally available from May through October, and cranberries are available during the holiday season.

Safety Check

Blueberries contain oxalates, which are naturally occurring substances. When oxalates become too concentrated in body fluids, they can crystallize and cause problems. Folks with kidney or gallbladder problems should avoid eating large amounts of blueberries. As always, if you have any suspected or diagnosed health issues, consult your physician before changing your diet.

Preserving Pointers

Sometimes berries used in baked goods take on a greenish tinge. This is not harmful. When the recipe calls for baking soda, this creates an alkaline environment, which causes the yellow pigments in the blueberries to turn green. The products are safe to eat.

Blueberries come in clear plastic cartons with ventilation holes. Cranberries come in plastic bags, also with ventilation holes. Both cranberries and blueberries should be loose inside the container. There should be no moisture, mold, or browning to the berries. Healthy blueberries have a whitish "blush" that protects them from breaking down.

There's no special handling involved, and preserving blueberries and cranberries couldn't be easier. Just put them in the freezer as is, and they'll keep for a year. Take out what you need as you go along. Don't wash the berries until you're ready to use them.

Soft Berries

Soft berries include blackberries, raspberries, loganberries (a cross between a raspberry and a blackberry), and boysenberries (a cross among a loganberry, raspberry, and the Pacific blackberry). There are many other soft berries, but most of them are the result of crossing various strains of blackberries and raspberries.

Pick-your-own berry farms have become popular places for families to gather all kinds of soft berries. Even if you live in the city, you'll probably not be too far from one.

If you're worried about thorns and getting scratches, most of these commercial, open-to-the-public places have thornless bushes and canes. Still, long sleeves are a good idea, and don't forget the sunblock and insect repellent.

You bring your own containers. They should not be too deep—you don't want to crush the bottom layer. Coffee cans work well. Berries are fragile, so handle with care. Blackberries and raspberries are ripe when they slip easily from their caps. The more you have to tug, the greener (less ripe) the berry.

To find a complete listing of all pick-your-own fruit and vegetable farms in the United States, Canada, Great Britain, and various other countries throughout the world, go to www.pickyourown.org.

Preserving soft berries is just one step more advanced than freezing blueberries and cranberries. It's time for those cookie sheets. Here are the step-by-step instructions:

1. Wash berries with cool water. The spray nozzle on your sink works well. You don't want to blast the berries, just give them a gentle shower.

2. Set berries aside to drain; you can spread them on paper towels to absorb any excess water. You'll use a dry pack (more about that in the next section) and want them to be dry for step 3.

3. Spread berries in a single layer on cookie sheets. Don't crowd them.

4. Pop the trays into your freezer. When the berries are hard, take the cookie sheets out of the freezer, use a spatula to loosen the berries, scoop them into freezer bags (prelabeled and dated), and seal. Return the sealed bags to the freezer.

Blackberries on cookie sheet.

When you need some, take out what you need and either thaw them in the microwave or let them thaw at room temperature. Use berries on cereal and yogurt and in muffins, fruit salads, and smoothies—or just eat them plain. When you're ready to make jams and jellies (see Chapter 18), you'll have a supply of berries on hand.

Strawberries

Strawberries are almost a category of their own. They're firm (but not hard) when ripe but require gentle handling and can become overripe (and too soft) very quickly. You can store them in the fridge for a few days, but they're best used quickly. Strawberries make excellent jams and jellies (see Chapter 18), and if your jelly doesn't set the way you'd like, you've got wonderful strawberry syrup.

Strawberries have a nice long season, and when you've eaten your fill, it's time to freeze a bunch to see you through the fall and winter seasons. You have a few options when it comes to preserving strawberries. The texture of thawed strawberries will differ depending on what method you choose, but the taste will be great. Choose whichever method fits your needs:

- **Dry pack.** This method of preserving food doesn't use any additional liquid, such as juice or water, when packing food in freezer bags or containers. Food is packed as is. You can use the cookie sheet method and dry pack strawberries the same way you freeze blackberries or raspberries, but the berries will tend to lose their shape as they thaw.

- **Sugar pack.** This option expands your preserving skill set. It's nothing more than rolling strawberries in *superfine sugar*, putting them on cookie sheets, and popping them into the freezer. When they're frozen, remove with a spatula, place in freezer bags, and return to the freezer. When thawed, the sugared berries will keep their shape better.

def•i•ni•tion

Superfine sugar (referred to as *castor sugar* in Great Britain) is finely granulated sugar that dissolves almost instantly without leaving a granular residue at the bottom of the bowl. It's manufactured by Domino Sugar and should be available at your local grocers.

◆ **Syrup pack.** The other method of putting up strawberries uses syrup, which is a mixture of differing proportions of sugar and water that are heated until boiling, then cooled and poured over fruit before the container is sealed. See Appendix C for instructions on making different strengths of syrups.

To prepare strawberries for a syrup pack, wash the berries and remove the green caps. Some people prefer to also remove the core, but it really isn't necessary. A short paring knife works well for this. Just make a circular incision and remove the stem and cap. Slice the berries directly into the freezer container (usually a hard plastic container with a tight-fitting lid) and cover them with the syrup of your choice, leaving about ½ inch of headroom to allow for expansion during the freezing process. Then secure the lid, label and date, and store in the freezer.

Fruits packed without added sugar or liquid, such as syrup or juice, need ½ inch of headroom. That applies to any container of any size. If you've puréed or crushed the fruit or packed it in liquid, allow 1½ inches for wide-mouth pint jars and 1 inch for wide-mouth quart jars. If you're using regular (narrow-mouth) jars, allow ¾ inch for pints and 1½ inches for quarts. And yes, those glass canning jars are also fine for freezing.

Once you've packed, sealed, labeled, and dated your containers, it's time to take them to the freezer. Spread your containers around in a single layer until the fruit has frozen. A good rule is to leave them spread out overnight and then stack them the next morning.

Cherries

Cherries are generally divided into sweet (eating) and tart or sour (pie). Both types can be frozen as well as canned. Cherries can be frozen by the cookie sheet method or packed in liquid. Frozen cherries don't need to be pitted, but the use you have in mind for them will determine if you pit them or not. For example, if you're going to be snacking, it's no trouble to spit out a pit. If you're going to make a pie, pitting is definitely the way to go.

Pitting used to be tedious work, but for under $20 you can have a lifetime of pitting ease. Cherry pitters are remarkable little devices. You drop cherries into the hopper, depress a plunger that neatly divests the

Safety Check

Always double-check to be sure the pits have been removed before proceeding to pack the cherries. Biting down on a pit can break a tooth.

cherries of their pits (two at a time), and the pits are pushed out into side trays while the pitted cherries slide down a little ramp and into your waiting receptacle. This is a great job for the younger apprentices in your preserving kitchen.

Cherry pitter.

If you've come home with a box of cherries, plan on putting them up right away. They have a habit of turning soft quickly. Wash and sort the cherries. Trim any bruised portions, toss the bruises, and set the trimmed fruit aside to make jam (see Chapter 18). Remove the stems and pits if desired. Pack into freezer containers.

Cherries in freezer containers.

If you've decided to pack the cherries in syrup, determine the strength of the syrup you'll use and prepare it according to the directions given in Appendix C's Syrup Chart. Cover the cherries with syrup, allowing enough headroom for expansion during the freezing process.

Adding syrup to cherries.

Wipe the rims of the containers to remove any syrup. Seal, label, date, and freeze them. When the cherries have frozen, you can stack the containers and store them in the freezer.

Frozen cherries ready for freezer storage.

Apricots, Peaches, and Nectarines

These fruits can be frozen, canned, or dried—and pickled peaches are a wonderful accompaniment to holiday meals (see Chapter 14). Each method produces a good product with different textures suitable for different uses.

Apricots

Apricots don't require any special preparation, and they hold their shape better if frozen with skins on. Wash them carefully, checking for bruises and blemishes. Trim out the damaged portions and set the trimmed fruit aside to make jam (see Chapter 18). Slice the apricots in half, remove the pits, and pack into freezer containers. Freeze without sugar or freeze using syrup in the strength of your choice. Allowing proper headroom, seal, label, date, and freeze.

Peaches and Nectarines

These fruits differ from berries and cherries in that they have skins that must be dealt with, and their pits are quite a bit larger. They also tend to discolor quickly when their cut surfaces are exposed to air. Taking one step at a time, however, makes the job easy.

Peaches are either clings or freestone. Clings do just that; the pits are firmly attached to the skin and can be difficult to remove without mangling the fruit. Freestones separate more easily. You slice around the fruit and then twist the two halves in opposite directions. Voilà! The fruit separates; one side has the pit and the other side is free. The pit should separate easily. However, if freestones are picked green, the pit may not work the way it's supposed to, and you'll be faced with a clinger.

> **Preserving Pointers**
>
> All fruits can be safely frozen without added sugar, but the quality may not be as good as those frozen using sugar or syrup.

Clings are the first peaches to come ripe in the spring, and unless you've got access to a commercial pick-your-own orchard, you'll probably not find them readily available. Most of them are marked for the commercial packers. Later on the freestones come ripe, and these are the ones you're more likely to find at the grocery store or farmers' market.

Nectarines are peaches that lack fuzz. In fact, it's possible for a peach tree to bear nectarines on a branch and vice versa. Once peaches and nectarines have been picked, sugar production ceases and the ripening process stops. The fruit will soften, but it will not ripen any further. All the more reason to buy tree-ripened fruit at the local farmers' market.

Ripe peaches are fragrant. Early Elberta, Elberta, Improved Elberta, and O'Henry are good varieties for freezing. Check with your local extension service for recommended peach and nectarine varieties in your area (see Appendix G). Ripe peaches also have a nice blush, and their skin should yield gently to the touch. They shouldn't be soft and definitely shouldn't be hard.

In Other Words

"Bruises are the sweetest part of the fruit." This is not true, just a handy old lie that children have been told to be sure they eat everything up. Bruises are damaged flesh. Cut them out and throw them away.

Removing Skins

Unlike apricots, which usually hold their shape better with the skin left on, peaches are frozen without their skins. If you're groaning at the prospect of peeling two or three boxes of peaches, you're in for a very pleasant surprise. You won't have to peel a single peach, and the skins will come off so easily you'll probably decide to go buy another box. But first, assemble your equipment. You'll need the following:

◆ At least 2 big bowls (about 15 inches in diameter and able to hold a gallon or more of liquid)

◆ Boiling water canner or a cooking pot of similar size

◆ Ascorbic acid, lemon juice, or a commercial antidarkening agent for light-colored fruits

◆ Slotted spoon

◆ Colander

◆ Paring knife

◆ Grapefruit spoon

◆ Prepared syrup

◆ Freezer containers (pints or quarts)

1. Wash and sort the fruit. Here's where having a couple of large bowls comes in handy. Perfect fruit goes into one bowl; fruit with blemishes goes in another. You'll be preserving your perfect peaches first. Later you can cut up the damaged fruit and save the good parts to make jam or purée it to make fruit leather (see Chapter 20).

Perfect peaches.

2. Fill your cook pot or canner about half full of water, turn heat on high, and bring to a boil.

3. Mix up your antidiscoloration solution (see the next section) in one of the large bowls and set it to one side of your sink. You'll be working with 2 to 3 pounds of fruit at a time.

4. Fill the sink with cold water and add ice cubes to get it even colder.

5. Once the water has come to a boil, use your slotted spoon to carefully lower peaches into the water. Leave the peaches in the water for 10 to 20 seconds. You'll see the skins begin to separate.

6. Once you've seen the first signs of the skins separating, use your slotted spoon again to remove the peaches and plunge them into the ice water.

7. Keeping each peach underwater as you work, gently rub the skin. The skin will separate easily from the peach.

8. Place each whole peach in the bowl containing the antidiscoloration solution.

9. Make a 360-degree cut around the peach, starting at the stem. Use your paring knife to gently coax the halves apart, and use your grapefruit spoon to nudge the pit away from the half it's still attached to. Then you can either cut the halves into slices or keep them as is. Hold them in the antidiscoloration solution until you're ready to put them into containers.

Peaches in antidiscoloration solution.

Most of the prep work is now done. You can use plastic freezer containers or glass canning and freezing jars. If you're planning on freezing halves and want to use jars, quart wide-mouth jars are an easier way to go. With slices it doesn't make much difference, although it's easier to arrange the slices neatly if you've got some room to work with.

Slice the peaches directly into the freezer containers and add syrup in the strength of your choice. There's one additional step to ensure that your peaches won't rise up and greet the air in the headspace. Tear off a small piece of plastic wrap, crumple it up, and place it on top of the fruit. This will keep the peaches in their place. Seal, label, date, and freeze.

Peaches with buffer protection.

Sealed frozen peaches.

Apples

You can freeze apple slices and use them later in pies. Put slices in boiling water for 2 minutes. Remove them from the boiling water, drain, and plunge them into ice water. When cooled, drain and pack in freezer bags.

That's one way, but if you have some extra room in the freezer, why not line a pie pan with foil—leave plenty for folding back over—arrange your apple slices in the pan until you're happy with the height, and then fold the foil securely around the apples? Place the pan with the apples in the freezer. When the apples have frozen, lift out the pie-shaped foil from the pan and return your preshaped pie to the freezer. When you're ready to bake your pie, all you need do is unwrap the foil, remove the frozen apples and transfer them to the crust, add spices, and bake.

You can freeze applesauce as well. Prepare by your favorite recipe (see Chapter 10 on canning fruits for some suggestions) and pack it into freezer containers, leaving ½ inch headroom. Seal, label, date, and freeze.

Pears

Good old Bartletts freeze nicely. They're by far the most popular and readily available pear and the one most used by both commercial and home food preservers. You can freeze them as halves or quarters or put them up as a purée. Wash fruit in several changes of cool, clean water. To pare pears is a matter of preference. They tend to hold their shape better if you leave the skins on.

Use your grapefruit spoon to gently remove the stringy center. A neat twisting motion followed by a scrape will clean up the pear half quite neatly. Pack halves or slices into freezer containers; add syrup (in your choice of strength) to cover, leaving proper headspace; seal; label; and freeze.

Plums

Plums freeze nicely whole, halved, or quartered. They hold their shape better if frozen with their skins on. If you're planning to make jam later, don't use a sugar or syrup pack. Choose plums with a deep, rich color. Wash fruit in several changes of cool, clean water.

To pack unsweetened, pack whole plums into containers, leaving proper headspace. Seal, label, date, and freeze.

To pack in syrup, slice plums in half or quarter. Remove pits. Select syrup strength of your choice. Cover fruit with syrup, leaving proper headspace. Seal, label, date, and freeze.

Citrus

If you have your own citrus trees, it's worth your time and effort to freeze these fruits, but it is a bit more work than putting up other kinds of fruit. Of course, this is why grapefruit spoons were invented. When you're freezing oranges, lemons, or limes, save some rind for making marmalade (see Chapter 18).

Grapefruit and Oranges

Wash the fruit, peel away the white membrane, and use a sharp knife to make the first cut and remove the first section. The rest will be easier. Separate each section and clean up the extra membranes that cling to the segments. Remove the seeds as you go along.

This is a juicy process, so be sure to collect the juice as you work and save it for packing. You can sweeten the juice to your taste or leave it unsweetened. Pack the fruit into freezer containers; cover with juice or a light or extra light syrup, leaving proper headspace; seal; label; and freeze.

If you want to freeze juice and have enough fruit to make it cost effective, consider investing in a juice extractor to make the job easier. Freezing juice in glass canning and freezing jars makes for a more attractive product. Leave appropriate headroom, seal, label, date, and freeze.

Lemons and Limes

You'll want to freeze lemons and limes for their juice. Use your juice extractor (or you can use the old tried-and-true hand juicer) and pour the juice directly into freezer containers. Leave appropriate headroom, seal, label, date, and freeze. No need to worry about these products darkening!

Grapes

Seedless grapes freeze well if you treat them the same way you do berries. They make great snacks and are good additions to fruit salads. Arrange them in a single layer on a cookie sheet and pop them in the freezer. When they're frozen, loosen them with a spatula and pack them into freezer bags. Return to the freezer.

If you're handling grapes with seeds, slice the grapes in half lengthwise and remove the seeds before committing them to the cookie sheet.

To freeze with liquid, pack freezer containers with grapes and cover with syrup in your choice of strength. Leave appropriate headroom, seal, label, and freeze.

> **Preserving Pointers**
>
> You can also freeze grape juice, of course. Wash grapes in several changes of cool, clean water. Remove the stems and use a potato masher to crush the grapes. Pour the mixture into a jelly bag and allow it to drip at its own pace. The sediment will settle to the bottom of the receiving container, so pour off the clear juice carefully so as not to disturb the sediment.

Melons: Cantaloupe, Honeydew, Casaba, and Watermelon

All of these freeze well with the exception of watermelon. You can try using your melon baller on watermelon, but this fruit tends to get mushy. After all, it's mostly water. If you do decide to give it a shot, take a close look at the thickness of the rind. If it's thick, put it aside to make watermelon rind pickles (see Chapter 14).

For other melons, you want to use the firm flesh for melon balls, so remove the seeds and any of the soft, flaky parts. Scoop away, arrange on cookie sheets in a single layer, and freeze. When the melon balls are frozen, use your spatula to loosen them and then pour them into freezer bags. Seal, label, date, and freeze. If you prefer slices or cubes, they'll do fine as well. Just be sure to cut off all the rind and any dark green coloring close to the rind.

Avocados

Preparation involves mashing. Think ahead to guacamole and bases for dips. Peel and smash away. If you're planning on using the avocados for something sweet, add $\frac{1}{8}$ teaspoon crystalline ascorbic acid (vitamin C) to each quart of purée. Otherwise, for guacamole or dips, 1 tablespoon of lemon juice for every 2 avocados will keep them from turning dark.

Coconut

Puncture the eye and pour out the coconut milk. Save. Crack open the shell with a hammer and separate the meat from the shell. You can grate it by hand or use the food processor. Put the coconut in the freezer container, cover with the milk, seal, label, and freeze.

Dates

Dates are the fruit of the date palm. They're a dark reddish brown, oval, and about 1½ inches long. Their skins are wrinkled and coated with a sticky, waxy film. They are very sweet when ripe. These are as easy to freeze as cherries. Wash, drain, dry, pit, and pack. Seal, label, date, and freeze.

Figs

Sort, wash, and cut off the stems. You can peel the figs if you prefer them that way. You can slice them or leave them whole. Pack them in a 35 percent syrup with ¾ teaspoon ascorbic acid per quart. (A 35 percent syrup uses 2½ cups sugar to 4 cups water.)

If you prefer the no-sugar method, you can simply use water. Cover the figs with water to which you've added ¾ teaspoon ascorbic acid per quart. Seal, label, date, and freeze.

Pineapple

A pineapple is ripe when the top pulls out easily. Pare the pineapple and dig out the eyes. Core it. Then decide how you want to freeze it. Slices? Cubes? Sticks? Pineapple freezes nicely in its own juice, but if you want a sweeter syrup, it's best to go with extra light or light syrup (see Appendix C). Ripe pineapple has a rich flavor already and is sweet enough. Pack pineapple into freezer containers, add liquid to cover, leave proper headroom, seal, label, date, and freeze.

Pie Fillings

The main ingredients of pie fillings are fruit and sugar, spices for interest and flavor, and a thickening agent. Thickening agents include tapioca, flour, or cornstarch.

Cornstarch has twice the thickening capacity of flour. You dissolve it in a small amount of cool water before adding it to your pie filling so that it won't lump up. Also, unlike flour, cornstarch won't add a white tint to your filling. It sets up clear. Flour and water, of course, make paste. Tapioca is another option.

Preserving Pointers

"A pint's a pound the world around" is one of the first rhymes a new cook learns. It comes in mighty handy when you're putting up food.

To make an 8- or 9-inch pie, plan on putting up a quart of filling. Equivalencies can be confusing. See Appendix B for clarifications.

- **Apple pie filling:** One apple pie uses about 6 to 8 apples, ½ cup sugar, cinnamon, nutmeg, and lemon juice.

- **Berry pie filling:** One berry pie uses 1 to 2 quarts of berries, ⅔ cup sugar, and 1½ tablespoons tapioca.

- **Cherry pie filling:** One cherry pie uses 1 to 2 quarts of sour cherries, 1 to 2 cups sugar, and 2 tablespoons cornstarch or flour.

- **Peach pie filling:** One peach pie takes about 1 to 2 quarts of peaches, 1 cup sugar, ¼ cup flour, cinnamon, nutmeg, and lemon juice.

Whatever your favorite pie recipe, you can freeze it. Mix all the ingredients together gently in a medium-size cook pot (see the preceding list for specific ingredients). Then cook over low heat until the juices begin to flow from the fruits and the mixture begins to thicken. Pack it into quart freezer containers or glass canning and freezing jars, allowing proper headroom. Seal, date, and allow the filling to cool down before placing in the freezer.

Recipes

Frozen berries, cherries, peaches, apples, and pears that have been dry packed all work well with these recipes. There's no need to thaw berries or cherries before using them in cooking, but if you want to use fruit that's been frozen in liquid, you'll want to thaw first and drain before using.

Blueberry Grunt or Slump

This was a colonial favorite, although this version uses baking mix, something colonial cooks didn't have unless they made their own. Some say the dessert got its name from the "grunts" of satisfied eaters or the fact that it didn't hold its shape when dished up!

Serves 8
Prep time: 10 minutes
Cook time: about 25 minutes

2 cups buttermilk baking mix

½ tsp. dried lemon peel

¼ tsp. nutmeg

⅔ cup milk

2 cups blueberries

1 cup water

½ cup sugar

Cream or ice cream (optional)

In a medium-size bowl, mix together baking mix, lemon peel, and nutmeg. Add milk and mix with a fork just until moistened. Put blueberries, water, and sugar in 10-inch skillet and cook just until mixture begins to bubble. Lower heat. Drop dough in 8 mounds on simmering blueberries and cook uncovered over low heat 10 minutes. Cover and cook 10 minutes longer. Serve with cream or ice cream.

Linda's Crispy Cobbler

This is a real crowd pleaser and very easy to make.

Serves 6 to 8
Prep time: 5 minutes
Cook time: 40 minutes

½ cup butter

1 cup sifted flour

1 cup sugar

2 tsp. baking powder

⅛ tsp. salt

¾ cup milk

4 cups fruit (blackberries, raspberries, peaches, apples, and pears are well-suited to this dish)

Vanilla ice cream (optional)

Melt butter in an 8"×10"×2" pan. Sift dry ingredients together in a medium-size mixing bowl. Stir in milk. Pour batter over butter. Spread fruit on top. Bake in a 375°F oven 40 minutes or until top is very brown. Serve with vanilla ice cream.

Chapter 5

Freezing Vegetables and Herbs

In This Chapter

- Choosing the best produce
- The importance of hot and cold
- Young versus old: young wins
- Icing herbs

Freezing vegetables definitely takes less time than canning them, and the flavor, texture, and quality are often superior to the canned product. If you choose varieties suitable for freezing, you'll be happy with the result and have a good supply to last the entire year. Chapter 3 explains the blanching and cooling process necessary to ensure a good product.

While you're at it, add some herbs to your preserving repertoire. Herbs give zip to soups, stews, and all kinds of meat dishes. They're a snap to freeze as well!

Asparagus

Asparagus is one of the taste treats of spring. Mary Washington is the standard variety and is great for freezing. Choose young, tender stalks with tips that haven't begun to blossom out.

Hold the stalk with one hand and grasp the base of the stalk with the other. Bend the end of the stalk until it snaps. This should leave you with the tenderest part of the stalk to freeze.

You can cut the stalk into sections or freeze it whole. Blanching times are as follows:

◆ Small stalks: $1\frac{1}{2}$ minutes

◆ Medium stalks: 2 minutes

◆ Large stalks: 3 minutes

After blanching and cooling, drain and pack the asparagus in labeled and dated moisture/vapor-resistant freezer bags or containers and freeze.

Beans

Beans have undergone an explosion as far as new varieties coming onto the market. Those that do well for freezing include Indy Golden (a yellow wax), Aquadulce broad bean, Roma II (Italian), Matador, and Provider (green).

Green Beans

These are also called snap beans or string beans, although you won't encounter strings anymore unless you're working with a batch of really old, tough beans—not recommended.

In addition to being virtually stringless, these beans come in a nice assortment of colors. There are yellow wax beans and purple beans that turn green while they cook. You can use Italian beans (flat and wide) as well.

Select green beans (or any of their relatives mentioned earlier) that are firm. They should snap when bent. Avoid beans that don't snap. They should be moist and full inside, not hollow (the sign of an old bean).

Beans have a bit of a fuzzy surface that tends to trap pieces of leaves and other garden debris. Washing them doesn't always take care of this, and you may need to pick these leaves off by hand.

Snipping tips and tails comes next. You may choose to do this one bean at a time, but that's time consuming and tedious. Instead, try this: pick up half a dozen beans and arrange them in your hand. Using your kitchen shears, snip off the tips. Turn the beans around, even them up, and snip off the tails. Then snap them into pieces, slice lengthwise, or leave whole.

Wash the beans in cool water and give them a final quality-control check. Next comes blanching. Blanching times for green beans and Italian pod beans are 3 minutes (2 minutes for green bean pieces). Then cool, drain, and pack in labeled and dated moisture/vapor-resistant freezer bags or containers and freeze. Beans also can well (see Chapter 11).

> **In Other Words**
>
> Green beans, or string beans as they are usually called, must be done till very tender—it takes nearly an hour and a half.
>
> —Sarah Josepha Hale, *The Good Housekeeper* (1839). Cooking times have certainly gotten shorter!

Lima Beans

Lima beans are treated like peas for freezing purposes. Select firm green pods without yellowing or blemishes. Snip off the blossom tip of the bean and open the bean along the seam. Remove the beans—there are generally three or four per pod. Blanching times are 1 minute for small, 2 minutes for medium, and 3 minutes for large beans. Pack in labeled and dated moisture/vapor-resistant freezer bags or containers and freeze.

> **Preserving Pointers**
>
> Succotash is one familiar vegetable combination, and you can make your own by combining lima beans and corn in one package. You can also create other combinations of vegetables to freeze for soups or stews.

Beets

Smaller beets, such as Cylindra or Rodina, are the best choice for freezing. Clip off the tops, leaving just enough to cover the beet, and clip most of the root, leaving about an inch. Wash the beets and cook them until tender. Small beets will cook in about 25 to 30 minutes, while bigger ones may take nearly 1 hour.

Remove the beets from the cooking pot and immerse them in cold water to slip the skins. Beets can be frozen whole, as slices, or as cubes. To slice beets, try using your egg slicer. It will give you uniform slices of just the right width.

Egg slicer slicing beets.

Broccoli, Cauliflower, Broccoflower, and Brussels Sprouts

The only difference among these is that broccoli stalks are also freezable. Blanching and cooling procedures for all are the same and so is the deworming procedure. These vegetables are often hosts for loopers, nasty little white or yellow worms. (They won't hurt you, but it's not the hallmark of a good dinner when a guest pulls a yellow worm from his broccoli and then pushes his plate away.)

Loopers are tough to find sometimes, so soaking the vegetables for half an hour in a saltwater solution can speed up the process of getting rid of them. Use 4 teaspoons of salt to a gallon of water. This kills the worms; they lose their grip and sink to the bottom of the sink.

Broccoli

Choose broccoli with dark green, tightly budded heads. Premium Crop and Arcadia are good choices for freezing. If the heads are beginning to open or yellow, the broccoli is past its prime. You can choose to freeze just the florets or the florets with stalks attached. Wash the broccoli and remove the leaves. The young, tender leaves are quite tasty, similar to collards.

If you are using the stalks as well as the heads, peel the hard outer skin away. Examine the heads carefully for worms. If the heads are overly large and difficult to separate into florets, you can split the stalk down the middle lengthwise and divide the head. Otherwise, break off sections of the head for florets. Blanching time is 3 minutes.

In packing stalks with florets, alternate head first with stalk end first. You'll get more in the container and won't crush the heads.

Cauliflower and Broccoflower

Broccoflower is a cross between broccoli and cauliflower. It looks like cauliflower, but it's green. Choose heads that are firm and all white for cauliflower and a lime green for broccoflower. Avoid heads with brown or black spots. Cut off the stem, peel away the covering leaves, and break off the florets. Soak them in the saltwater solution (see the beginning of the section) to remove worms. Blanching time is 3 minutes. When cool, pack in labeled and dated moisture/vapor-resistant freezer bags or containers and freeze.

Brussels Sprouts

If you find these at a farmers' market, they may still be attached to the stalk. That is good. Leave them that way until you're ready to deal with them. They'll stay fresher, and you'll be happier with the flavor.

The heads should be firm and compact. They should be a nice even green without signs of yellowing or drying. Wash and remove the outer leaves. Soak them in the saltwater solution (see the beginning of the section) to remove worms. Blanching time is 4 minutes for small heads and 5 minutes for bigger ones. When cool, pack in labeled and dated moisture/vapor-resistant freezer bags or containers and freeze.

Carrots

Carrots are fairly straightforward to freeze. Touchon is a good variety for freezing. Cut off the tops and any trailing root. Scrub or scrape, as it suits you, and slice into pieces or lengthwise, depending on their future intended use. Blanching time is 2 minutes.

When cool, pack in labeled and dated moisture/vapor-resistant freezer bags or containers and freeze. Carrots also can and root cellar well (see Chapters 11 and 23).

Corn

There are many good varieties for freezing, and corn that matures in mid- to late summer generally is better than the earlier-ripening varieties. Corn should be picked and processed quickly. The sugars turn to starch faster than you can blink. If you must hold the corn for a day or so, keep it refrigerated. Ears should be well filled with kernels that should not be overly large. Large kernels generally indicate old, tough corn.

In Other Words

Plough deep, while Sluggards sleep; and you shall have Corn, to sell and to keep.

—Benjamin Franklin

Shucking corn is messy business that is best done outside. After the corn is shucked and most of the silk removed, haul the lot inside and give it a good washing under cool, running water. This should help get the last of the silk.

Blanching comes before cutting. Blanch for 4 minutes and then plunge the ears into cold water.

When the corn has cooled, use a sharp knife or corn slicer to cut the kernels from the ears. Don't scrape all the way to the cob. If you aim for about two thirds of the kernel, you'll get plenty.

Safety Check

Keep the board dry when you're slicing corn off the cob. You'll decrease the chances of the cob slipping out from underhand and you getting a nasty cut with the knife.

For creamed corn, cut from the cob at about one half of the kernel and then use a kitchen knife to scrape the milk and the rest of the kernel pieces from the cob.

For corn on the cob, blanching times are 7 minutes for small ears, 9 minutes for medium ears, and 11 minutes for large ears. Cool the corn quickly and thoroughly, and you'll help prevent it from having a "cobby" taste.

Then pack the corn in labeled and dated moisture/vapor-resistant freezer bags or containers and freeze. Corn also cans well (see Chapter 11) and makes excellent relish (see Chapter 16).

Greens

Some plants are grown strictly for their tender leaves (chard, spinach, collards, and kale). Mustard, beets, and turnips are dual-use vegetables, with the leaves being a tasty bonus. Regardless of the type of greens you'll be harvesting, try to pick them early in the morning when they're at their freshest. As the day wears on, the sun's heat causes them to wilt, dry, and otherwise be less than perfect for picking.

Whether picking your own or buying at the farmers' market, choose young, tender leaves. It doesn't make sense to struggle with tough, spotted, insect-damaged greens. What you work with is what you'll have available to eat, and the freezing process won't improve the quality.

Wash the greens thoroughly in a few changes of cool water. Greens are sand magnets, and you don't want to taste grit with your greens. Grits, perhaps; grit, no. The easiest way to get the job done is to fill the sink with cool water, add an armful of greens, and swish them around. Repeat this until you don't see any telltale grains at the bottom of the sink. Then drain the greens in a colander. They don't have to be dry; after all, they're headed to boiling water shortly. You just want to remove the excess water that will lower the temperature in the blanching pot.

Preserving Pointers

If you cut off the chard stems, put them aside to use in a stir-fry. They slice easily and add a good crunch.

During the rinsing process, check for yellowed leaves or other blemishes and discard them. You can trim the stems on chard if your family isn't partial to them, but it's not necessary.

Next comes blanching. The boiling water canner works very well as a blanching kettle, so fill it two thirds full of water, put the lid on, and turn on the heat. When the water has reached a boil, take a double handful of greens and submerge them in the boiling water. You can help them take the dive by pushing them underwater with a large spoon.

Don't overfill the pot; it will take too long for the water to return to a boil, and you'll end up with cooked mush. Replace the lid and wait for the water to boil again. Then set the timer. Blanching times for greens are as follows:

◆ Beet greens: 2 minutes

◆ Chard: 2 minutes

- Collards: 3 minutes

- Kale: 2 minutes

- Mustard: 2 minutes

- Spinach: 1½ to 2 minutes (depending on the size of the leaves)

- Turnip: 2 minutes

Greens going into the blanching pot.

While the greens are blanching, rinse out the sink and refill it with cold water. You can add some ice cubes to help lower the temperature. When the timer buzzes, remove the lid from the canner (being careful to turn it away from you to avoid a steam burn) and use a slotted spoon, fried food lifter, or whatever handy kitchen utensil will help you lift the greens from the pot and transfer them to the cold water in the sink.

Swish the greens around in the cold water. You want to stop the blanching process as quickly as you can. It generally takes as long to cool veggies as it does to blanch them. While the veggies are cooling down, you can label your freezer bags or freezer containers.

Greens coming out of the blanching pot.

When the greens are sufficiently cool, transfer them to a colander and allow them to drain. You can press gently to remove excess water, but be careful not to mash the greens. When they've drained, transfer them to freezer containers.

As you gain experience, you'll find it easy to develop a good rhythm. You'll have one batch in the blancher, another in the cool water, and another draining.

Safety Check

When you've blanched the last load, turn off the heat, replace the lid on the canner, and allow it to cool down. Don't move it unless you absolutely have to. Remember, you've got a very big pot of boiling water, and it takes time to cool down—just like an Olympic athlete.

Kohlrabi

Kohlrabi belongs to the cabbage family, although in this case we eat the stem rather than the flower. Kohlrabi comes in white, green, and purple varieties.

Choose young kohlrabi for freezing. Cut off the top and the roots. Scrub, peel, and either leave whole or cut into cubes. The blanching time for whole kohlrabi is 3 minutes and just 1 minute for cubes. When cool, pack in labeled and dated moisture/vapor-resistant freezer bags or containers and freeze.

Mushrooms

Select mushrooms without spots or any signs of decay. Wash them in cool water. Cut off the stem ends and either leave the mushrooms whole if small or cut them into slices or quarters. Mushrooms more than 1 inch in diameter should be cut or sliced.

To prepare for blanching, mushrooms should be treated to prevent darkening. Use either 1 teaspoon of lemon juice or 1½ teaspoons of citric acid per pint of water. Immerse the mushrooms in the solution for 5 minutes.

Then either *steam blanch* or sauté. Steam blanching times are as follows: 5 minutes for whole mushrooms, 3½ minutes for buttons or quarters, and 3 minutes for slices.

def•i•ni•tion

> **Steam blanching** takes longer than regular blanching, but if you prefer not to partially cook your vegetables, you may find this is a good alternative. You place a single layer of vegetables in a basket and hold the basket in place over boiling water. The steam generated by the boiling water blanches the veggies. This method works for broccoli, pumpkin, sweet potatoes, winter squash, and mushrooms.

If you prefer not to steam blanch, you can sauté the mushrooms in butter until they're nearly done. Then cool them. With either method, when cool, pack in labeled and dated moisture/vapor-resistant freezer bags or containers and freeze. Mushrooms are also suitable for canning (see Chapter 11).

Okra

If you love gumbo, you need okra. Wash and cut off the stems. Be careful not to cut too deep and expose the seed cells. Blanch small pods for 3 minutes and large pods for 4 minutes. Cool and pack in labeled and dated moisture/vapor-resistant freezer bags or containers and freeze.

Peas

Peas are a spring vegetable and are one of the first to become available at the grocery store or farmers' market. There are three basic types of fresh peas: pod peas, snap peas, and snow peas. All can be frozen. Good varieties of shelling peas include Frosty, Green Arrow, Wando, Mr. Big, and Dakota. Oregon Sugar and Oregon Dwarf Sugar Pod are excellent varieties for pod peas.

If you disliked peas as a youngster, it may be because the ones you were served were tough and mealy. This does the pea a disservice since it's tender and delicious when picked young. The English may be to blame for this travesty since sprouted peas (peas so old that they're actually trying to get about the business of reproducing) are a staple of their cuisine.

Young peas come from young pods. When you're selecting peas for freezing, choose pods that are a uniform green with no yellowing. Pods that are an intense green generally are immature. The peas should be bumps you can feel on the outside but shouldn't be so big that the pod looks like it's stretched to the max trying to hold them in.

You can expect about 7 to 9 peas per pod, and opening the pod is simple to do if the peas are at the right stage of ripeness.

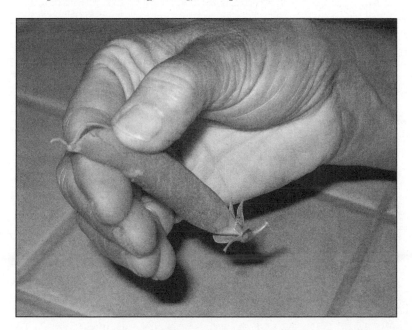

Pea pod popping.

Hold the pod in your palm and press down at the seam by the tail tip. The pod will pop open, and you can then split it the rest of the way down the seam and run your finger along the back of the pod to evict the peas.

You don't need to wash pea pods before shelling them unless they're absolutely filthy for some reason. It just makes them difficult to handle. They get slippery or slimy, and it's quite frustrating. If they are that dirty, it's probably best not to buy them anyhow. If you've grown them, hose them off before bringing them into the kitchen.

Preserving Pointers

Snap peas should snap firmly when bent. If they bend but don't break, look elsewhere. They should be plump and juicy on the inside. Snow peas should be a nice green with barely visible little pea bumps showing through the outer skin.

Shelling peas is a great way to get your family involved in home food preservation. You get the job done, and at the same time you get to talk together—something that's tough to come by these days. The most streamlined process for shelling involves three pans: one to hold the pea pods, one to hold the shelled peas, and one to hold the empty pods. It actually works like a shell game!

While the shelling is going on, get the boiling water canner ready for blanching and the sink ready for cool down. When the peas have been shelled, place them in a colander or steam basket and submerge them in the boiling water. Replace the lid on the canner and wait for the water to return to a boil. When it's boiling, set the timer for 1½ to 2 minutes, depending on the size of the peas. Snow peas and snap peas also blanch for 1½ to 2 minutes.

When the timer buzzes, remove the lid, lift out the basket or colander, and dump the peas into cold water. Swirl the peas around a bit to get them started cooling. When cooled, snare the peas with a slotted spoon and return them to the colander to drain. Then place them in labeled and dated freezer containers or moisture/vapor-resistant freezer bags and freeze. Peas also can well (see Chapter 11).

Peppers

Peppers are easy to freeze. Look for thick-walled peppers—Orange Sun is a good variety. It starts out green and turns orange as it matures. They require no blanching. Wash the peppers, cut them open, and remove the seeds and pith. Then slice and package them in labeled and dated moisture/vapor-resistant freezer bags or containers. They are a bit soft when thawed, but they do quite well in stir-fry and other recipes calling for cooked peppers.

Summer Squash

There are many varieties of summer squash, although crookneck and zucchini are the most popular. They do freeze, although they tend to get watery and are best used in soups and stews after thawing.

Select young squash. Do not peel or you'll end up with mush. Cut off the blossom end and stalk end and discard. Slice or cube the squash. Blanching time is 2 minutes. When cool, pack the squash in labeled and dated moisture/vapor-resistant freezer bags or containers and freeze. If you have an abundance of zucchini or other summer squash, consider shredding it for future service in zucchini bread.

Use your food processor or the vegetable shredder. Shred the squash (skin on) and pack it in 2-cup portions in moisture/vapor-resistant freezer bags or containers. (A recipe for zucchini bread follows at the end of the chapter.)

Shredding zucchini.

Freezing Herbs

Get out a cookie sheet! You can freeze herbs using the cookie sheet method. This works especially well for the more tender herbs with a higher water content. Mint, basil, and tarragon do very well frozen. Clip the herbs and place stems with leaves on the cookie sheet. When they're frozen, pick leaves from the stems and pack the leaves in labeled and dated moisture/vapor-resistant freezer bags or containers and freeze.

Another option is to place herb leaves in ice cube trays, fill the trays with water, and pop them in the freezer. When the cubes have frozen, tip them out of the ice trays and pack them into freezer bags.

Freezing herbs.

Recipes

Here are two recipes: one for dessert and one for dinner. Both use previously frozen vegetables.

Zucchini Bread

Zucchini bread is moist and dense. When accompanied by a scoop of vanilla ice cream, it's a complete rich, chewy, and flavorful dessert. The squash adds moisture and texture.

Makes 1 loaf
Prep time: 20 minutes
Cook time: 40 minutes

3 cups flour

1 tsp. salt

2 tsp. baking soda

2 tsp. cinnamon

$\frac{1}{2}$ tsp. nutmeg

$\frac{1}{4}$ tsp. ground cloves

3 eggs

2 cups sugar

1 cup oil

2 tsp. vanilla

2 cups shredded zucchini

1 cup cranberries or raisins

1 cup chopped walnuts

1. Preheat the oven to 350°F. Combine flour, salt, baking soda, cinnamon, nutmeg, and ground cloves in a large mixing bowl.

2. In a separate bowl, beat eggs until light. Add sugar, oil, vanilla, and zucchini to the egg mixture and stir well. Combine with dry mixture and stir until all ingredients are moistened. Fold in cranberries or raisins and nuts. Pour into 8$\frac{1}{2}$×4$\frac{1}{2}$×2$\frac{1}{2}$-inch loaf pan. Bake until loaf tests done—about 1 hour.

Asparagus Beef Stir-Fry

Flank steak or round steak is not the most tender cut of beef, but this recipe turns it into gourmet fare. You can use broccoli or bok choi instead of asparagus. Slice these on the diagonal before combining them with the rest of the ingredients. As with most Asian fare, most of the work is in the preparation with minimal cooking time. That makes it a good company dish—get everything ready ahead of time and spend just a few minutes dazzling your company with your presentation!

For beef marinade:

2 TB. soy sauce

1 clove garlic, minced

1 tsp. sugar

1 TB. cornstarch

½ tsp. baking soda

2 TB. water

For the stir-fry:

½ lb. flank, round, or sirloin steak

1 lb. asparagus spears or 1 pt. chopped asparagus stalks

4 TB. peanut oil

1 large slice ginger

½ TB. dry sherry

¼ tsp. baking soda

½ tsp. salt

2 TB. water

Serves 4	
Prep time: 45 minutes	
Cook time: 10 minutes	

1. Prepare marinade by combining soy sauce, garlic, sugar, cornstarch, baking soda, and water. Slice meat thinly across the grain. Add to marinade. Let stand for 30 minutes.

2. Slice asparagus into 2-inch pieces.

3. Heat the wok and add 2 tablespoons oil. When hot, add asparagus, ginger, sherry, baking soda, and salt. Stir quickly. Add water. Reduce the heat to medium. Cover the wok and steam for 2 minutes. Turn off the heat, remove the food to a bowl. Cover it to keep it warm.

4. Place 2 tablespoons oil in the wok. When hot, add meat. Spread meat evenly in the wok and do not stir until meat has slightly browned (about 2 minutes). Turn meat and allow other side to brown (1 minute). Reduce the heat and add asparagus. Stir to mix well. Serve with rice.

Chapter 6

Freezing Meat, Poultry, Seafood, and Game

In This Chapter

- Getting the most for your food dollar
- Choosing the right cuts of meat
- Chicken little, chicken big
- Fresh fish frozen fast

These are the items that make the biggest dent in your food budget. Buying in bulk can be an excellent cost-cutting decision, and knowing how to properly wrap and store these foods will ensure that your purchases are fresh and flavorful when you're ready to use them.

Checking Out the Sources

Farmers grow fruits and vegetables, and ranchers grow meat. If you want the best beef, pork, or lamb, go straight to the place these products are grown and buy direct. You don't even have to visit them in person since many ranches have a virtual presence on the web. You contract with the grower and make arrangements with the butcher, where you pick up the cut and wrapped meat. Check to see if the supplier is a member of the Better Business Bureau and ask for references from customers who have patronized the supplier.

Another method is to contact your local Cooperative Extension Office (the number is in your phone book) for information on 4-H and Future Farmers of America (FFA) county fair livestock auctions. You can support the youngsters who participate in 4-H and FFA by buying an animal they've raised for sale. Again, you make arrangements with the butcher (you'll be provided a list of names in your area), and you'll pick up the cut and wrapped meat there.

Preserving Pointers

Allow 1 cubic foot of freezer space for each 35 to 40 pounds of cut and wrapped meat. Not all packages will be uniformly sized, and odd-shaped packages may require slightly more space.

Finally, you can contact your local meat locker. It often has special purchase plans for families interested in buying a quarter, half, or whole animal.

Meat is probably the most expensive item in your household budget. The preceding options help you eliminate the costs incurred with the middle man. You can also take advantage of buying in bulk at warehouse clubs and stocking up on specials at your local grocers.

Making the Decision

You can buy beef, pork, and lamb as a whole, half (side), or quarter. You can also purchase special cuts (which are more expensive) either wholesale or retail. You may find it economical to go in with someone else, and each of you gets a side. If a quarter is sufficient for your family's needs, then you'll want to have a few people involved in the purchase.

The main factor is buying cuts of meat your family enjoys. It doesn't make sense to buy a whole beef, hog, or lamb if your family only likes rump roast, leg of lamb, or spare ribs. However, if your tastes are more varied and you're open to creating new recipes, then buying the whole, side, or quarter may be the logical and economical choice.

Safety Check

When you buy a beef or part of a beef, you'll be getting ground beef made from that one animal, whereas a package of ground beef purchased at the store may have been made from many animals. The meat is done up in big lots. That raises the possibility of contamination as well as of lesser-quality meat in that package.

For example, when considering a beef, if you use a good amount of ground beef, a front quarter may be the best choice. If you prefer roasts and steaks, then the back quarter provides the better cuts.

It's a Wrap!

If your meat comes to you via the butcher or meat locker, it will already be wrapped for you. If you buy in bulk at the grocery store or super foods warehouse, you'll need to do your own wrapping. It's the same basic procedure as wrapping a gift. Double-wrapping helps prevent freezer burn. This means first wrapping in moisture/vapor-resistant wrap (usually plastic) and then overwrapping with freezer wrap or aluminum foil.

First place the cut of meat in the center of the moisture/vapor-resistant wrap. Wrap the meat securely, pressing out any air.

If you're wrapping chops, put a piece of freezer wrap between them so they'll separate more easily when you want to defrost them. If there's a sharp bone in the cut, place a wadded piece of wrap around it so it doesn't puncture the freezer paper when you wrap the entire cut.

At this point, you're ready for the overwrap. The following illustrations show the "diaper wrap" as done by a butcher. When the butcher processes and wraps your beef, pork, or lamb, the final step is to stamp the cut of meat, the date processed, and then affix a closure tape that says "Not for Sale." This ensures that your meat doesn't get mixed in with the commercial cuts that are offered for sale to the public.

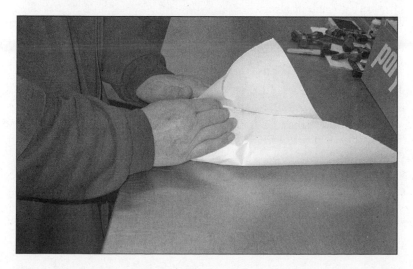

Beginning the diaper wrap.

Wrapped meat ready for securing with tape.

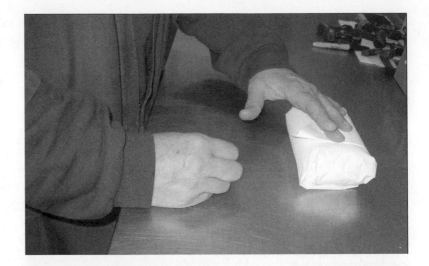

Meat as you will see it when you pick it up at the butcher shop.

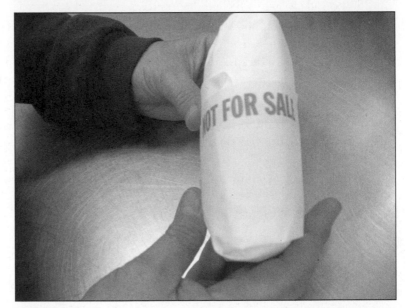

The other method is the familiar gift-wrapping method. Position the meat in the center of the foil or freezer paper. Next, bring the two ends of the wrap together over the center of the meat. Fold them together and then fold again, this time bringing them down to the meat and making a tight fit. Secure this with a piece of freezer tape.

Then fold each other edge by pressing the top layer of wrap toward the bottom and creasing each edge, making a triangle. Bring each folded edge up and secure it with freezer tape. Label, date, and freeze.

About Beef

On average, a beef carcass weighs around 600 pounds. That means a side (the hanging weight, or the weight of the beef right after slaughter) is going to be in the vicinity of 300 pounds. It's the carcass after the head, hide, and entrails have been removed. If you buy a whole, half, or quarter beef, you'll be paying hanging weight price. Also, you'll be charged for cutting and wrapping. You may also pay a kill fee.

After hanging, the meat is cut, trimmed, and wrapped. You can expect around 25 percent weight loss during this process. That means you'll wind up with about 350 pounds from a whole and about 225 pounds from a side. You'll get about one third of this meat in steaks, one third in ground beef and stew meat, and one third in roasts.

Coming to Terms

There's some basic terminology that's helpful to know:

- *Beef* refers to meat from fully grown cattle about 2 years old.

- *Calf* and *baby beef* refer to young cattle weighing around 700 pounds. They have been raised on milk and on grass.

- *Veal* refers to meat from a calf weighing about 150 pounds that has been mostly milk fed.

A cow is a female who's given birth, a heifer is a cow in training, a steer is a castrated male, and a bull is the daddy. Since most purchases involve either a steer or a heifer, it's referred to as beef for simplicity's sake.

All cattle are grazed on grass initially. Some continue on grass until slaughter, while others are transported to feedlots where they are finished on grain. This involves feeding them grain, usually free choice, in concentrated rations. The goal is to get them to market weight as quickly as possible.

Consumer Concerns

One important consideration for many people is whether or not the beef they are purchasing has been exposed to hormones, antibiotics, or additives. The Food and Drug Administration (FDA) is the government agency that regulates meat and inspects all cattle.

Antibiotics are used to prevent or treat disease in cattle. However, there is a specific withdrawal time required before the animals can be legally slaughtered. The Food Safety and Inspection Service (FSIS), which is the public health agency of the FDA, conducts random tests to sample tissues from cattle at slaughter to ensure the law is complied with.

Hormones are permitted to be used in cattle to promote efficient growth. Estradiol, progesterone, testosterone, zeranol, and trenbolone acetate may be implanted in the animal's ear. These are time released over a period of 90 to 120 days.

Melengesterol acetate, used to prevent cows from coming into heat or to improve weight gain and efficient use of feed, is permitted to be used as a feed additive. For additional information, consult the FDA website at www.fda.gov.

Making the Grade

While USDA inspection of all meat is mandatory under the law, grading of the meat is voluntary. A meat plant must pay a fee to have its meat graded. USDA grades of beef are prime, choice, and select. Other grades include standard, commercial, utility, cutter, and canner—cuts used primarily in ground or processed meat products.

USDA prime is the most tender and flavorful cut with the most *marbling*. Choice or select are the most commonly found grades of beef sold in stores.

def•i•ni•tion

> **Marbling** is the term given to the white flecks of fat in the muscle. Higher grades have more marbling, which increases the tenderness and flavor of the meat.

Cuts

Beef has four primal cuts: chuck, loin, rib, and round. When you buy a package of beef at the store, you'll generally see two terms. The first refers to the cut and the second to the product—for example, "chuck roast" or "loin chops." Chuck and round are less tender cuts; loin and rib are more tender.

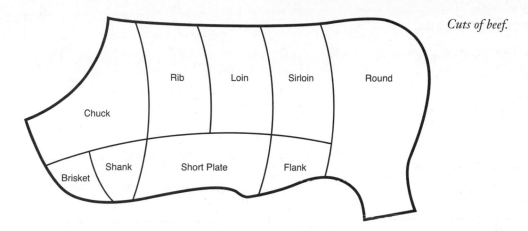

Cuts of beef.

You may be used to hearing a cut of meat called by a certain name. This is regional, and if you went to a different location, that same cut might be called something quite different. For example, if you went looking for a boneless top loin steak, you might be stumped unless you realized that it could also be called a strip steak.

Chuck produces the following:

- Chuck eye roast
- Boneless top blade steak
- Arm roast
- Boneless chuck roast
- Cross rib roast
- Blade roast
- Under blade roast
- 7-bone roast (so named because it's shaped like the number 7)
- Short ribs
- Flanken-style ribs

Loin produces the following:

- Boneless top loin steak
- Top loin steak
- T-bone steak

- Tenderloin roast
- Porterhouse steak
- Tenderloin steak
- Sirloin steak (pin, flat, round, wedge, boneless)
- Top sirloin steak

Rib produces the following:

- Rib roast
- Rib eye roast
- Rib steak
- Rib eye steak
- Back ribs
- Skirt steak

Round produces the following:

- Round steak
- Top round roast
- Top round steak
- Boneless rump roast
- Bottom round roast
- Tip roast
- Eye of round roast
- Tip steak

The brisket and shank are cuts from the lower chest below the shoulder and the neck, short plate is located below the primal rib, and flank is cut from the belly.

In addition, there are the liver, kidneys, heart, and tongue.

The Skinny on Beef

Beef is a marbled meat, which means it contains fat. The leaner the beef, the less fat it has, of course, but fat is what adds flavor and tenderness. The amount of fat in ground beef is based on what cut of meat was ground up. For example, ground chuck or ground round will generally have a lower fat content than ground scraps of various other cuts.

The difference between ground beef and hamburger is simple: ground beef doesn't contain added beef fat; hamburger does. The cuts are generally not trimmed of excess fat before grinding, and the USDA has established a maximum amount of fat that may be added. Hamburger or ground beef can have *up to* 30 percent fat by weight. That means it's 70 percent meat.

Both hamburger and ground beef can have seasonings added but not water, phosphates, extenders, or binders. Both must be labeled according to federal standards and carry a USDA-inspected label. Even though most ground beef is made and packaged at the local grocery store, it still must comply with federal labeling laws on fat content.

Safety Check

Because ground beef has more surface area exposed to air than solid cuts of beef, there is greater opportunity for bacterial contamination. This is why you should never eat raw or partially cooked ground beef and never use it to make jerky.

What About Color?

Freshly cut meat is a purplish color. That bright red color you see on prepackaged meats comes about when oxygen reacts with pigments on the surface of cut meat. Underneath the surface, the meat is generally a gray-brown color. If the meat in the package is more gray or brown than red, spoilage could be underway. Dispose of the package.

Pork

An average hog at butchering time weighs about 250 pounds. The hanging carcass will weigh about 180 pounds. From that you can expect to get about 145 pounds of meat for the freezer. Pork can give you fresh cuts in addition to smoked cuts. The smoked cuts will give you hams, ham hocks, and bacon. Bacon comes from the side of the hog.

Many people have the hind quarters smoked for hams and leave the forequarters for roasts. A whole ham is rather large and, unless you have an army to feed, probably will do best if you have it cut in half. From this you can have ham, ham slices, and ham cubes (for stir-fry, kabobs, or casseroles and soups).

Cuts of pork.

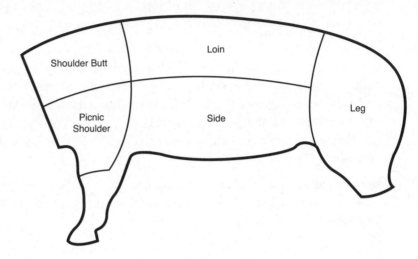

Shoulder produces the following:

◆ Shoulder butt, roast, steak

◆ Blade steak

◆ Boneless blade Boston roast

◆ Smoked arm picnic, picnic shoulder

◆ Smoked hock

◆ Ground pork for sausage

Loin produces:

◆ Boneless whole loin

◆ Loin roast

◆ Sirloin roast

◆ Tenderloin

◆ Chops

◆ Country style ribs

If you're partial to roasts and chops, consider purchasing a whole bone-in or boneless loin cut. The loin is located between the leg and the shoulder and weighs around 15 to 18 pounds. The center loin gives you center-cut chops and roasts and is usually a good value. You'll need to tell the butcher how many chops you want in each package and how thick you like them—generally about an inch thick works well so that the chops don't dry out when you're cooking them. This can happen if they're either too thin or they need to be cooked to death to be safe because they're too thick.

Consumer Concerns

All pork sold in stores has been either USDA inspected or inspected by state agencies with standards equal to that of the federal government.

Antibiotics may be given to hogs to treat or prevent disease. A withdrawal period is required before slaughter to ensure that the drugs are no longer present in the animal's system. The FSIS conducts random samples at slaughterhouses to ensure the law is complied with.

No hormones are permitted in the raising of hogs.

Making the Grade

The grading process is simple for hogs: they're either acceptable or utility. Acceptable quality is the only grade sold in retail stores.

Lamb

Lamb refers to a sheep that is less than 1 year old. Mutton refers to an animal older than 1 year. A lamb at slaughter weighs about 125 pounds and yields about 60 to 75 pounds of meat. Lamb doesn't hog the freezer. You'll need about 2.5 cubic feet of freezer space per lamb.

Lambs aren't very difficult animals as far as cuts of meat are concerned. Shoulder, leg, shank, rack, and loin are referred to as the primal cuts. Unlike pork, where you can have bone-in or boneless hams, lamb legs keep the bone. This gives added flavor.

Cuts of lamb.

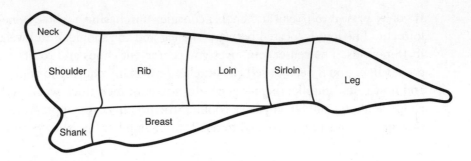

Shoulder produces the following:

◆ Shoulder roast (bone-in or boneless)

◆ Shoulder steaks and chops

◆ Shoulder arm chop

◆ Ground lamb or cubes

◆ Shoulder blade chops (bone-in and boneless)

Leg produces the following:

◆ Leg roast or steaks

◆ Cubes or strips

◆ Ground

The neck is the cut above the shoulder.

The rib is the cut directly behind the shoulder and next to the loin. It produces rib roast and rib chops.

The breast is the cut below the rib and loin.

def•i•ni•tion

The **fell** is a thin, paperlike cover on the outer layers of fat on roasts and legs. It seals in the juices and helps these cuts keep their shape during cooking.

The loin is the cut between the rib and the leg and produces chops and roast. The sirloin is the cut directly behind the loin.

Shank is the cut below the shoulder and below the leg.

When packaging lamb for the freezer, trim the excess fat from chops and other smaller cuts, but don't remove the *fell* from roasts or legs.

Consumer Concerns

All lamb is USDA inspected.

Antibiotics may be given to prevent or treat disease in lambs. A withholding period is required before the animals can be slaughtered. This is to permit the antibiotics to pass through the animal's system. The FSIS conducts random samples at slaughter to ensure compliance with the law.

The synthetic hormone zeronal is permitted to be used as an implant to promote efficient growth in feedlot lambs. The hormone is time released over a 30-day period. A withholding period of 40 days is required by law before the animals can be slaughtered. This withholding period allows the hormone to pass out of the animal's system.

Making the Grade

There are five grades of lamb: prime, choice, good, utility, and cull. Prime and choice are the grades you will usually find at the meat counter. Prime has more marbling than choice, but both grades give good-quality meat.

Game Meat

The essentials of preparing game meat for the freezer involve strict cleanliness and cold temperatures. Game meat must be cooled to a temperature below 40°F (preferably 32°F to 36°F) within 24 hours after harvesting to prevent souring or spoiling. For more information, HGIC 3516, "Safe Handling of Wild Game Meats," can be downloaded from http://hgic.clemson.edu/factsheets/hgic3516.htm.

Poultry

We generally think of chicken or turkey when the word "poultry" comes to mind; however, the term is a bit broader than that and includes domestic duck and goose as well.

Coming to Terms

The local market may have a super sale on poultry (chicken usually), and you want to stock up while the price is right. Poultry is usually a good buy at food warehouse outlets as well. However, is the bird fresh or frozen? It could be tough to tell.

Safety Check _____

Never stuff a bird before freezing it. It takes too long for the internal temperature of the bird to reach a safe level, and in the meantime, the stuffing becomes a bacterial breeding ground and could make you extremely ill.

The USDA allows any poultry that has never been below 26°F to be labeled "fresh." It could be worth your while to ponder that for a moment in light of the fact that freezing occurs at 32°F. Frozen or previously frozen refers to poultry that has been held at 0°F. If the poultry has been stored at temperatures between 0°F and 25°F, the label doesn't have to tell you. You can ask the butcher or the person behind the counter, but he or she probably won't know. So the truth is that you won't know if your bird was killed yesterday or two weeks ago.

Consumer Concerns

Antibiotics may be used to prevent disease. They also may be used to increase the poultry's efficient use of feed. This means the grower wants the most return in poundage of bird per pound of grain consumed.

Chickens that have been given antibiotics must be held from slaughter until the antibiotics have passed out of their system. FSIS conducts random samples of poultry at slaughter to ensure compliance.

No hormones are permitted to be used in the raising of poultry.

Bacterial Concerns

Bacteria associated with poultry can include *Salmonella enteritidis*, *Staphyloccus aureus*, *Campylobacter jejuni*, and *Listeria monocytogenes*. To deal with these bacteria, the FSIS has approved use of an antimicrobial agent called trisodium phosphate (TSP). It's either sprayed in a dilute solution on chickens or is used as a dip at slaughter to reduce levels of bacteria that may be present. TSP falls into the category of substances "generally recognized as safe" by the FSIS.

Irradiation

Irradiation exposes foods to radiation or radiant energy in order to control bacteria that may be present. This practice was approved for poultry by the USDA in 1992. Irradiated chicken sold in stores must carry the international symbol for radiation and must bear the statement "treated with irradiation" or "treated by irradiation."

To learn more about how irradiation works, consult www.extension.iastate.edu/foodsafety/irradiation/.

You can also help protect your family's health by observing strict cleanliness when preparing poultry. Keep poultry juices from coming in contact with other foods. Avoid cross-contamination by cleaning and sanitizing your cutting board and utensils after working with poultry and wash your hands frequently. See Chapter 2 for more information.

Freezing Poultry

You can freeze chicken in the grocery store bag, but it's better to clean the bird and repackage it. You'll see that the bag contains an absorbent diaper that's been placed in the vicinity of the bird's posterior. This is to sop up the moisture that develops during the chilling process after slaughter. There may be a slight pink tinge to this liquid, but it's mostly water. Birds that aren't bled thoroughly after slaughter are condemned and do not continue on the path to your grocery store.

Remove the bird from the bag and dispose of the paper diaper. Clean and rinse out the cavity to remove all the internal organs. Next round up a plastic bag big enough to accommodate the bird—be sure there aren't any holes in it—and put the bird inside. You're going to force out nearly all the air.

Dip the bag into a dishpan filled with enough water to nearly cover the bird, but don't let the water seep into the bag. Rest the bird on the bottom of the dishpan and gently press the air out of the bag, starting from the bottom and working up. Then secure the top with a twisty tie. After this, pack the bird in a moisture/vapor-resistant freezer bag and label, date, and freeze. Package the heart, gizzard, and liver separately.

It's easy to turn a whole chicken into parts. It's generally a lot cheaper than buying select parts, and cutting and/or boning a chicken takes only a few minutes. All you need is a sharp knife and a little patience. YouTube has an excellent video on the process; you can find it at www.youtube.com/watch?v=sy6P3E84Dqs.

Game Birds

Game birds, such as quail, duck, dove, or pheasant, should be field dressed and gutted as quickly as possible. They should then be cleaned thoroughly and cooled immediately. Removing excess fat from wild duck and goose helps prevent the bird from turning rancid. They're frozen in the same manner as poultry. For additional information on processing game birds, consult HGIC 3515, "Safe Handling of Game Birds," which can be downloaded from http://hgic.clemson.edu/factsheets/HGIC3515.htm.

Freezing Seafood

Seafood is always best served fresh, but proper freezing techniques can give you an excellent product. For best results, freeze seafood as soon as possible after the catch. Fish is highly perishable.

Fish

The initial procedures are the same, regardless of how you'll eventually freeze the fish. First wash it in cool water. Then scale it and remove the entrails, gills, head, and fins. After that you can freeze the fish whole or cut it into steaks (cutting across the body) or fillets (making lengthwise slices). Usually small fish are frozen whole.

Safety Check

Take a hint from Ben Franklin: "Fish and visitors smell in three days." Process your seafood ASAP!

You can then wrap the fish in moisture/vapor-resistant freezer wrap and place it in a labeled and dated freezer bag, or you can choose to first glaze the fish. This helps prevent drying out and flavor loss. To glaze it, simply place the fish on a cookie sheet and put the sheet in the freezer. When the fish is solidly frozen, remove it from the freezer and dip the fish into cold water for about 20 seconds. The water will freeze; this is called an ice glaze. Return the fish to the freezer to ensure the water has frozen. Then you can wrap the fish for freezing as previously described.

See Appendix E for recommended freezer storage times for different varieties of fish.

Freezing Smoked Fish

Wrap the fish for freezing as soon as they come out of the smoker. You can apply a thin coat of olive oil to help retard oxidation and moisture loss during freezing. Wrap as previously discussed.

Freezing Roe

Roe is the term for fish eggs. Wash the roe in cool, running water. Pack it in freezer containers, leaving ¼ inch of headspace. Label, date, and freeze.

Scaling

Fish tend to be slippery, so you don't want to use a sharp knife for scaling. If the fish slips out of your grasp, you could end up with a nasty cut. A regular dinner knife or even a teaspoon works fine. Grasp the fish by the tail and, with the knife blade or edge of the spoon, scrape down the fish. You may find this easier to do under cool, running water.

Gutting

To gut the fish, make a knife cut along the length of the fish's belly. Then spread the sides apart, scoop out the innards, and rinse the cavity thoroughly.

Removing Head, Backbone, and Fins

Off with their heads! This is the easy part. Just slice through above the collarbone. You can give the backbone a sharp smack on the counter or cutting board; that will break it so it will be easier to ease out.

You may be accustomed to clipping off the fins with your kitchen shears, but this leaves some bones still stuck to the fish where the fin attached. It's better to make a small incision alongside each fin and lift it out.

Crab

Crab purchased from the store has already been cleaned. That is to say, it's been scrubbed to remove sea debris. If you've harvested your own crab, you'll find it much easier to scrub it after you've killed it. That brings us to the pressing issue of how to humanely kill a crab.

Tossing the crab into a pot of boiling water has been a traditional method of both killing and cooking the crab, but it's not all that humane. If you've used this procedure, you may have noticed that occasionally one or more of the legs will detach from the body. That's caused by the crab going into shock. If the water isn't at a rolling boil, it's neither a quick nor a pleasant death.

So what do you do if you're concerned about this? You'll need a screwdriver. Really. Using tongs, flip the crab over onto its back. You'll notice a triangular flap near the base of its shell. Lift the flap and, with a sharp motion, jam the screwdriver all the way in and then shove it toward the head. Immediately, fluid will be released, and the crab will be dead.

You can then scrub it before putting it in the hot water.

It may help to keep in mind that a crab doesn't have an evolved nervous system, just a mess of ganglia, so it doesn't experience pain the way a human does. Still, it doesn't hurt to be humane.

Boil the crab for 10 minutes, remove it from the water, and allow it to cool. You don't need to pick it before freezing. When cooled, pull off the legs and the back shell. Then remove gills and entrails. Wrap the prepared crab securely in moisture/vapor-resistant freezer wrap and then put it into a labeled and dated freezer bag. Be sure to press out as much air as you can. Crab has a relatively short freezer life, about 3 months.

Lobster

Freezing lobster uncooked is the best choice, and it's also the best way to kill the lobster humanely. Put the lobster in a bowl or pan that's freezer friendly and place it in the freezer. After about 20 to 30 minutes, remove the lobster, which by now is very, very cold and not feeling much of anything. Then insert a sharp knife into the abdomen just behind the smallest set of legs and push down hard. Slice from this point up through the head and sever the body in half. Then rinse the lobster, wrap it in moisture/vapor-resistant freezer wrap, place it in a freezer bag, label, date, and freeze. Freezer life is about 4 to 6 months.

> **Preserving Pointers**
>
> Lobsters are on par with crab. Their nervous system is rudimentary, and they're also cold blooded. That's why popping them into the freezer is a more humane way of dispatching them.

Scallops

Scallops are frozen after being shucked. To shuck a scallop, hold the scallop in the palm of your hand and then insert a thin, strong knife into the slit close to the hinge. Twist. Don't force it open or you'll damage the muscle. Open the shell carefully and cut the muscle free from the top shell. Cut the muscle free from the bottom shell and remove the white scallop meat. Rinse in cool, running water to remove all the sand, pieces of shell, and viscera.

You can place the scallops on a cookie sheet and freeze them. When the scallops are frozen, remove them with a spatula, place them in moisture/vapor-resistant freezer bags, label, date, and freeze. Freezer life is about 4 to 6 months.

Shrimp

You can freeze shrimp raw or cooked and also in the shell or shelled. They'll keep longer in the freezer if you remove the heads but keep the shells on.

Shrimp you buy at the store may be shelled and deveined or not. If not, you'll need your kitchen shears. Hold the shrimp in one hand so that the swimmerettes are on the bottom. Insert the shears into the sand vein and cut straight upward so that the shell comes off. The bluish vein will peel right off. Then rinse the shrimp in cool, running water. You can freeze shrimp by the cookie sheet method. Then package them in labeled and dated moisture/vapor-resistant freezer bags or containers and freeze. Freezer life is about 4 to 6 months.

Clams and Mussels

You can freeze these shellfish in their shells, but you may be disappointed with the result. There's air inside those shells, and your shellfish can dry out.

Clams and mussels should be shucked before freezing. Wash them in cool, running water. Then holding the shell in the palm of your hand, insert a thin, sturdy knife into the slit. Twist. Then remove the meat. Clean out the contents of the stomach. Rinse the meat. Place the clams or mussels on a cookie sheet and place them in the freezer until they've frozen solid. Then remove them from the freezer and dip them in cold water. Return them to the freezer until they are firmly frozen. Then repackage them in moisture/vapor-resistant freezer bags. Label, date, and freeze. Freezer life is about 4 to 6 months. Freezer life for clams in the shell is only about 1 month.

Oysters

The same principle that applies to clams and mussels applies to oysters. If you freeze them in the shell (and you can), prepare to be disappointed with the result. Air trapped in the shell can cause the oysters to dry out. In any case, frozen oysters lack the mystery and sensuous nature of their raw counterparts. You'll probably want to use them in dishes where they're just one of several ingredients, as they tend to be a bit tough.

It's best to shuck them. First, be sure you're dealing with live oysters. If the oyster is live, the shell will be closed, or it will close immediately when you handle it. Discard dead oysters. Then rinse the live oysters in cool, running water. You'll need your oyster knife because these shells are tough nuts to crack. You'll also need a pan to work over since you definitely want to capture the liquor that's inside the shell.

Insert the oyster knife into the dip by the hinge. Twist. This severs the hinge. You may need some help getting the oyster knife into the shell. A wooden mallet works well to help you make the first incision.

Then slide the knife around the oyster until you have cut the abductor muscle that controls the shell movement. Take off the upper half of the shell and cut the muscle away from the bottom half of the shell. Remove any pieces of shell from the oyster.

Place the shucked oysters and liquor in a freezer container, leaving ½ inch of headroom. Label, date, and freeze. You can also freeze the oysters in ice cube trays. Add water to cover them and then pop them in the freezer. When they've frozen, repackage them in moisture/vapor-resistant freezer bags. Label, date, and freeze. Freezer life is about 4 to 6 months.

Recipes

Meat, poultry, and seafood provide the structure around which meals are built. With a freezer full of choices, the possibilities are endless.

Fillet of Sole Veronique

This is an elegant fish dish that does well accompanied by roasted red potatoes and a hearty cole slaw.

Serves 6
Prep time: 10 to 15 minutes
Cook time: 15 to 20 minutes

6 fillets of sole

½ cup dry white wine

Salt and pepper to taste

2 TB. butter

2 TB. flour

1 cup milk

1 cup white grapes, sliced

1. Preheat the oven to 350°F. Arrange fillets in a single layer in a buttered, ovenproof casserole dish suitable for serving. Pour wine over fish and sprinkle with salt and pepper to taste. Cover with foil and bake for 15 minutes.

2. Make a roux by melting butter in a medium-size saucepan. Add flour and whisk until roux begins to turn a golden brown. Then add milk and whisk over medium heat until sauce becomes thick.

3. Remove fish from the oven. Pour off juice from fish and add to cream sauce. Mix well. Add ½ cup sliced grapes to sauce and pour mixture over fish in ovenproof dish.

4. Turn the oven to broil and place casserole under the broiler just until surface is browned. Remove from the oven and arrange remaining grapes around the fish before serving.

Curried Chicken

Curry is flavorful, hearty, and an excellent way to use up leftover chicken or other poultry. You can also use tuna. This dish is excellent with rice and chutney.

1 apple, pared and diced

1 cup cooked carrots, diced

1 to 2 small onions, chopped

1 clove garlic, minced

1 stalk celery, diced

¼ cup butter or olive oil

2 TB. flour

1 tsp. salt

1 tsp. curry powder

½ tsp. dry mustard

1½ cup chicken broth or stock

1 bay leaf

½ cup milk

3 cups cooked, chopped chicken

Serves 4
Prep time: 15 to 20 minutes
Cook time: 10 minutes

1. Sauté apple, carrots, onions, garlic, and celery in butter or olive oil until onions have become transparent (about 5 minutes).

2. Add flour, salt, curry powder, dry mustard, broth or stock, and bay leaf. Heat to boiling. Add milk and chicken and stir well.

Chapter 7

Freezing Dairy Products, Eggs, and Bakery Products

In This Chapter

- ◆ Texture matters
- ◆ Daily bread and dealing with crumbs
- ◆ Baking in big lots
- ◆ American pie

Here's where you can really take advantage of bulk sales, supermarket specials, and day-old bakery markdowns. The secret to keeping these items fresh is proper packaging and storage. If you're freezing your own baked desserts, doubling or tripling your batches will make good use of your freezer space.

Dairy Products

Freezing will change the consistency or texture of many dairy products, and these items also have a shorter freezer life. Previously frozen dairy products generally are fine in cooking but may not be satisfactory for table use.

Freezing eggs and dairy in amounts required for specific recipes will give you a head start on holiday baking, and you won't have to run out to the store for last-minute supplies.

Butter

Whenever you see butter on sale, grab as much as you can and freeze it. You don't need any special packaging. Just transfer the waxed boxes to your freezer, being careful to spread them around until they're thoroughly frozen. Then stack them up.

If you buy solid 1-pound blocks as opposed to quarters, you can cut them into usable portions first. Wrap with moisture/vapor-resistant plastic wrap and then place in a plastic freezer bag.

Unsalted butter has a shorter freezer life than salted butter, and margarine and whipped spreads don't freeze well because they tend to break down. Some brands work better than others, so if you prefer margarine to butter, you'll need to experiment.

Milk, Cream, and Homemade Ice Cream

Quarts or half-gallons of milk are the best sizes for freezing, and you can freeze them in their original containers. Gallons take too long to freeze and too long to thaw. You will need to pour out about 1½ inches of milk from the container to allow adequate headroom. Then close the container securely before placing it in the freezer. Pasteurized and homogenized milk may separate out their water content during freezing. When the milk has thawed, use a whisk to thoroughly remix it. You may be disappointed in the texture for drinking, although it certainly won't hurt you.

Preserving Pointers

Once you've opened a container of commercially produced ice cream, air enters the container and can cause that rubbery, dried-out surface and also ice crystals to form. Plastic wrap smoothed down over the surface of the ice cream can help prevent this from happening.

Heavy cream with 40 percent or more butterfat freezes well, although if you're planning on using it for whipping, you may be disappointed in the volume. Plan to use it in cooking or in coffee. To freeze, heat to 170°F for 10 minutes. Add ⅓ cup sugar to each quart, pour into rigid freezer containers, and leave 1 inch of headspace. Seal, label, date, and freeze.

One way to solve the decreased volume problem is to sweeten and whip the cream first. Then haul out your cookie sheet and drop dollops of the whipped cream on it, being sure to keep some space between each dollop. Place it in the freezer and, when frozen, remove the dollops and place them in a labeled and dated plastic freezer bag.

Changes in texture are the biggest problems when you freeze sour cream, buttermilk, or yogurt. They may not be palatable for eating because they get grainy and can separate. They are fine for cooking.

Homemade ice cream doesn't freeze well. It gets grainy. Commercially processed ice cream has milk solids and gelatin included in the ingredients, and these are responsible for its smooth texture.

Cheeses

Hard and semihard cheeses tend to crumble when thawed, and this can make slicing frustrating. If you're going to use them in cooking (macaroni and cheese, for example), then this isn't a problem.

Creamed cottage cheese can separate after thawing and get mushy.

Ricotta, processed cheeses, cheese sauce, cream cheese (again, better when used in cooking), and cheese dips freeze well.

Eggs

Eggs keep very well for up to a month in the refrigerator, but if you want to freeze some with specific recipes in mind, you can prepare whole eggs, egg whites, and egg yolks. You can't freeze eggs in the shell because expansion while freezing will rupture the shell. The following directions are based on using a dozen eggs.

◆ **Whole eggs**—Mix whites and yolks thoroughly with a fork, being careful not to whip air into the mixture. If you will use them in desserts, add 1 tablespoon of sugar to the mix. If you will use them in cooking, add ½ teaspoon salt to the mix. This keeps them from getting grainy or gummy. Strain the mixture through a colander, food mill, or sieve to get good uniformity of texture. Pour into rigid freezer containers, leave ½ inch of headspace, seal, label, date, and freeze.

Safety Check

Thaw all dairy products and eggs in the refrigerator to prevent bacterial growth and plan on using them within a few days.

♦ **Yolks**—Separate eggs and stir gently. It's best to have certain recipes in mind as you freeze these. If you'll be working with something sweet, add 2 tablespoons of sugar. If the yolks are destined for a recipe that's less in the dessert realm and more in the main course arena, add 1 teaspoon of salt. Strain and pour into a rigid freezer container, allowing ½ inch headspace. Seal, label, date, and freeze.

♦ **Whites**—Separate eggs and stir gently. Strain and pour them into a rigid freezer container, allowing ½ inch headspace. Seal, label, date, and freeze. Two tablespoons of egg white mixture equals one egg white.

Preserving Pointers _____

Three tablespoons of the beaten egg yolks and whites is the equivalent of one egg. Pour 3 tablespoons of the mixture into each cell of an ice cube tray and place it in the freezer. When frozen, transfer cubes to a plastic freezer bag and seal, label, date, and return them to the freezer. When your recipe calls for an egg, thaw the cube and you're ready to go!

Breadcrumbs

Breadcrumbs come in handy for all kinds of dishes, from toppings to breading mixtures, and you can make your own breadcrumbs for a fraction of the store price. This is an excellent, thrifty use for end slices or for bread that's gone too stale for regular use. There are a couple of ways to go about making breadcrumbs; one is messy and the other isn't.

The messier method involves dumping chunks of stale bread into your food processor or blender, whirring away, and then pouring the crumbs into gallon freezer bags. There are a couple of problems with this method:

♦ You may find that the bread on the bottom has pulverized into fine dust, while the chunks still floating on top are way too big to be called crumbs.

♦ You've got to clean the processor or blender container, which means soap and water and drying.

♦ Some crumbs may end up on the kitchen counter or on the floor, and that means more cleaning.

The less messy and more convenient way consists of just one step and involves putting chunks of stale bread into the gallon freezer bag. Don't overfill it; you want plenty of room inside. Close the freezer bag, place it on a bread board or other hard surface, get out your rolling pin, and roll away.

You can move the contents around easily to be sure you're getting to all the bread chunks. When you're satisfied with the result, press out as much air as you can, seal the bag, and put the freezer bag, labeled and dated, in the freezer. No mess and nothing to clean up.

> **Safety Check**
>
> You can store stale bread in a covered bowl until you're ready to get to it, but always check to be sure none of the slices are moldy. If you see any signs of mold, discard that piece of bread.

Quick Breads

Quick breads encompass an entire family of baked foods that includes, in addition to loaves: scones and biscuits, muffins, waffles, popovers, cornbread, spoon bread, and donuts. Quick breads differ from regular breads in that they don't use yeast to make them rise—a process that takes some time. Instead, they use either baking powder or baking soda to achieve loft while they're baking in the oven. In fact, they begin to rise as soon as the baking soda or powder meets the liquid in the recipe. They rise again while they're baking, and this is why you'll see the "double-acting" note on the baking powder label.

> **Preserving Pointers**
>
> If you've run out of baking powder, you can make your own! Mix together 2 teaspoons cream of tartar and 1 teaspoon baking soda. If you decide that you want to make a big batch, add 1 teaspoon cornstarch to the mix before you store it in a covered container in your pantry or cupboard.

Quick breads are also quick to assemble, and that's an excellent reason to make double or triple batches when you're in the mood to bake. You can eat one batch and freeze the others for future use.

Preparing for the Freezer

When your quick breads have thoroughly cooled, wrap them securely in plastic wrap and then wrap them again in aluminum foil. This double wrapping keeps them fresh. You can then put them in labeled freezer bags, if you're so inclined, but the double wrap should be sufficient.

If you wrap them in foil first, you'll find that little pieces of the foil may stick to the quick breads, and picking them out is a chore. You'll probably only do it that way once!

Using Quick Breads

Everything about quick breads is quick, and so is their storage life. For best quality, you'll want to keep them in the freezer from 2 to 4 months. Muffins max out at about 3 months. After that they'll still be safe to eat, but you may be disappointed in their texture and flavor.

Preserving Pointers

You can use all kinds of left-over baked goods to make crumbs for use in toppings. Don't limit those crumbs to just stale breads.

Remove them from the freezer and allow them to thaw wrapped at room temperature. If you slice quick breads before they're entirely thawed, you'll reduce crumbling.

For biscuits or muffins, preheat the oven to 350°F and warm biscuits and muffins for 15 to 20 minutes. If you want to use the microwave, it takes about 10 to 15 seconds per biscuit or muffin (depending on size).

Pie Crusts and Pastries

Pie crusts are generally made with flour, salt, fat, and water, although you'll find a wide selection of different possibilities as you rummage through cookbooks. The secret to a good pie crust is gentle, quick handling and ice water. General procedures for making pie crusts are similar, and you'll find a recipe for a great pie crust at the end of this chapter.

Baked pie crusts and pastries yield better results when frozen than unbaked ones. First of all, they'll freeze more quickly than the raw dough because they're less dense, and the quicker you can freeze something the better the quality will be. They also keep twice as long in the freezer as their unbaked counterparts.

You can freeze pie crust dough, but it will need to be thawed (but still chilled) before you can roll it out. Overhandling the dough will make the crust tough. Freeze dough in portions that will make either an 8-inch or 9-inch pie, whichever suits your pie pans. You can keep it rolled up or flatten it to size. The flattened dough will thaw more quickly.

Wrap each piece individually with moisture/vapor-resistant plastic wrap. You can stack flattened crust dough to save freezer space. Place a sheet of freezer wrap between doughs to help you remove each one easily. Place in gallon freezer bags and press down to expel the air before sealing.

Another potential difficulty with freezing unbaked pie crusts is that the water in them will expand during the freezing process and will play havoc with the crust. If you must freeze pie crusts unbaked, use a fork to prick a few holes in the bottom and sides first. The key is in secure packaging so that your pie crust doesn't fall apart during storage. These have a relatively short freezer life, about 2 months, so be sure to use them while they're at their prime.

Since foods get jostled around in the freezer, even in the best storage conditions, you'll be happier with your pie crusts if you freeze them in their pans—that's why saving those aluminum pie pans that you accumulate from purchases at the grocery store comes in handy. Foil pans also work well.

Wrap each pie crust securely with plastic wrap that's moisture and vapor resistant and then wrap in foil. You can stack pies to save storage space. An optional final step would be placing your wrapped crusts in labeled gallon freezer bags for extra cushioning. To further protect the crusts, you can stack them inside a box, which will keep other foods from intruding on their space.

Preserving Pointers

Graham cracker crusts also freeze well, with or without pie filling. Add the whipped cream when you're ready to serve.

Pies

You can freeze filled, unbaked pies, but the crust will most likely get soggy if you do. It's best to lightly coat both top and bottom crusts with shortening to help prevent sogginess. Don't cut air holes in the top crust until you're ready to bake the pie. Add an additional 1 tablespoon of flour or tapioca or 1 teaspoon of cornstarch to fruit pie fillings before freezing. This keeps them from boiling over as they bake.

Baking pies first, however, will keep the crust flakier. Fruit pies, including mince-meat, freeze very well, as do vegetable pies (pumpkin and squash) and pudding pies. Many standard cookbooks recommend that you allow 1 pint of filling for an 8-inch pie, although this can be really skimpy. If you like flat pies that may be enough. However, if you prefer pies with some height, especially if you're dealing with fruit pies, 1 quart of fruit filling will give you a substantial, eye-appealing pie.

If you want to freeze a lemon meringue pie, freeze the lemon pie and add the meringue just before serving. Meringue tends to separate from the edge and adhere to the wrap. Custard and cream pies do not freeze well. Chiffon pies will need to include ½ cup or more of whipped cream if they're to freeze satisfactorily.

You'll take unbaked pie crusts directly from freezer to oven. Don't allow the crust to thaw before baking. Bake at 425°F for 12 to 15 minutes or until light brown.

To bake frozen, filled pie crusts, remove the freezer wrap and place the unthawed pie on the bottom shelf of an oven that's been preheated to 450°F. Bake for 15 to 20 minutes and then reduce heat to 375°F for about 45 minutes or until the pie is done.

To serve a frozen, baked pie, allow the pie to thaw at room temperature if you're serving it cool. This would include pudding pie, pumpkin or squash pie, and chiffon pie. If you want to serve the pie warm, as in fruit pie, remove the freezer wrap and transfer the pie directly to an oven that's been preheated to 400°F for 30 to 40 minutes or until thoroughly warmed.

Cobblers and Crisps

Fruit cobblers are a baked fruit with a pastry base or topping like dumplings, while crisps are a baked fruit with a crumble/streusel topping. Both are sweet. See Chapter 4 for a fruit cobbler recipe that's rich and flavorful. In both desserts, fruit is either sliced (as in peaches and apples) or left whole (in the case of berries).

Both of these desserts can be made with frozen fruit, and frozen berries work especially well. Don't thaw the fruit. Just take out what you need, arrange it in the baking pan, add the pastry batter or the streusel mix, and bake.

Streusel adds texture and crunch to crisps and coffeecakes. A basic streusel topping consists of flour, sugar, and butter. There are many variations on this, so consider adding oats, substituting brown sugar for white, and adding a bit of cinnamon (for apples) or nutmeg (for peaches). You mix the butter with the sugar, a process called creaming. Then add the flour, spices, and oats. Work it with your hands until you've got a good mix of small- and medium-size clusters. Sprinkle this on top of your fruit and bake.

To freeze cobblers and crisps, cover the baking pan securely with aluminum foil and place it in the freezer. When frozen, remove it from the freezer and remove the dessert from the pan. Wrap the frozen dessert in moisture/vapor-resistant plastic wrap and then wrap it in foil. Label, date, and return it to the freezer.

When you're ready to use these desserts, remove them from the freezer and remove the wrap. Return them to a baking pan and bake, unthawed, at 375°F for 40 to 60 minutes or until thoroughly warmed.

Cookies and Cookie Dough

Cookies are easy to freeze. Commercial products can be frozen in labeled and dated plastic freezer bags. Home-baked cookies can be frozen in either plastic freezer bags or rigid freezer containers. Place a sheet of waxed paper or freezer paper between rows of cookies to keep them from sticking together.

When you're ready to use the cookies, remove them from the freezer and allow them to thaw in their packaging for about 15 to 20 minutes.

You can also freeze cookie dough. If you're making refrigerator cookies, just roll up the dough, wrap it in moisture/vapor-resistant plastic wrap, and then place rolls in freezer bags. Label, date, and freeze.

Freezing unbaked drop cookies is similar to freezing berries. Drop dough onto a cookie sheet and place it in the freezer. When the dough has frozen, remove it from the freezer and drop it into freezer bags. Label, date, and return them to the freezer. When you're ready to bake, transfer the cookies to a cookie sheet and bake 10 to 15 minutes without thawing at 400°F.

An alternative to freezing individual drop cookies is freezing the batch of dough all at once. Just pack it into the appropriate-size freezer container and label, date, and store. When you're ready to bake cookies, thaw the dough at room temperature. When you can insert a teaspoon into the dough, it's ready to use. Drop by teaspoonfuls onto a cookie sheet and bake according to your recipe.

Recipes

Finding the perfect pie crust recipe can be difficult, but this one comes close. Next, an applesauce loaf can fill the house with the wonderful aromas of spices and fragrant apples, especially during the holidays.

Ramona's No-Fail Pie Crust

This may seem too good to be true, but it's as close to perfect as you can get! There's practically no way to make this come out any way less than wonderful.

Makes 2 9-inch pie crusts

Prep time: 10 minutes

Cook time: 8 to 10 minutes

---

1 cup Crisco (now comes in convenient 1-cup packages)

2 cups flour

1 tsp. salt

6 TB. ice water

Cut fat into flour/salt mixture. When well mixed, add water (a tablespoon at a time) while mixing in flour, salt, and fat mixture. Roll pie crust and put into a pie pan. Bake in a 400°F oven for 8 to 10 minutes. Remove from oven and place the pie pan on a cooling rack.

Applesauce Raisin Loaf

This is a quick bread that's rich and flavorful. Freezing small loaves will get you extra mileage out of one recipe, and they make good gifts.

Makes 1 loaf

Prep time: 15 minutes

Cook time: 1 hour

½ cup golden raisins

½ cup regular raisins

½ cup butter

1 cup sugar

1 tsp. vanilla

1 egg

1½ cup applesauce

¾ tsp. apple pie spice

2 cups flour

2 tsp. baking soda

1. Preheat oven to 350°F. Place raisins in a small saucepan and cover with water. Simmer until raisins plump—about 5 minutes. Remove from heat and drain.

2. Cream butter and sugar, add vanilla and egg. Add applesauce, apple pie spice, flour, and baking soda and mix thoroughly. Bake in medium-size loaf pan for 1 hour or until loaf tests done. Remove from oven and allow to cool 5 to 10 minutes. Remove from loaf pan and place on cooling rack.

Chapter 8

Freezing Convenience Foods and Meals

In This Chapter

- Designer food on the cheap
- The end of leftovers
- Cooking with a plan in mind
- Fast food lunches

Saving time, saving money, and making the most of your freezer space are just a few reasons why freezing your own convenience foods makes sense. Concerned about the high sodium and high fat contents of commercially prepared foods? Learn to make your own and eat healthy!

There are two ways to approach freezing complete meals. You can think in terms of single servings or make plans to feed a crowd. You can also freeze baby foods and foods with special dietary requirements in mind.

Soups and Stews and Stock

Take a look at the nutritional information of canned or packaged soups or soup mixes, and the sodium content is enough to make you put the item back on the shelf. Even with reduced-sodium offerings, you still may not be satisfied.

Another problem with commercially available soups is that there is frequently much too little of the ingredient you're looking for. So if you're tired of fishing for those little bits of beef in the canned beef stew, there is a simple remedy. Make your own recipes, freeze them, and have them on hand. They'll keep in the freezer for up to a year.

Soups and stews start with stock, and there are just four basic types. If you haven't made stock before, you're in for a treat. It's very easy, freezes beautifully, and best of all, you control what goes into it.

Meat Stock

Meat scraps (with the fat trimmed off) and bones are a wonderful foundation for meat stock. After you've finished up the roast, chops, or ribs, toss the bones into a stock pot (actually a large saucepan whose size will be based on how much meat and bones you have), add cold water to cover, and turn the heat on medium. Usually about 5 pounds of meat and bones make a good stock.

Some cooks roast the bones in a hot oven (400°F to 450°F) for half an hour first. This makes for a darker, richer stock. You can also crack the bones if you're dealing with a shank or leg.

Then add the following:

- 1 bay leaf

- 1 to 2 cloves garlic, minced

- 2 carrots, chopped into 2- to 3-inch pieces

- 2 onions, chopped into quarters

- 2 stalks celery, chopped into 2- to 3-inch pieces (include the leaves)

- 2 tomatoes, chopped

- 1 tablespoon each of whichever of the following you are partial to: parsley, sage, rosemary, thyme, basil, and/or oregano

- 1 tablespoon ground black peppercorns

Bring all ingredients to a boil, then reduce heat and simmer for 4 to 6 hours. Skim off the gray scum that forms on top of the water during the early cooking. Add water as necessary to keep everything covered.

Remove from the heat. Pour the contents through a colander, capturing all the liquid stock in a large bowl or saucepan. Dispose of the solids. Place the stock in the refrigerator until all the fat has congealed at the surface. Skim off the fat.

Pour the stock into labeled and dated freezer containers or ice cube trays and freeze. If using ice cube trays, after the stock has frozen, pop out the cubes and package them in labeled and dated moisture/vapor-resistant freezer bags. Return them to the freezer.

Poultry Stock

After everyone has picked through the Thanksgiving turkey carcass and there aren't any more meals to be coaxed out of it, it's time to make stock. (This applies to chicken carcasses as well.)

Save the necks and backs (freeze them until you've got a good supply) and gather up the bones and you're good to go.

You'll want about 5 pounds of poultry bones and parts for the stock pot. Then add the following:

- 1 bay leaf
- 1 large onion, chopped into quarters
- 2 large carrots, chopped into 2- to 3-inch pieces
- 2 celery stalks, chopped into 2- to 3-inch pieces (include the leaves)
- 1 to 2 cloves garlic, minced
- 1 tablespoon ground black peppercorns

Preserving Pointers

Including poultry livers, hearts, and gizzards in stock is a matter of personal taste. They tend to have a stronger flavor, so if your family doesn't want to eat them when they're first cooked, it's probably best to omit them from the stock.

Add water to cover. Turn the heat on medium and bring the mixture to a boil. Then reduce the heat and simmer for 4 to 6 hours, adding water as needed to keep everything covered. Remove the pot from the stove and pour the ingredients through a colander, capturing the liquid stock in a bowl. Dispose of the solids.

Place the bowl in the refrigerator to chill. When the fat has congealed at the top, skim it off. Pour stock into labeled and dated freezer containers or into ice cube trays. When frozen, pop out the cubes and pack them into labeled and dated moisture/vapor-resistant freezer bags. Return them to the freezer.

Seafood Stock

Rich, creamy chowders get their aroma and flavor from hearty seafood stocks. Whenever you serve fish with bones, save the bones along with whatever scraps are left over. You can also use shellfish shells such as crab, lobster, or shrimp.

Fish stock is easy to make. You'll need about 5 pounds of shells, bones, and scraps for the stock pot. Place the fish parts in a large cooking pot, cover with water, and add 1 to 2 teaspoons of salt. Turn the heat on medium and bring to a boil. Then reduce the heat and simmer 1 to 2 hours. Skim off any foam that gathers around the edges of the top of the pot. Remove the pot from the stove and pour the ingredients through a colander, capturing the liquid stock in a bowl. Dispose of the solids.

Safety Check

Strain the stock carefully and thoroughly. Small fish bones can cause serious damage if swallowed.

Place the bowl in the refrigerator to chill. When the fat has congealed at the top, skim it off. Pour the stock into labeled and dated freezer containers or into ice cube trays. When frozen, pop out the cubes and pack them into labeled and dated moisture/vapor-resistant freezer bags. Return them to the freezer.

Vegetable Stock

This is not for the faint of heart. You're going to clean out the refrigerator and dump every vegetable that's still edible into the stock pot. This also means using potato peels, beet skins, corn cobs, and just about anything else you can dredge up.

If you're aiming for a generic vegetable broth without any distinguishing flavor or aroma giveaway, consider doing without cabbage or cauliflower. Also a little broccoli and a few tomatoes go a long way. They're powerful.

Add all the vegetables to the stock pot, cover them with water, and then add 1 bay leaf, 1 to 2 cloves of minced garlic, and 1 tablespoon of ground black peppercorns. Add other spices to suit your tastes (for example, parsley, thyme, basil, or other herbs). Turn the heat on medium and bring the ingredients to a boil. Then reduce the heat and simmer 1 to 2 hours, checking frequently to be sure vegetables aren't sticking to the bottom of the pot. Add water as you need to. Then remove the pot from the heat and strain all the ingredients through a sieve. This will catch the bay leaf!

Safety Check

Bay leaves have sharp, spiny edges that can catch in your esophagus and cause damage. Always count the bay leaves as you're putting them in a dish and always keep count as you remove each one before you serve that dish. Swallowing a bay leaf can be serious business.

Casseroles

There certainly is no end to the possibilities when it comes to creating casseroles. Casseroles generally are entire meals cooked and served in the same ovenproof dish. They're great timesavers and are convenient ways to use up odds and ends of foods that might otherwise be consigned to the refrigerator until they either dry up or turn green and have to be discarded.

Consider mini casseroles. Use those microwavable divided dinner trays you may have accumulated and create your own customized meals. Wrap them in moisture/vapor-resistant freezer wrap and then overwrap in foil or place in a large freezer bag. Label, date, and freeze them, and you've got dinner ready for the microwave.

For the price of an additional baking dish, you can save yourself some time and make more economical use of your oven. Cook your favorite casseroles in batches, and you can eat one and freeze the rest. Here are some tips:

♦ Slightly undercook a casserole destined for the freezer. This keeps the food from becoming overdone while it's reheating. If you'll be including pork or chicken, be sure to allow enough time to finish cooking it thoroughly when you're ready to use it.

♦ Add breadcrumb topping as you are preparing the casserole for reheating. Freezing breadcrumbs on top of the casserole will cause them to get soggy.

♦ Add cheese toppings as you are preparing the casserole for reheating. Freezing cheese makes it dry and brittle.

Preserving Pointers

Think small! Freeze lemon zest and orange rind for puddings and pies. Crumble left-over bacon and freeze it for topping baked potatoes. Little bits of this and that come in handy, as long as they're easily marked and readily accessible in a specifically designated section of the freezer.

◆ If you're freezing a stew, leave the potatoes out. Cook them when you're ready to reheat the stew and add them just before serving. This keeps them from turning to mush.

◆ If you're freezing a pasta dish, such as lasagna or macaroni and cheese, make sure the sauce completely covers the noodles. This prevents freezer burn and tough, dried-out pasta.

To prepare casseroles for the freezer, line the casserole dish with heavy-duty aluminum foil, then add the ingredients and bake. When the food is done, remove it from the oven and allow it to cool. Then place the covered casserole in the freezer. When frozen, you can lift the food out of the dish, wrap it securely in foil, and then return it to the freezer. Casseroles have a relatively short freezer life of about 3 months.

When you're ready to use the casserole, remove it from the freezer, unwrap it, and place the casserole back in the dish. Take it directly to the oven to reheat. No need to thaw it first.

Meat Loaf and Fish Loaf

To freeze these unbaked, prepare them according to your favorite recipes. Do not top with bacon strips, if that is your usual *modus operandi*. Add that when you're ready to cook the loaves.

Line a loaf pan with heavy-duty aluminum foil, then place the food in the pan and cover it with foil. Place it in the freezer. When frozen, pop the loaf out of the pan, wrap it securely in moisture/vapor-resistant freezer wrap, overwrap with foil, label and date it, and return it to the freezer. Freezer storage time is 1 to 2 months.

When you're ready to use a loaf, remove it from the freezer, unwrap it, place it in a loaf pan, cover it with plastic wrap, and allow it to thaw overnight in the refrigerator. When thawed, add bacon strips if desired and bake as usual.

To freeze a baked loaf, wrap it securely in moisture/vapor-resistant freezer wrap and overwrap in foil. Label and date it. When you're ready to use it, allow it to thaw in the refrigerator. Serve it cold or remove the foil and freezer wrap, place the loaf in a loaf pan, cover it loosely with foil, and reheat it in a 350°F oven.

Gravies

There's almost always gravy left over after the roast or turkey is finished. You can freeze that gravy for future use. Pour it into labeled and dated freezer containers and store it in the freezer. It'll keep well for 3 to 4 months.

Preserving Pointers _____

To prevent milk sauces and gravies from curdling or separating, the University of Missouri Extension Service recommends using "mochiko" in their preparation. This is a waxy rice flour available at many oriental food stores. You can learn more at http://extension.missouri.edu/xplor/hesguide/foodnut/gh1505.htm.

When you're ready to use the gravy, remove the desired containers from the freezer and allow them to thaw in the refrigerator overnight. You can also take the gravy directly to the sauce pan, turn the heat on low, add a tablespoon or so of water to keep it from scorching, and place the lid on the pot. Check frequently and stir to keep ingredients from scorching or sticking. If you find that the gravy is watery or has separated, grab your whisk and set to work to regain a smooth consistency.

Fried Chicken

Fried foods tend to lose crispness during the freezing process. Still, if you've got a bunch of leftover fried chicken, it's worth your while to freeze it. You can also partially fry foods and then freeze them. When you're ready to use them, you may find that the final frying process crisps them up nicely.

To freeze, wrap them in moisture/vapor-resistant freezer wrap and then either overwrap in foil or place in labeled and dated freezer bags. Freezer storage life is 1 to 3 months.

Cooked Meats and Poultry

Trim as much fat as possible before freezing cooked meats. The fats can turn rancid, and this will have a bad effect on the meat. It's best to keep the pieces as large as possible. This reduces the amount of surface area contacting the air and helps prevent freezer burn. For poultry, remove the meat from the bones to help it cool more quickly.

You can choose to freeze cooked meat with or without gravy. Freezing it with gravy helps keep it from drying out, although this makes using a freezer bag difficult. The gravy slops all around, and as the package freezes, it can take on some rather strange shapes if you don't store it flat. Freezer storage life is 2 to 4 months.

When you're ready to use the meat, remove it from the freezer and allow it to thaw in the refrigerator. Depending on the size of the package, it may take anywhere from a few hours to overnight. When thawed, reheat the meat in the microwave or in a saucepan on the stove over low heat.

To freeze stuffing, cool it quickly in the refrigerator and then pack it into rigid freezer containers. Label, date, and freeze it. Storage life is about 1 month. To use, allow it to thaw in the refrigerator. Then place it in a saucepan with a tablespoon of water and reheat over low heat, fluffing occasionally. Keep an eye on it to prevent it from sticking or scorching.

Baked Beans

Baked beans freeze well, provided you slightly undercook them and use bacon, ham, or salt pork sparingly in their preparation. Prepare by your favorite recipe, then cool quickly in the refrigerator and pack in rigid freezer containers. Be sure the beans and any meat are covered with liquid. Leave appropriate headspace. Label, date, and freeze them. Freezer storage life is about 6 months.

When you're ready to use the beans, remove them from the freezer and allow them to thaw in the refrigerator. Heat them in a saucepan over low heat.

Pizza

Prepare by your favorite recipe but do not bake it. Wrap it securely in moisture/vapor-resistant freezer wrap and overwrap in foil. Label and date it. Freezer storage life is about 1 month.

When you're ready to use the pizza, remove it from the freezer and place it directly in a preheated 450°F oven. Bake for 20 minutes or until the crust is browned, the cheese has melted, and the toppings are cooked.

Sandwiches

If soggy sandwiches don't appeal to you, you're not alone. You can take some steps to prevent this. First, freeze the loaf of bread. Place it in the freezer in its store wrap or wrap a homemade loaf securely in freezer wrap and place it in the freezer.

While the bread is freezing, make the spreads or prepare the meats. Ham, chicken, bologna, tuna (not prepared as tuna salad), and other cuts of lunch meats freeze well. Peanut butter and jelly also does fine. So do cheese spreads or cream cheese with nuts and olives or bits of fruit.

When the bread has frozen, remove it from the freezer and spread a thin layer of butter or margarine across each slice (except in the case of PB&J sandwiches).

Then make the sandwiches. Avoid mayonnaise or other oil-based ingredients such as salad dressings. Wrap them securely in freezer wrap, then place them in labeled and dated freezer sandwich bags. Freezer storage life is about 1 month.

When you're ready to use the sandwiches, remove them from the freezer and allow them to thaw in their wrap. Add lettuce or tomato slices just before eating. No soggy bread!

Vegetable Stir-Fry Mix

Make your own vegetable stir-fry mix. You'll have the ingredients you like and won't have to pay grocery store prices. Slice fresh vegetables to your own specifications and follow the blanching times recommended in Chapter 5. Suggestions include carrots, green beans, broccoli, peas, cauliflower, or summer squash. (Peppers do not need blanching.) Cool and package them in labeled and dated moisture/vapor-resistant freezer bags.

Potatoes (White or Sweet)

Raw potatoes don't freeze well, but they do root cellar beautifully (see Chapter 23). Cooked potato dishes are easy to freeze, and having a variety of these on hand will help you assemble a tasty and nutritious meal on short notice.

Baked

For baked potatoes, scrub large potatoes to remove all dirt. Then make a couple of incisions into the skin to allow the steam to escape and to prevent the potato from exploding in the oven. This is a mess you don't even want to contemplate having to clean up.

Safety Check

Baked potatoes left at room temperature have resulted in cases of botulism. Always store foods in the refrigerator if you're not going to be able to get to them within 2 hours.

Rub lightly with butter or shortening, place them on an oven rack, and bake them at 350°F until a knife inserts easily all the way through. Cool quickly in the refrigerator. Then wrap them in labeled and dated moisture/vapor-resistant freezer wrap. Over-wrap with foil and freeze. Freezer storage life is 1 to 2 months.

When you're ready to use the potatoes, remove them from the freezer and transfer them to the oven. Reheat at 375°F until heated through.

Stuffed

Bake large potatoes. When done, cut them in half lengthwise and scoop out the white portion. Mash with milk, salt, pepper, shredded cheese, and sour cream. Return the mixture to the hollowed-out potato. Place the potatoes on a cookie sheet and place them in the freezer. When frozen, remove them from the cookie sheet and wrap them in moisture/vapor-resistant freezer wrap. Overwrap in freezer bags or foil. Freeze. Freezer storage life is 1 to 2 months.

When you're ready to use the potatoes, remove them from the freezer and transfer them to the oven. Reheat at 375°F for 30 to 40 minutes or until thoroughly heated.

Hash Browns

For cubes: Scrub, peel, and cut potatoes into ½-inch cubes. Blanch them in boiling water for 5 minutes. Drain and cool. Package them in freezer bags or freezer containers.

For shredded: Scrub and cook whole potatoes with the skins on until almost done. Cool, peel, and grate them with a vegetable grater or food processor. Package them in freezer bags or freezer containers.

Freezer storage life is 1 to 3 months.

French Fries

Scrub the potatoes, peel them, and cut them into strips. Blanch them using either the oven or oil method.

Oven method: Place the strips on a cookie sheet. Brush them with melted butter or margarine and bake them at 450°F until the potatoes begin to brown, turning the potatoes with a spatula occasionally. Remove the potatoes from the oven and allow to cool. (You can cool them quickly in the refrigerator.) Package them in freezer bags or freezer containers.

Oil method: Blanch the strips in oil heated to 370°F until the strips are tender but not browned. Remove them from the oil and drain them. Allow to cool, or cool them quickly in the refrigerator. Package them in freezer bags or freezer containers.

Freezer storage life is 1 to 3 months.

Potato Patties

This is a good use for leftover mashed potatoes. Make patties and season them with salt and pepper as desired. Place the patties on a cookie sheet and place it in the freezer. When frozen, remove the patties with a spatula and stack them in a freezer container. Place a sheet of freezer wrap between the patties to prevent sticking. Freezer storage life is 1 to 3 months.

When you're ready to use the patties, remove them from the freezer and bake them on a greased cookie sheet at 375°F until heated through.

In Other Words

… If a fellow really likes potatoes, he must be a pretty decent sort of fellow.

—A. A. Milne, beloved creator of Winnie the Pooh

Recipes

Both of these hearty meals can be prepared to enjoy now and have plenty left over to freeze for later meals.

Karen's Vegetable Beef Soup

This is a great way to use your home-frozen vegetables. There's really no limit on what you can put in or leave out, so tailor this recipe to suit your family's tastes. This soup is fine the first day, better the second, and great the third. If you want to freeze the soup, omit the potatoes, as they change texture when frozen. You can add them later, when you're planning to serve the soup.

Serves 8
Prep time: 15 to 20 minutes
Cook time: 4 to 6 hours

1 lb. stew meat

1 clove garlic, minced

1 TB. olive oil

1 qt. whole tomatoes

1 pt. corn

1 qt. green beans, cut into 2-inch slices

1 large onion, cut into eighths

3 large carrots, sliced

3 large potatoes, cut into 1-inch cubes

Salt, pepper, spices to taste (parsley, sage, rosemary, thyme, oregano, basil—whatever you like)

4 to 6 beef or vegetable stock cubes

1. Place stew meat and garlic in large cooking pot. Add 1 tablespoon of olive oil. Turn heat on high and brown meat, turning as necessary to sear in the juices and get an even browning.

2. Reduce heat to medium. Add tomatoes, corn, green beans, onion, carrots, and stock cubes. Add water to cover all ingredients. Bring to a boil. Then reduce the heat, add salt, pepper, and spices, and simmer for 4 to 6 hours. Add water as necessary to keep ingredients covered and to create a rich broth. Add potatoes 1 hour before serving.

Barbara's Baked Beans

This is just the right dish for a cold winter day. Soak the beans the night before. Serve with brats or hot dogs and potato salad.

1 (16 oz.) package white beans

1 tsp. baking soda

½ to ¾ cup light brown sugar

Small piece salt pork or bacon

1 small onion, chopped

1 tsp. dry mustard

Salt to taste

Serves 6
Prep time: 25 minutes
Cook time: 6 to 8 hours

Wash and sort beans. Soak overnight in cold water. In the morning, add 1 teaspoon baking soda and boil for 10 minutes. Drain. Add more cold water to cover beans and boil until soft (30 to 45 minutes). Pour beans and the liquid they cooked in into bean crock and add brown sugar, salt pork or bacon, onion, mustard, and salt. Bake in a very slow oven (200°F to 250°F) for 6 to 8 hours. Check each hour. Add water if needed to keep beans covered.

Part **3**

Canning

Canning is an economical way of putting up all kinds of foods—fruits, vegetables, meats, and combination dishes. It's not as complicated as you may think. If you can follow a recipe, you *can* can! It's simply taking one step at a time. Canning used to involve using actual cans, but today they've more or less gone the way of the dodo bird. Glass canning jars are in! In Part 3, you'll learn safe canning procedures and follow specific research-based recipes designed to please.

Introduction to Canning

In This Chapter

- ◆ The invention of canning
- ◆ What you need to get started
- ◆ How to care for and use your equipment
- ◆ Making sure you get the best product
- ◆ Troubleshooting common problems

Certain varieties of fruits and vegetables can better than they freeze. Canning uses heat and occasionally pressure to drive out air that can cause food spoilage. If you've got a pantry or can find a space to install a cupboard with sturdy shelves, you can eat well for pennies on the dollar.

The Science Behind Canning

We have the French to thank for the invention of canning and a candy-maker by the name of Nicholas Appert to be precise. When Napoleon Bonaparte offered a prize of 12,000 francs to whoever could develop a system for keeping food fresh for his soldiers, Appert bit. It took him years, but he learned that if he put food in a bottle; kept out as much air as possible through a system of corks, wires, and sealing wax; and heated the foods in hot water, the food didn't spoil.

Napoleon was impressed with Appert's canned (or bottled) soups, fruits, vegetables, and gravies and awarded Appert the prize. The army got to eat unspoiled food, and the food canning industry was born. In 1811, Appert published a book explaining his process. Since that time much has changed, but the basic principles remain: sealing jars to keep out air and then heating the contents of the jars to destroy microorganisms that can cause the food to spoil. Appert didn't know why the process worked—that discovery was to come later.

Preserving Pointers

Nicholas Appert is considered the father of canning, and his birthday, October 23, is National Canned Foods Day. It's a good day to put up some canned food and honor Nicholas and his contribution to the home arts. Incidentally, Appert is also the inventor of peppermint schnapps.

Nicholas Appert would be quite impressed with the innovations and equipment now available to the home food preserver. We now know the science behind why his process worked and how to use both heat and acidity to create a safe product.

Supplies and Equipment for Canning

Gathering the essential supplies for canning is a bit like organizing a scavenger hunt: some things you already have, and some you'll need to get. If you're new to home canning, the process may seem rather overwhelming and perhaps a bit frightening. It's important to relax. Take a deep breath and approach canning with curiosity, enthusiasm, and a touch of respect. It's called a process because that's exactly what it is. Just take one step at a time, follow the directions carefully, and you'll end up with a safe, delicious product.

Boiling Water Canner

Without a doubt, this is the most versatile, handy, wonderful, and indispensable piece of equipment for the home food preserver. You can use it for blanching, making soups, and a host of other tasks—in addition to its primary function as a canner for acidic foods (discussed later in this chapter). In fact, as you get inspired by the possibilities, you may find that one isn't enough. They're reasonably priced, starting at around $60 new.

The boiling water canner (sometimes referred to as a water bath canner) is essentially a large cooking pot. It's made of aluminum or porcelain-coated steel, has a lid with a handle, and comes with a removable rack that holds jars in place while the water boils and also keeps the glass from coming into direct contact with the bottom of the canner.

Boiling water canners have either flat or ridged bottoms. If you're working with an electric range, you'll want the flat bottom. For gas ranges, the ridged one works well.

These canners come in different sizes, with the standard size able to accommodate 7 quarts or 9 pints with room for the required 1 to 2 inches of water needed above the tops of the jars.

Pressure Canner

This is an essential item for canning low-acid foods. It's probably the most intimidating appliance for a novice, but it's actually simple to use. Pressure canners come in different sizes and are rated by the volume of water they can hold. The standard size pressure canner is a 16-quart model. This means it will hold 16 quarts of water. For canning purposes, it will hold 7 quart jars or 9 pint jars (just like the boiling water canner).

Pressure canners have undergone considerable streamlining over the last few decades. They're more lightweight for sure! Older models are heavy affairs.

Models made before the 1970s have thick walls with lids that either clamp or turn on. They have a dial gauge in the lid, along with a vent (either a petcock or counterweight) and a safety fuse.

Safety Check

Whether you have an older-model canner or a newer one, take some time to become familiar with its features before you can your first load. Knowledge is power!

Newer models have thinner walls and generally have turn-on lids. The lid has a gasket, either a dial or weighted gauge, an automatic vent/cover lock, a vent port that's closed with a counterweight or weighted gauge, and a safety fuse. Compared to an older model, it has more safety features built in.

An older–model, dial-gauge pressure canner.

A newer-model, weighted-gauge pressure canner.

Here's how those parts work:

◆ **Vent port, petcock, or steam vent.** These names all refer to the same thing. The vent is the escape hatch for air trapped inside the canner, and it also releases steam during processing. It's part of the pressure-regulating system.

◆ **Weighted gauge.** This is a round piece of solid aluminum with three holes drilled into the side. Each hole corresponds to a different pressure: 5, 10, or 15. If you are processing foods at 10 pounds of pressure, you put the number 10 hole on top of the vent port.

The weight jiggles back and forth during processing, releasing steam and keeping the pressure steady. The major drawback to the weighted gauge is that you can't easily adjust for altitude (see the discussion later in this section). If you need to process at 12 pounds of pressure to adjust for altitude, you have no choice but to use the number 15 hole. This can be overkill, and you may overprocess your foods. Going below to the number 5 hole isn't an option since your foods could be underprocessed and potentially unsafe.

◆ **Dial gauge.** More user-friendly than the weighted gauge, you can easily adjust for altitude since the gauge has increments of 1 pound. You'll need to keep a close eye on a canner with a dial gauge and turn the heat up or down as necessary to maintain a constant temperature.

Dial-gauge canners also have a petcock but no weight to put on it. You have the petcock open (in the straight-up position) during *venting* and close the petcock (flick it to the side) after venting has been completed and processing has begun.

def•i•ni•tion

Dial gauges should be checked for accuracy at the beginning of each canning season and more frequently if you turn it into a workhorse. Contact your Extension Office for information. (You'll find its number in the phone book.)

> **Venting** is the process by which air is expelled from the canner. Once the air has been expelled, the petcock is closed or the weight is placed on the vent and processing begins.

◆ **Safety fuse, safety plug, safety release plug, or overpressure plug.** These names all refer to that little rubber plug or thin metal insert that releases pressure from the canner if the pressure gets dangerously high. You'll notice that there is a red zone on the dial gauge. You want to stay out of the red zone at all costs. Think of it as the RPM gauge on your car. Red is bad. Very, very bad. Fortunately, if you're paying attention, this shouldn't ever be a problem.

◆ **Gasket.** This is round and made of rubber or other space-age material and is designed to fit perfectly inside grooves or slots in the lid. Not all canners use gaskets. Check the gasket at the beginning of each canning season to be sure it is still pliable, hasn't stretched, and has no cracks. If you detect any damage, purchase a new one. They are available at many hardware stores and also through the company that made your canner (another good reason to keep the instruction book handy). It's helpful to keep the instruction booklet in the canner when you're storing it for the season. That way you'll never have to search for it and you'll be more inclined to refer to it when you should.

Safety Check _____

Some people fear that their pressure canner will explode. The horror story in your family history probably has more to do with Aunt Mabel heading out to the garden and spending the afternoon there (forgetting she had a canner full of green beans on the stove) than any equipment malfunction. If you follow the directions and attend to business, there's no reason on this earth for explosions. Pay attention and all will be well.

◆ **The rack.** Not a medieval torture device, this is a handy part of the canner that keeps the bottom of the glass jars from coming in contact with the hot, hot bottom of the canner. The rack for a pressure canner is constructed differently from one for use in a boiling water canner. It's a molded piece of aluminum with holes punched in it to allow water to circulate.

Boiling water canner rack.

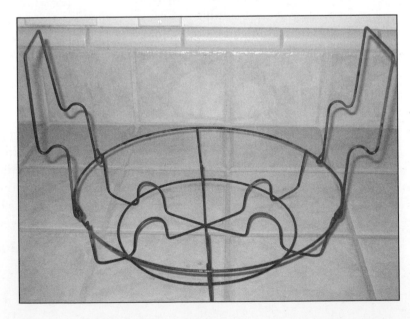

Pressure canner rack.

Glass Canning and Freezing Jars

These jars are specially designed and manufactured to withstand temperature and pressure changes. See Chapter 3 for a detailed discussion of the various types and sizes of these jars, as well as information on rings and lids.

Nifty Gadgets

A jar lifter is essential. Potholders become wet, and when they're wet you can quickly get burned. Jar lifters are available at most hardware stores.

A lid wand is a fun gadget. It's not essential, but it keeps your hands out of hot water when you're reaching for a lid to place on a jar. It's a wand with a small magnet at the end that captures the lid.

A canning funnel is a must. It's wider at the base than a regular funnel and fits nicely into quart or pint jars. It keeps hot foods at a respectful distance from your hands. You'll find these at hardware stores or other stores that sell canning supplies.

Canning funnel.

Caring for the Equipment

Both at the beginning of the canning season and after each load has been processed, the canner should be carefully cleaned. Washing the boiling water canner is a simple process. Wash it in regular dish detergent, rinse, and dry. Be especially careful with the wire rack, which loves to rust if given any opportunity to do so. When you've finished with the canner for any length of time, be sure it's completely dry before storing it. Placing a crumpled sheet of newspaper in the bottom of the canner will help draw any moisture away from the rack.

Washing the pressure canner is a bit trickier. If you've got a dial-gauge lid, you can't submerge the lid in water. Also, be careful not to invert the lid while there's still water on it, as that water can work its way into the dial and wreak havoc.

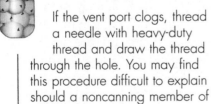

Preserving Pointers

If the vent port clogs, thread a needle with heavy-duty thread and draw the thread through the hole. You may find this procedure difficult to explain should a noncanning member of your family happen to pass by.

Wash the base in regular dish detergent, rinse, and dry. Avoid using scouring powder or baking soda because they will cause the aluminum to turn dark. You can use fine steel wool if you come across some stubborn stuck-on food. Aluminum does have a tendency to pit, so don't leave food or water in the canner. Also, the canner may absorb odors from food. What this means in simple language is that you shouldn't use the pressure canner for storing food.

If the petcock is removable, you can wash it as you need to. With either model, be careful not to scrape away at the vent. The rubber material can be damaged if you get too industrious with the cleaning.

Using Your Canners

Boiling water canner: Fill the canner one half to two thirds full of water. Raise the jar rack and secure it on the rim of the canner by hooking the handle slots on the rim.

Rack positioned on canner rim.

Turn the heat on high and set the lid in place. When the water has come to a boil, use a jar lifter to place jars in the rack slots. Then lift the rack handles and reposition the rack inside the canner. Replace the lid. When the water returns to a boil, begin timing. When the processing time has been completed, turn off the heat, remove the lid (being careful to turn it away from you to avoid a steam burn), and use the jar lifter to remove jars from the canner. Place them on a clean, dry dish towel. Do not touch them again until they have sealed. You may hear a distinctive "ping" as the seal sets. Leave the jars undisturbed overnight.

Pressure canner: Place the rack in the canner. It will sit on the bottom. Put 2 to 3 inches of hot water in the canner. The water will come through the holes in the rack and fill the bottom of the canner. Turn the heat on high. When the water begins to boil, use a jar lifter to position the jars on the rack inside the canner. One jar will go in the center of the rack. The rest will form a circle around the center jar. Try to keep them from touching each other. Secure the lid. Leave the petcock in the open position. When steam begins escaping through the vent in a steady stream, set the timer for 10 minutes. After the canner has vented for 10 minutes, close the petcock or place the weighted gauge on the vent.

The pressure will now begin to build inside the canner. If you are using a weighted gauge, the gauge will begin to rock and jiggle when the correct pressure has been reached. Check your owner's manual to find out how often the gauge should jiggle. You can control the frequency by controlling the heat on the stove. For example, if the weight is jiggling too often, reduce the heat. If it's not jiggling often enough, increase the heat. Once you've found the correct heat and the gauge is operating correctly, begin to time the processing.

If you are using a dial gauge, you will see the pressure begin to climb. When the pressure has reached the correct level, turn down the heat as necessary to maintain that temperature. With an electric range, begin reducing the heat just before the needle indicator reaches the correct level. Gas ranges respond more quickly. Then begin to time the processing. It may take a little finessing to arrive at a steady pressure, but be patient. You control the heat. You control the pressure. You are in control!

When processing time is up, turn off the heat and do *nothing else!* The canner will gradually lose pressure, and you should do *nothing* to try to speed up the process. There are several good reasons for this:

- You could warp the canner.
- You could cause the jars to break.
- You could prevent the jars from sealing.
- You could draw liquid from the jars.
- You could get a really nasty burn.

Newer-model canners have vent locks that relax and return to the normal position when pressure reaches zero. When the pressure has reached zero, it's time to remove the weighted gauge, if your canner has one, and wait an additional 2 minutes. Then open the lid and remove the jars. Always turn the lid away from you to prevent a steam burn. The contents will still be boiling hot, even though the pressure part of the processing has been completed.

Use a jar lifter and place the jars on a flat, dry surface. A folded, dry kitchen towel works well. Allow the jars to cool and form their seal. Again, this is a process you mustn't rush. Once you've negotiated your first load of canning, celebrate! You've made the grade!

Getting the Best Product

Each load you process represents hard work and a financial investment. In addition to obtaining and caring for your equipment, there are some things to learn about the process to make sure your results come out top notch. Two of these must-know topics are acidity and heat.

Understanding Acidity

Acidity is the most important factor in determining how foods should be processed. Foods are divided into acid and low acid, for purposes of canning. Their level of acidity is determined by the pH scale, which ranges from 0 to 14 with 7 being neutral. For foods to be considered acid, they must have a pH of 4.6 or lower.

Acid foods contain enough natural acidity to prevent the growth of heat-resistant bacteria, or they are able to destroy them more rapidly during processing. Foods that can be safely canned using the boiling water bath are acid, have acid added to them (citric acid, lemon juice, or vinegar), or are fermented.

Safety Check

Over the years new varieties of foods have been introduced, and older varieties have been hybridized. In some cases, this has resulted in a change in their acidity. Tomatoes are a case in point. No longer as acidic as they used to be, it's necessary to add lemon juice to the jar before processing to ensure a safe product. Exact amounts are indicated in individual recipes.

Low-acid foods, those with a pH above 4.6, must be processed in a pressure canner to ensure a safe product. They don't have the natural acidity to prevent heat-resistant bacteria from growing. They need help. They need a heat boost, and that's delivered with pressure.

What You Need to Know About Bacteria

Bacteria are microscopic organisms that are present everywhere—in the air, in the soil, even on your skin. Some are beneficial (such as the bacteria in milk that help produce yogurt), but many are harmful, including those that cause botulism.

The common bacterium *Clostridium botulinum* is found in soil everywhere in the world. Soil in the western United States is particularly high in the type of this bacterium (type A) that is especially dangerous to people.

You've no doubt read about cases of botulism, but just how rare are these occurrences? The answer is fairly rare, because certain factors have to be in place for people to become sick. The bacterium has to be present in the food, the food has to be low-acid, and the food has to have been improperly processed.

The home food preserver can take measures to prevent this bacterium from contaminating home-preserved foods. The procedure is simple: always pressure-can low-acid foods and follow research-based, approved recipes. For added safety, boil low-acid home-canned foods for 10 minutes at sea level before serving. The *botulinum* toxin is destroyed by boiling. This is why previous generations of home food preservers boiled the heck out of their vegetables before putting them out on the table for dinner. You don't have to cook your veggies until they're mush, however, for them to be safe. Just do the job right and don't take shortcuts.

Turning Up the Heat

Water boils at 212°F at sea level. As the altitude increases, atmospheric pressure drops, and the temperature at which water boils also drops. This means that no matter how long you boil the water, its temperature will not increase.

In the case of low-acid foods, this is a problem. *Clostridium botulinum* spores are not killed at the normal temperature of boiling water. In order to kill them and prevent botulism, you must raise the temperature of the food being processed to 240°F to 250°F. This is accomplished with pressure. As you increase the pressure, the temperature rises. Enter the pressure canner, your number one food safety insurance policy.

The length of processing time depends on a variety of factors: the level of acidity of the food, the size of the jars, and how tightly you've packed those jars, for starters. That's why you'll find specific times and pressures for each food in the directions for processing that food.

Altitude Adjustments

You read in the last section that water boils at 212°F at sea level. If you live at 4,000 feet, water boils at 204°F, and if you're on top of the mountain at 8,000 feet, it's a mere 197°F. To make sure your food is safe, you'll need to adjust your pressure reading to reflect your own altitude. For example, if you live at 5,000 feet, you'll need to up the pressure from 10 pounds to 12½ pounds. This is much more easily done if you've got a pressure canner with a dial gauge.

Go to www.topozone.com/findplace to determine your altitude. Consult your canner instruction book for the chart that tells you what pressure you'll need to use. The general rule is to add 1 pound of pressure for each 1,000 feet above sea level. Processing times remain the same, regardless of your altitude.

Hot Pack vs. Raw Pack

These terms refer to the temperature of the foods you're putting in the jars. In hot pack, you'll heat the food in boiling water, syrup, or juice before you pack it into jars. In raw pack, you pack the food into jars without heating it and then add liquid to cover. Both hot pack and raw pack have advantages:

The advantages of hot pack are as follows:

◆ The food is softer and easier to fit into jars.

◆ More food can fit in the jar. Foods may contain up to 30 percent air. Cooking releases this air.

◆ There's less of a problem with floating food.

◆ Color and flavor may be better than raw pack after time in storage.

◆ It increases the vacuum in sealed jars.

Safety Check

The open kettle method was an older way of putting up fruits such as peaches. The peaches were heated in juice or water to boiling and then packed boiling hot into glass canning jars. Lids were adjusted and then left to seal on their own. Sometimes they did, and sometimes they didn't. Sometimes they unsealed during storage. It's not the recommended way to ensure a good seal and can result in a whole lot of spoiled food.

Here are the advantages of raw pack:

- It's better for foods that tend to lose their shape after cooking.
- It's perhaps less time-consuming than hot pack, depending on the food.

Measuring Correct Headspace

The headspace is the area in a canning jar between the top of the food and the bottom of the lid. Since many foods expand during processing, it's important to leave the correct headspace for the food you're canning. Each recipe will tell you how much headspace to leave.

Measuring correct headspace.

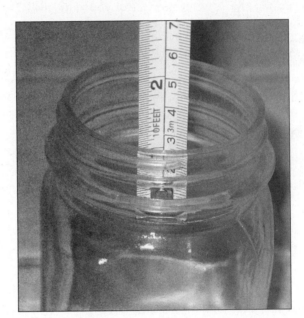

Troubleshooting

Most of the time everything turns out fine. Sometimes, though, in spite of your best efforts, weird things happen. There's always a logical reason why. Here are some of the most common problems, along with their causes and solutions.

Why Jars Break

In addition to using jars not suited for canning (such as mayonnaise jars), having the bad luck to have a jar with an imperfection, or using old jars, there are three basic causes of breakage: thermal shock, pressure, and impact. Canning jars are tough, but they do have their limits.

Preserving Pointers

Nothing lasts forever. Canning jars have a limited life expectancy. After about 12 years, it's time to take them to the recycling bin.

Thermal shock, as the name implies, has to do with temperature extremes. The jar generally breaks into a few large sections. You may encounter this if you forget to put the rack in the bottom of the canner, if you decide to cool the jars by running cold water over them, or if you take a cold jar and dump it into boiling water.

Solution: Avoid subjecting jars to temperature extremes and do a checklist of procedures before you commit the canner to the stove. This includes checking to be sure you've put the rack in the bottom of the canner!

Pressure breaks occur when the pressure takes some wild swings during processing because you've forgotten to keep an eye on the dial gauge. This can also happen if you give in to temptation and try to hasten the depressuring process by nudging the petcock. If you screw the jar lids on so tightly that nothing can escape—not even the air that needs to—or pack the jar to the tippy top and forget about headspace, you can also have a pressure break. These breaks can result in spidery lines along with big cracks.

Solution: Follow procedures to the letter. Don't try to rush the process at any point, and always attend to what you're doing. This means staying in the kitchen while you're processing foods with the pressure canner.

Impact breaks happen if you drop, bang, or otherwise subject the jar to some sort of insult. Interestingly enough, using a sharp knife to remove air bubbles can also cause these kinds of breaks if the knife tip jabs into the side of the jar. These breaks have a central hole with radiating cracks.

Solution: Use a rubber spatula to remove air bubbles. And, of course, try not to drop the jars. Always inspect jars carefully for nicks, scratches, or cracks before using them. Recycle the ones that fail the test.

Failure to Seal

Why didn't my jar seal? This is the most plaintive cry of the home food preserver. After everything you did for it, it repays you by doing absolutely nothing. It just sits there.

Usually, after you've given it more than enough time to do the right thing, you'll unscrew the band and remove the lid to find a bit of food stuck to the adhesive compound. That's the most common culprit. Here are some other possibilities:

◆ Using old lids for which the adhesive compound has degraded

◆ Not leaving the correct headspace

◆ Not following correct processing times or procedures

◆ Screwing the band on too tightly or not tightly enough

You can either reprocess the food right then and there or put it in the refrigerator to use within a few days.

Explaining Liquid Loss

Often this occurs when the pressure fluctuates during processing or if someone has opened the petcock prematurely. In these two pictures, the jar of peaches on the right has the correct amount of liquid. The peaches are nestled nicely in syrup. The jar on the left has lost so much liquid that the peaches are almost certain to turn brown. Which jar would you be proud to claim as your own?

Liquid loss from too little headspace.

In a boiling water bath, the water must be 1 to 2 inches above the tops of the jars or water will be sucked out of them during processing. In a pressure canner, you can get liquid loss by not letting the pressure canner exhaust for 10 minutes before beginning processing. What this means is that there's still air inside and you've not completely pressurized your canner. That air sucks out the liquid.

Other possibilities include the following:

♦ Not taking the jars out of the canner when processing has stopped, but allowing them to cool down with the canner. This most often happens when you've decided to do one last load before bedtime and figure you'll just take out the jars in the morning. The solution here is to plan your day and keep to the plan.

♦ Not removing all the air bubbles from the jar before processing. You'd think that just pouring the liquid into the jar would fill in all the spaces between the pieces of food, but it isn't so. Air gets trapped in the smallest depressions—for example, in the hollow of peaches where you've removed the pit. When you place the peach, pitted side down, in the jar, you've left an air pocket. The solution here is to gently use a rubber spatula to lift the fruit to allow the liquid to fill the space. You can't see into the middle of the jar and it's likely there are small air pockets there as well. Run the spatula around the edges of the jar. This will move the food that's in the center of the jar and allow the liquid to penetrate thoroughly.

♦ Packing the jars too tightly or too full. This often happens when you're down to your last jar to make a full canner load and you've got more food than the jar should take. You're trying to use every bit of food, so you cram it all in; however, food expands during processing and this drives out the liquid in the jar. As the jar cools down, that liquid loss becomes depressingly apparent. Always leave the necessary headspace. You have options for that extra food. You can eat it, of course, or you can refrigerate it overnight and add it to the next day's processing load.

♦ Starchy foods in the jar absorbed the liquid. Corn is a real culprit here. As the processing time bubbles along, the corn cooks and plumps beautifully. This plumping, however, happens because the corn has availed itself of the liquid you so thoughtfully provided it. Follow the directions carefully for correct headspace for starchy vegetables.

When faced with liquid loss, what do you do? If the jar has sealed, the food is safe to eat, although you should eat it as soon as possible. The top layer is likely to darken, but you can remove this before using the rest of the contents.

When to Reprocess

The decision is up to you. If the additional processing time (and you've got to redo the whole time) won't turn the food to mush, go ahead and reprocess it. Decide then and there. You've only got about 24 hours, with the food kept under refrigeration, to make up your mind before the spoilage microorganisms wake up and get to work. If you don't want to spend the time or energy, just make plans to eat the food.

Food that's been sealed and stored and then unseals should not be reprocessed. Toss it. Common sense should be your best indicator when it comes to determining whether you've got a problem or an irritation.

If you detect mold, a strange odor, or if the liquid has turned cloudy in the jar, discard the food. If your food is bubbling, this is definitely not a good sign. Your food should not be moving under any circumstances. Don't taste it. Destroy it.

Safe Disposal

The Centers for Disease Control (CDC) has guidelines for proper ways of disposing of foods that are suspected of harboring the *botulinum* toxin. It recommends extreme care, since even a small amount of the toxin is dangerous and can be absorbed through a break in the skin or through the eye. Their recommendations are found on their website (www.cdc.gov/botulism/botulism_faq.htm) and are as follows:

◆ Place any food that you think is contaminated in a sealable bag, wrap another plastic bag around the sealable bag, and tape it tightly. Place the bags outside in a trash receptacle for nonrecyclable trash. Make sure they're out of reach of people and pets.

◆ Never discard the food down a sink, garbage disposal, or toilet.

◆ Avoid contact with the skin. Wear rubber or latex gloves when handling open containers of food that you think may be contaminated. Wash your hands with soap and running water for at least 2 minutes after handling food or containers that may be contaminated.

◆ Clean up any spills using a bleach solution (use ¼ cup bleach for every 2 cups of water). Completely cover the spill with the bleach solution; then place a thick layer of paper towels on top of the bleach solution. Let the towels sit for at least 15 minutes, then dispose of them in the trash. Wipe up any remaining liquid with new paper towels. Clean the area with liquid soap and water to remove the bleach. Wash your hands with soap and running water for at least 2 minutes.

◆ Discard any sponges, cloths, rags, gloves, and containers that may have come into contact with contaminated food.

Putting Canning to Work for You

Putting up food by canning is fun, thrifty, and healthy when you do it right. Start with the freshest ingredients, follow strict guidelines for cleanliness and procedures for processing, and you'll fill your pantry with fruits, vegetables, meats, and all manner of tasty products to last you the year.

The Least You Need to Know

◆ A boiling water canner is used for canning acid foods and a pressure canner is essential for canning low-acid foods. These are your two essential pieces of equipment.

◆ Glass canning and freezing jars are specifically designed to withstand a wide range of temperatures and pressure. They're necessary supplies for home canning.

◆ Make adjustments for your altitude when using either the boiling water bath or pressure canning.

◆ Never take shortcuts with your pressure canner; always play it by the book.

◆ Pressure canning raises the internal temperature of foods to destroy spoilage microorganisms.

◆ To get the best product, start with the freshest ingredients, prepare them according to research-based, approved recipes, and process them properly.

Chapter 10

Canning Fruits and Fruit Products

In This Chapter

- ◆ General preparation tips
- ◆ Canning step-by-step
- ◆ Creating beauty in a jar: the best fruits for canning
- ◆ Creating combinations
- ◆ Making fruit juices, purées, and pie fillings
- ◆ Canning tomatoes

The beauty of home-canned fruits is that you control the amount of sugar that's used. That's a real bonus if you or someone in your family has special dietary needs, you want to put up some baby food, or you just want to cut back on calories. You can even can fruits without sugar and still create a tasty product.

The Adventure Begins

If you're new to canning, beginning with fruit and fruit products will give you confidence quickly. It's a good way to get started. Preparing food for the boiling water canner, loading the canner, monitoring the processing time, and removing jars after processing for a proper cool down are essential skills you'll need when it's time to move on to using the pressure canner.

In Other Words

I am not a cook. I hate to cook, but there's something about canning that gets me enthused about food. I can point to all those jars and say, "I did that!" I'm doing something good for my family, and I feel proud.

—Melanie, novice canner

It may seem that there's a great deal to learn, and there is. But as mentioned in the last chapter, it's called processing because it's a process. One step at a time. Make haste slowly and enjoy the experience. You'll emerge an expert!

General Procedures

Select firm, ripe fruit without blemishes or bruises. It's best to use slightly underripe fruit. Overripe fruit will break down during processing and leave you with strings and mushy places and a product that's too soft. Wash the fruit and remove stems, pits, and peels as necessary. Decide how you'll use the fruit since this will determine if you leave it whole, halved, sliced, chopped, or made into juice, purée, or sauce. So many choices!

Generally, it's easier to work with small batches. This means using about 3 pounds of fruit per canning session. It's a manageable amount, and you'll finish quickly.

A Word About Syrup

You'll need to use some type of liquid to accompany the fruit in the jars, and you have options here as well. You can make syrups in various strengths using sugar and water (see Appendix C for measurements), you can use fruit juice, or you can use water. Sugar helps fruit stay bright and colorful and also helps it hang on to its texture, but it's not necessary.

Tastes change over time, and whereas syrups used to be thick and sticky sweet, today they've gone lighter. Heavy syrup, containing 50 percent sugar, used to be the norm; today, it's light (30 percent sugar) or extra light (20 percent sugar). The decrease in the amount of sugar lets the flavor of the fruit come through. It cuts calories, and it's cheaper to make! If you'll be making syrup, use whatever strength suits your dietary needs and tastes.

To make the syrup following the measurements given in Appendix C, place the sugar and water in a large saucepan, turn the heat on high, and bring it to a boil. Reduce the heat and let it simmer while you pack fruit into jars.

You can use honey or corn syrup for part of the sugar requirement in syrup if you wish. Use 1 cup of honey, 1½ cups of sugar, and 3 cups of water to get about 5 cups of syrup. When using corn syrup, use 1 cup with 1½ cup of sugar and 3 cups of water to get about 6 cups of syrup.

Preserving Pointers

It's perfectly fine to make up a double or triple batch of syrup to save time. Refrigerate what you don't use. It will keep for several days. You can also freeze it. Pour it into rigid freezer containers, label it, date it, leave ½ inch of headroom, and freeze. When you're ready to use it, remove it from the freezer and allow it to thaw.

Antidarkening Solutions

Light-colored fruit (such as apples, peaches, or pears) should be dipped in an antidarkening solution while they're waiting their turn to be packed into jars. See Chapter 3 for more on how to use ascorbic acid (vitamin C) or a commercial preparation to keep the color of the fruit bright.

Estimating the Amount of Fruit to Use

Kitchen scales are useful for helping you eyeball how much fruit you'll need. Working with small amounts at a time is easiest. Think 2 to 3 pounds. Prepare the fruit and then work with the next 2 to 3 pounds. A rough rule is that altogether you'll need about 10 to 12 pounds per canner load for pints and nearly double that for quarts.

Slipping Skins

Dip peaches or tomatoes into boiling water for about 20 seconds and then plunge them into very cold water. Their skins will slip off easily.

Canning the Fruit

You've done all of the following:

1. The fruit is clean, slipped, cut, and dipped or peeled.

2. You've run the glass canning jars through the dishwasher, and they're keeping warm.

3. The rings and lids are simmering in hot water, and the lid wand and jar lifter are at the ready.

4. The syrup is made and simmering on the stove.

5. There's a clean, folded dish towel on the kitchen counter ready to receive the processed jars. You've made sure it's not in a drafty location and is away from any possible contact with cold water.

6. The boiling water bath is half-filled with water, the lid is in place, and the heat under it is turned on. The water is starting to boil.

7. You've checked the processing time for your altitude for the particular food you're canning.

Now it's time to go over the steps involved in producing a jar of canned fruit:

1. Pack the fruit into jars, using either raw pack or hot pack (see Chapter 9).

2. Add syrup or some other liquid to cover, leaving appropriate headroom.

3. Insert a spatula into the jar to remove any air bubbles.

4. Wipe the rim of the jar to remove any pieces of fruit.

5. Adjust the lids. (This is the phrase used for putting on the lid and screwing on the band.)

6. Using the jar lifter, pick up the jar by the neck and place it in one section of the rack in the bottom of the canner.

7. Place the lid on the canner.

8. Begin timing when the water has returned to a full boil.

9. Remove the jars from the canner with a jar lifter after time is up and place them on a clean, dry dish towel.

10. Allow the jars to cool undisturbed.

11. Listen for the sound that's music to your ears—the "ping" of lids sealing.

12. The next day, remove the rings and inspect the seals.

13. Wash the jars in warm water to remove any syrup or food residue.

14. Dry jars and store without rings in a cool, dark place.

Safety Check

Store your jars without the rings on. The rings can mask a seal that has failed. They can also stick like glue if there is any moisture or syrup stuck in the threads.

Now it's time for some recipes.

Goodness in a Jar

The best peach varieties for canning include Red Haven, Red Globe, Elberta, and Fairhaven. Freestones are much easier to work with than clings (see Chapter 4 for a discussion of the differences).

Apricots, nectarines, and peaches can beautifully, and a large part of the appearance is the arrangement in the jar. Layer the fruit with their insides facing down, and you'll get an interesting overlapping pattern. Even with slices, if you take a moment to position the fruit attractively, the result is almost art. You'll also get more fruit in each jar this way as opposed to just ladling it in haphazardly.

Preserving Pointers

Some varieties of fruits are widely available, but each region has its own specialties suited to canning. To find the best varieties of fruits for canning in your area, check with your extension service. You'll find its number in the phone book.

Apricots

Wash the fruit and leave the skins on. Apricots tend to fall apart without their skins to keep them company. Remove the pits. Apricots are usually canned as halves. You'll get quite a few in a pint jar. Raw pack is best, as they tend to break down in hot pack. Pack the jars and add syrup to cover. Leave ½ inch of headspace. Remove air bubbles, wipe rims, adjust lids, and process in a boiling water canner. See Appendix D for times. Remove them from the canner and allow them to cool on a flat, dry surface.

Nectarines and Peaches

These are essentially the same fruit. Wash the fruit. Slip skins on peaches and nectarines. Trim away any bruised portions. Slice the fruit in half and remove the pits. Use a grapefruit spoon to remove peach pits, if they're stubborn. Slide the serrated tip of the spoon under the stem end and continue on under the pit to loosen it. Lift the pit out. Treat the fruit with antidarkening solution.

Removing a peach pit with a grapefruit spoon.

If you'll be using this fruit for cobblers or pies, you'll want to use quart jars as opposed to pints. Use either hot pack or raw pack. Pack the jars and add syrup to cover. Leave ½ inch of headspace. Remove air bubbles, wipe rims, adjust lids, and process in a boiling water canner. See Appendix D for times. Remove them from the canner and allow them to cool on a flat, dry surface.

Soft Berries

Berries tend to get very soft with canning, but if you don't have room in the freezer for them, this is better than nothing. Fill the jars with berries. They'll settle with processing, so shake them down to give them the general idea of what they're supposed to do. *Never, never, never* bang the jar on the counter to force the berries down. Remember that glass jars are strong, but they're still glass and can break. (See Chapter 9 for more on pressure breaks.)

Cover the berries with syrup in the strength of your choice, leaving ½ inch of headspace. Remove air bubbles, wipe rims, adjust lids, and process in a boiling water canner. Process 10 minutes for pints and 15 minutes for quarts. Remove them from the canner and allow them to cool on a flat, dry surface.

Cherries—Sweet or Pie

To pit or not to pit, that is the question with cherries. Definitely pit cherries that are destined for pie. Unpitted cherries hold their shape better than pitted, but if you have a nifty cherry pitter and want to use it, go right ahead and pit away. If you do pit, remember to check each cherry before it goes into the jar to be sure no stray pits are trying to sneak past your vigilant eye.

Choose either raw pack or hot pack. Pack them into jars and add syrup to cover, leaving ½ inch of headspace. Remove air bubbles, wipe rims, adjust lids, and process in a boiling water bath. See Appendix D for times.

Fruit Cocktail (Compote)

This is a great way to use up the odds and ends of fruits you accumulate at the end of a canning session. Think variety! There's no law that requires you to pack just one kind of fruit in a jar. Mix them up! Try peaches and pears together or combine several different fruits to create your own fruit cocktail. Fruit cocktail you purchase commercially is often cut into tiny cubes, but you can make your pieces any size you like.

You'll need a variety of mixed fruits (peaches, pears, grapes, cherries, and perhaps a few maraschino cherries—whatever you have) and syrup in the strength you prefer.

Make the syrup and prepare the fruit. Wash, sort, and cut the fruit into slices or cubes. This recipe is more easily done hot pack than raw pack since it self-mixes while it's in the syrup. Add the fruit to the syrup and cook it until everything is hot all the way through. Ladle into jars, leaving ½ inch of headspace. Remove air bubbles, wipe rims, and adjust lids. Process in a boiling water bath for 20 minutes for pints and 25 minutes for quarts. Remove the jars from the canner and allow them to cool on a flat, dry surface.

Preserving Pointers

Try packing fruit in apple juice or white grape juice instead of syrup. It's lighter and has a delicious flavor.

Figs

Figs are lower in acid than most other fruits, so they need acid added and also require a longer processing time. Kadotas are a good variety for canning.

Wash the figs. Leave the stems on and don't peel. You'll use hot pack for figs and do them whole. Pack them into jars and add syrup to cover, leaving ½ inch of headspace. Add 1 tablespoon of bottled lemon juice to each pint and 2 tablespoons of lemon juice to each quart. Pack them into jars and add syrup to cover, leaving ½ inch of headspace. Remove air bubbles, wipe rims, adjust lids, and process in a boiling water bath. See Appendix D for times.

Grapefruit and Orange Sections

These are very nice combined for a citrus salad. You'll use raw pack for these. Wash and peel the fruit, being careful to snag all the white, spidery membrane as you go. Use a small, sharp knife to make the first incision between sections and then pull all sections apart. Clean any extra membrane or skin and remove any seeds. Pack them into jars and add syrup to cover, leaving ½ inch of headspace. Remove air bubbles, wipe rims, adjust lids, and process in a boiling water bath. See Appendix D for times.

Grapes

Use the seedless variety please. Eating your way through an entire jar of grapes, spitting out seeds as you go, gets tedious. Thompson seedless white grapes are a good choice. Use either raw or hot pack. Pack them into jars, leaving ½ inch of headspace. Remove air bubbles, wipe rims, adjust lids, and process in a boiling water bath. See Appendix D for times.

Pears

Bartlett pears are the best choice for canning. They hold their shape well and don't tend to get mushy. Wash the fruit. Peel and cut the pears in half. Using a grapefruit spoon, remove the center strings and seeds. Cut in halves or slice. Hold in antidarkening solution while you prepare the batch. Use either hot pack or raw pack. Pack the jars and add syrup to cover. Leave ½ inch of headspace. Remove air bubbles, wipe rims, adjust lids, and process in a boiling water canner. See Appendix D for times. Remove them from the canner and allow them to cool on a flat, dry surface.

Pineapple

Pineapple may not come quickly to mind when you're thinking about canning fruit, but if you've gotten a good deal at the grocery store, it's easy to put some up. The biggest deterrent for most people is the peeling and the coring and the digging out of all those indented "eyes." Actually, however, it's not any more time-consuming than peeling potatoes. Approach it with enthusiasm!

Whack off the top and the bottom and position the pineapple on a cutting board. Using a sharp knife, cut down each side, rotating the pineapple as you go along. It's rather like peeling a banana. Then you need to decide if you want rings or wedges.

For rings, slice across the diameter. Then use your apple corer to remove the core. If the core is wider than the corer, you'll need to overlap some coring or use a small, sharp knife to make an oval cut. For wedges, cut the pineapple in half lengthwise and then cut in half lengthwise again. The number of cuts will depend on the size of the pieces you want. Then cut away the core from the center pieces.

Hot pack usually gives a better result than raw pack, so simmer the pineapple in syrup until tender—about 3 to 5 minutes. Then pack it into jars, leaving ½ inch of headspace. Remove air bubbles, wipe rims, adjust lids, and process in a boiling water bath. See Appendix D for times.

Plums

Choose slightly underripe plums, as the riper ones are so juicy that they'll come apart during processing. Wash the plums, remove any stems, cut them in half, and remove the pits. You can process them with the pits if you want, but make a few pricks in the skin with a table fork to keep it from bursting during processing.

Use either hot pack or raw pack. For hot pack, simmer plums for 2 minutes in syrup. Pack them into jars and add syrup to cover, leaving ½ inch of headspace. Remove air bubbles, wipe rims, adjust lids, and process in a boiling water bath. See Appendix D for times.

Fruit Juices

Making your own fruit juices for babies or for anyone in the family is a good use for surplus fruit. There is a wide variety to choose from—apple, berry, cherry, and peach or apricot—called nectars (such a delicious term!).

Preserving Pointers

Apple juice is best if you mix several varieties of apples in the batch. The flavor is complex and rich.

Prepare these as you would if you were going to be making jelly and were ready to extract the juice. See Chapter 18 for detailed instructions. When you've prepared the juice, pour it into hot, sterilized jars, leaving ¼ inch of headspace. Wipe rims, adjust lids, and place in the boiling water canner. Process for 5 minutes for pints or quarts and 10 minutes for half-gallons.

Fruit Purées (Including Applesauce)

An excellent way to begin the process of making fruit leathers (see Chapter 20), purées are excellent foundations for fruit desserts and for baby food.

Wash, stem, and pit fruit as necessary. Peeling isn't mandatory, but it will make the purée easier to manage in the food mill. Use your potato masher to crush the fruit a bit before measuring it. Then place the fruit in a large saucepan. Add 1 cup of water to each 4 cups of fruit. Turn the heat on high, bring it just to a boil, and then reduce the heat and simmer until the fruit is tender. You can have at it with the masher again if you like.

Remove the saucepan from the heat and run the fruit through the food mill. The food mill is a handy food preparation tool. It's made of stainless steel and consists of two pieces. The bottom part is bowl-shaped with slots that allow you to position it securely over a medium-size cook pot or bowl. Instead of a solid bottom, however, it's a sieve with a small slot in the center. This slot supports a paddle that you operate by a hand crank. You pour food into the bottom of the food mill and turn the hand crank. This forces cooked soft foods through the sieve.

After milling, return the purée to a clean saucepan. Sweeten it to taste if you like. Reheat the purée to boiling. If you've added sugar, be sure it's all dissolved before you remove the purée from the heat. Then pour it into hot, sterilized jars, leaving ¼ inch of headspace. Wipe rims, adjust lids, and place in the boiling water canner. Process 15 minutes for pints or quarts.

Using a food mill.

Pie Fillings

A major problem with making canned pie fillings is that they tend to separate or get gummy if you use tapioca, flour, or cornstarch for thickening. A chemically modified food starch has been developed to solve this problem, and it's the only thickening agent approved by the USDA for canning. It can be a challenge to find, however, and you're not likely to find it at the grocery store. The National Center for Home Food Preservation has a link to sources: www.uga.edu/nchfp/how/can_02/canpie.html.

If you're not willing or able to go on the hunt, you have other options. You can always can the pie filling without any starch and then thicken it with tapioca, flour, or cornstarch before putting it in the pie shell.

You can also prepare the pie filling by your favorite recipe. Using your usual thickening agent, process quarts in a boiling water bath for 20 minutes. When you're ready to make a pie, reheat the filling and stir it to reblend the ingredients.

Preserving Pointers

One quart of pie filling will make a rather flat pie. Two quarts may be too much. Why not put up some quarts and some pints, too? Or you can use the extra filling to make individual apple tarts.

Tomatoes

Tomatoes are treated the same way as fruit, which they technically are. They're probably the most versatile fruit/veggie you'll work with.

Regardless of what your intended product is, begin by sorting, removing stems, and washing the tomatoes. Then fill your boiling water canner about half full of hot water, put the lid on, and turn on the heat. When the water boils, use a slotted spoon or fried food lifter to place the tomatoes in the boiling water. Leave them about 20 to 30 seconds, then remove them from the canner and plunge them into very cold water. The skins will peel right off (just like peaches).

Safety Check

It's important to use bottled lemon juice. Fresh lemon juice varies in its amount of acidity, but bottled is constant.

If you have plenty of tomatoes, crush some of them for juice to pour over the tomatoes you'll be canning. Salt is not necessary, so only add it if you want to. If you prefer your tomatoes unsalted, bully for you! You will need to add some bottled lemon juice, however. Today's tomatoes aren't as acidic as in years gone by, and to make them safe with a boiling water bath, some extra acid is necessary.

Canning Wholes or Halves

Wide-mouth jars are the easier way to go for tomatoes. Choose hot pack or raw pack. Hot pack will allow you to get more tomatoes in the jars. If you're canning whole tomatoes, first put a couple of tablespoons of tomato juice or hot water in the bottom of the jar. You'll be wedging two or three tomatoes in the bottom, and the liquid will help prevent a giant air bubble from forming. Add 1 tablespoon of bottled lemon juice per pint of tomatoes. Fill the jar and cover the tomatoes with juice or boiling water, leaving ½ inch of headspace. Wipe rims, adjust lids, and process in a boiling water canner. See Appendix D for times.

Tomato Sauce

Place peeled tomatoes in a large cooking pot and use your potato masher to crush them a bit. Turn the heat on low and allow the tomatoes to simmer. Stir occasionally. As they simmer, the cells will break down, causing the tomatoes to soften and the juice to be released. When the tomatoes are cooked sufficiently, remove them from the heat and put them through the food mill.

Return the sauce to a clean cooking pot and allow it to simmer. At this point, you can add spices according to your favorite recipe or can the sauce unseasoned after it has reached the desired consistency.

Add 1 tablespoon of bottled lemon juice per pint of tomato sauce. Then pour it into jars, leaving ¼ inch of headspace. Wipe rims, adjust lids, and process in a boiling water canner for 35 minutes for pints or 40 minutes for quarts.

Tomato Juice

Straining the tomatoes after they've simmered will give you fresh, flavorful tomato juice. Pour it into jars and add 1 tablespoon of bottled lemon juice per pint. Process in the boiling water canner for 40 minutes for pints and 45 minutes for quarts.

When the jars have cooled, you'll notice that the juice is beginning to separate. This is normal for home-canned juice. Commercial procedures are able to heat the tomatoes nearly to boiling in just seconds. This destroys enzymes that are responsible for the separation. The solution? Shake that jar before you pour!

Recipes

Cranberry sauce is a good accompaniment to all kinds of poultry, and while the whole berries freeze very well, sometimes you just want to reach for a jar of already made-up sauce. It's easy to can, so you can be ready for a last-minute change of menu! Canned fruits also make wonderful desserts. Here are two tasty desserts using canned fruits. One is hearty, and the other is light.

Cranberry Sauce

The following recipe is reprinted courtesy of Ocean Spray Cranberries, Inc. and has been adapted for canning. Recipe can be doubled.

Makes 2 pints
Prep time: 5 minutes
Cook time: 25 minutes (includes processing)

1 cup sugar

1 cup water

1 (12 oz.) package Ocean Spray whole cranberries

1. Wash and sort through berries. Bring water and sugar to a boil in a medium saucepan. Add cranberries and return to a boil. Reduce heat and boil gently for 10 minutes, stirring occasionally.

2. Ladle sauce into jars, leaving ⅛ inch headspace. Remove air bubbles, wipe rims, adjust lids, and process pints in a boiling water bath for 5 minutes to ensure the seal.

Broiled Pears

When you're in a hurry and want something quick and easy, this is a good dish to rely on. As a bonus, it's also elegant!

Serves 4
Prep time: 5 minutes
Cook time: 5 minutes

2 pears, peeled, halved, and cored

2 TB. brown sugar

¼ tsp. nutmeg

2 tsp. butter

Arrange pear halves in an oven-proof casserole dish with low sides. Sprinkle with brown sugar, nutmeg, and dot with butter. Broil until butter has bubbled and pears are a light brown. Serve with whipped cream.

Pineapple Upside-Down Cake

This is an old-time favorite. Many young cooks got their start by being allowed to place the maraschino cherries in the center of the pineapple rings. Crunchy, rich, and packed with flavor, it's sure to please.

½ cup butter	4 eggs, separated
2 cups dark brown sugar	1 cup sugar
1 qt. canned pineapple slices	1 cup flour
Maraschino cherries	1 tsp. baking powder

Serves 6 to 8
Prep time: 25 minutes
Cook time: 30 minutes

1. Preheat oven to 350°F. Melt butter in a 10-inch cast-iron skillet. Sprinkle brown sugar evenly across butter. Place one pineapple ring in the center of the skillet and arrange slices around it, covering the bottom of the skillet. Place a maraschino cherry in the center of each ring.

2. Beat egg whites until stiff. Set aside.

3. Make sponge cake. Beat egg yolks with sugar until fluffy. Combine flour and baking powder and sift. Fold gently into egg and sugar mixture, ½ cup at a time. Fold in beaten egg whites. Pour batter over pineapples and spread evenly with spatula. Bake 25 to 30 minutes or until cake tests done. Remove the skillet from the oven (use mitts!) and place it on top of the stove. Run a knife around the rim of the skillet. Then invert the skillet onto a serving platter.

Chapter 11

Canning Vegetables

In This Chapter

- ◆ Safety first
- ◆ Taking the procedure for a test drive
- ◆ From asparagus to winter squash: filling the pantry
- ◆ Mixing it up

If slicing and dicing and chopping don't sound like your idea of fun, take heart! There are some nifty gadgets on the market that make preparing vegetables so much easier than before. From green bean frenchers to corn slicers, canning vegetables has never been quicker and more fun. Never canned vegetables before? Once you hear those lids snapping shut, indicating a good seal, you'll be hooked. (Tomatoes are fruits, and they're covered in Chapter 10.)

General Principles

Vegetables are low-acid foods, which means they have a pH value above 4.6, and that means they must be processed in the pressure canner. All the skills covered in Chapter 10 apply here—all that's different is the manner of processing.

Whether this is your first canning season or your fifteenth, reviewing safety procedures and rereading the instructions that came with your pressure canner is the smart way to begin. Most mistakes are made by veterans. It's the rookies who play by the book. Getting comfortable with the process is the goal, but getting sloppy, careless, and taking shortcuts is not the way to get there. Take your time and do it right.

Taking a Test Drive

Still a little nervous? That's natural. Let's deal with the worries that may be making you nervous.

Worry #1: The pressure canner could explode.

Reality: Remember the story about Aunt Mabel in Chapter 9? You're not Aunt Mabel. You're going to stay in the kitchen and monitor the canning. You control the heat, and you control the pressure. If the pressure starts to creep up, simply turn the heat down.

Worry #2: All the jars will explode inside the canner.

Reality: Place 2 to 3 inches of water in the canner, monitor the heat and the temperature, and all will be fine.

Worry #3: I won't do it right, and I'll kill my whole family.

Reality: You will do it right because you are going to follow the directions and the proper procedures. You are going to give your family healthy, safe food.

Worry #4: There's too much to remember all at once.

Reality: If you've used your boiling water canner to process fruit (see Chapter 10), you have 90 percent of the procedures already under your belt. It's time to take a test drive:

1. Place your pressure canner on the stove and add 2 to 3 inches of water to it.

2. Put on and secure the lid. Be sure the petcock is open. Check the diagram in the instruction manual if you need to.

3. Turn on the heat.

4. When the steam starts to flow in an uninterrupted stream from the vent, set the oven timer for 10 minutes.

5. When the timer buzzes, either put on the weight or close the petcock, depending on the model of your canner.

6. If you have a weight gauge canner, pull up a chair and listen for the sound of it gently rocking back and forth and releasing steam. You don't have to do anything else. When it starts rocking, set the oven timer for 5 minutes. When the timer goes off, turn off the heat under the canner and wait for all the noise to stop. Then wait 2 more minutes, remove the weight, and remove the lid.

   If you have a dial gauge canner, pull up a chair and watch the pressure gradually climb to 10 pounds. Turn down the heat as needed to keep the pressure at 10 pounds. This may take a little finessing. Don't panic if the pressure climbs a bit more while you're learning how to adjust the heat. After you've been able to hold the heat at 10 pounds of pressure for 10 minutes, turn off the canner and wait. When the pressure reaches zero, open the petcock. Wait 2 more minutes and then remove the lid.

The test drive has been successfully completed. Nothing blew up, and you survived. You're ready to go for the real thing.

About Salt

You'll come across many recipes for canning vegetables that include salt. Feel free to omit it. It's not used as a preservative, only as a flavoring agent. If you're interested in reducing your salt intake, you can start here.

About Altitude

All vegetables are processed at 10 pounds of pressure at sea level. Follow the recommendations outlined in Chapter 9 with regard to increasing the pressure at which you'll process food at your particular altitude. Processing times do not increase, but pounds of pressure do.

About Quality

Canning will not improve the quality of the vegetables you're putting up, so it's important to use the best produce you can find. Each region has varieties of vegetables suited for canning. Check with your Extension Office for varieties for your area. Its number is in the phone book.

Preserving Pointers _____

Slightly underripe veggies are better than slightly overripe for canning purposes. You'll be cooking them hard during processing, and you want them to hold up. That's difficult to do when you're past your prime, especially if you're a vegetable.

Getting Started

Review the directions for loading the canner, securing the canner lid, venting, and placing the weight on the vent port or closing the petcock. Set the pressure canner on the stove and add 2 to 3 inches of water. Turn on the heat. Have the lid to the side so that it doesn't get jostled while you're preparing the food. While you're monitoring the first load in the canner, review proper cool-down procedures covered earlier in step 6 of your test drive.

Asparagus

Asparagus freezes better than it cans, but if you need to can some, it looks lovely when it's carefully arranged in a canning jar, so take the time to bring out your inner artist. Select young stalks and wash them thoroughly. Hold the stalk in one hand and grasp the bottom of the stalk with the other. Bend from the bottom to snap off the tougher bottom joint.

Measure one spear against the height of the jar minus ½ inch for headroom. Use this spear as a template for cutting the other spears to the proper height. You can use either raw pack or hot pack, although raw pack is much, much easier. Processing times are the same for either method.

For raw pack, place the spears upright (tips up) in the jar. You can fill another jar with the cut pieces and use them for stews or other casserole dishes.

For hot pack, arrange a bundle of spears to stand (tips pointed up) in a wire basket and place the basket in boiling water for 3 minutes. Do not get the tips in the boiling water. It can be quite a balancing act. Then remove them from boiling water and arrange the spears, tips pointed up, in the jars. They'll be hot and a bit flexible. It's sort of like trying to stack rubber bands.

Fill the jars with boiling water, leaving ½ inch of headspace. Wipe rims, adjust lids, and process in a pressure canner. See Appendix D for times.

Green Beans

Green beans and yellow wax beans can very nicely if you use varieties that hold up under processing. These include Contender, Topcrop, Tendercrop, and Kentucky Wonder. Wash them thoroughly to remove any stuck leaves or other garden debris. Remove the tips and tails and either can whole or cut into pieces. If you prefer French-style beans, you can find *frenchers* through vegetable seed catalogs or at kitchen specialty shops.

As with asparagus, you can stand the beans upright in the jar. This allows you to maximize the amount you put in each jar, and it also looks very appealing. You can also fill jars with cut pieces, and these work well in soups, stews, and casserole dishes.

For raw pack, arrange the beans in jars and cover with boiling water, leaving ½ inch of headspace. For hot pack, add the beans to boiling water and boil for 5 minutes. Then pack into jars and cover with the boiling water, leaving ½ inch of headspace.

def•i•ni•tion

A green bean **frencher** is a small device that clamps onto a counter or table top. You feed the beans into a hopper at the top and then turn a small hand crank that feeds the beans from the hopper to internal stainless steel blades that slice the beans lengthwise— a procedure called *frenching*.

Wipe rims, adjust lids, and process in a pressure canner. See Appendix D for times.

Lima Beans

Shell the beans and sort according to size. Lima beans come in different sizes, and while the smallest ones are the most desirable for canning, the larger ones also do fine. Limas tend to expand exponentially during processing, so they require considerably more headspace than other vegetables. You can use raw pack or hot pack, but hot pack will reduce the amount of headspace you need somewhat.

For raw pack, fill jars but don't pack the beans in too tightly. Cover with boiling water. Headspace for smaller beans is 1 inch for pints and 1½ inches for quarts. For larger beans, use ¾-inch headspace for pints and 1¼ inches for quarts.

For hot pack, add the beans to boiling water and cook for 1 minute. Drain. Fill the jars, leaving 1 inch of headspace for both pints and quarts.

Wipe rims, adjust lids, and process in a pressure canner. See Appendix D for times.

Beets

Beets are accommodating vegetables. Small beets work very well canned whole, and larger beets do fine as slices. Leave a portion of the top on—an inch or two—and about an inch of the root as well. If you don't, the beets will bleed while you're preparing them, and you'll end up with a rather anemic pink ball.

Use hot pack for these since they'll be doing a bit of cooking during skin removal. Wash the beets and sort them according to size. Work with one size group at a time. Place them in boiling water and cook for about 20 minutes. Then remove them from the water and place them in cold water to slip the skins, tops, and root pieces. Don't keep them in so long that they cool down.

Pack whole beets or slices in jars and add boiling water to cover, leaving ½ inch of headspace. Wipe rims, adjust lids, and process in a pressure canner. See Appendix D for times. Beets also root cellar if you have one (see Chapter 23), and it's the first choice for preserving them.

Carrots

An essential component of stews and soups, carrots are excellent keepers in a root cellar. If you want to put some up to have in the pantry, however, they also do well canned. Scrub them with a vegetable brush. That will get off the garden dirt and the skin, if the carrots are young. Older carrots have thicker skins. If they're a bit older, dip them in boiling water for about 30 seconds and then plunge them into cold water. Then slip off the skins. If you prefer to leave the skins on, it's perfectly acceptable.

Safety Check

For added safety, always boil low-acid canned vegetables for 10 minutes before serving. This will destroy toxins that may be present but which are undetectable to the naked eye.

Cut the carrots into slices (either vertical or horizontal), cubes, or leave them whole if they're tiny. Use either raw or hot pack.

For raw pack, pack carrots into jars and leave a full inch of headspace. Then add boiling water to cover, leaving ½ inch of final headspace.

For hot pack, add carrots to boiling water and allow the water to return to a full boil. Remove the carrots and pack into jars, leaving ½ inch of headspace. Cover with boiling water, still leaving ½ inch of headspace.

Wipe rims, adjust lids, and process in a pressure canner. See Appendix D for times.

Corn

Canned corn has a crunchier texture than frozen corn, and some people prefer it. It's certainly a handy item to have on hand, and if you've got a corn slicer, you can save wear and tear on your hands.

Using a corn slicer.

Husk the corn outside if you can. It's a messy process, with silk distributing itself all over the kitchen if given half a chance. Wash the ears under cool, running water to remove any remaining silk. Then either cut the kernels from the cob with a sharp knife or run the ears across the corn slicer, being careful to keep fingers out of the way.

The corn slicer is adjustable. You can set the blade to cut about two thirds of the way through the kernels for whole kernel or about halfway through if you're planning on making creamed corn.

Whole Kernel

Use either raw or hot pack. For raw pack, fill jars loosely leaving 1 inch of headspace at the top. Then add boiling water to cover, leaving a final headspace of ½ inch.

For hot pack, add corn to boiling water and allow it to return to a boil. Pack into jars and add water to cover, leaving 1 inch of headspace. Wipe rims, adjust lids, and process in a pressure canner. See Appendix D for times.

Creamed Corn

After cutting the kernels off the cob, run a table knife down each row to capture the milk. Add this to the corn. Creamed corn is quite dense and should only be processed in pint jars. Pack jars with kernels and milk, leaving 1 inch of headroom. Wipe rims, adjust lids, and process in a pressure canner. See Appendix D for times.

Greens

Greens (such as chard and spinach) freeze beautifully, but canning tends to turn them a murky shade of greenish gray. The length of time required for processing will generally make them mush. However, you *can* can them.

Use hot pack only. Wash greens in several changes of cool water to remove all the grit they love to harbor. Then trim the stems if you like. You can either blanch the greens for 2 minutes or steam them for about 10 minutes to get them wilted enough to be able to stuff them into jars.

Pack them into jars and cover them with water, leaving ½ inch of headspace. Wipe rims, adjust lids, and process in a pressure canner. See Appendix D for times.

Mushrooms

These freeze nicely, but if you're running out of freezer space or want some in the pantry to grab on the run, you can put them up in pints or even half-pints. You'll need a great many mushrooms to make a canning load: about 14½ pounds for a full load of pints.

Soak mushrooms in cool water for 10 minutes to loosen any dirt or sterilized manure. Remove them from the water, inspect for spots or damage, and trim away. Wash thoroughly and then slice, dice, or leave whole. Place in a saucepan and cover with water. Boil 5 minutes.

Safety Check

Do not can wild mushrooms. No safe processing times have been developed for them.

Pack into pint or half-pint jars, leaving 1 inch of headspace. To protect against discoloration, add ⅛ teaspoon of ascorbic acid powder or one 500 mg vitamin C tablet to each pint jar. Wipe rims, adjust lids, and process either pints or half-pints in a pressure canner. See Appendix D for times.

Okra

No Southern cook would even think of making stew without okra. You want young, tender pods without black spots. You'll be using hot pack.

Wash the okra but leave the caps on. Add them to boiling water and boil for 2 minutes. Drain. Then cut into slices or use whole. Pack into jars, leaving ½ inch of headroom. Wipe rims, adjust lids, and process in a pressure canner. See Appendix D for times.

Peas

Select fresh pods without yellowing. Peas should fill the pods without crowding them or showing signs of sprouting. Shell the peas and pack them into jars, leaving 1 inch of headspace. Peas expand as they process. Use either raw pack or hot pack.

> **In Other Words**
>
> "Many hands make light work" and "Too many cooks spoil the broth" are words of wisdom in the food-preserving kitchen. Enlist all the help you can get for husking corn and shelling peas, but once the canner is loaded, shoo the help out and take sole command.

For raw pack, add boiling water but don't cover the peas. Come to ½ inch of the top of the peas.

For hot pack, fill the jars and cover the peas with boiling water, leaving 1 inch of headspace. Wipe rims, adjust lids, and process in a pressure canner. See Appendix D for times.

Peppers—Hot or Sweet

You want firm peppers for canning. Avoid peppers with dark spots or other signs of damage. You can either use raw or hot pack for these. If they're small, you can process them whole. Bigger peppers can be cut into halves or quarters. Wash the peppers. If canning them whole, make several small slits in each pepper to allow air to escape. If not canning them whole, remove the seeds and pith.

You have a few options for blanching these. Place them under the broiler in the oven or arrange them on the middle oven rack with the oven heated to 400°F until the

Safety Check

Always wear plastic gloves when working with hot peppers. Be careful not to touch your face, especially your eyes, until you've washed your hands in soap and water.

skins blister. Then remove them from the oven and allow them to cool. Place a damp cloth over them for a few minutes to make peeling easier.

Smooshing comes next. Collapse whole peppers by pressing your palm against the side until they're flat. Pack them loosely into jars and add boiling water to cover, leaving 1 inch of headspace. Wipe rims, adjust lids, and process in a pressure canner. See Appendix D for times.

Potatoes

Uncooked white potatoes do not freeze well, but you *can* can them and have a good product. Of course, the canning cooks them, but you're starting out with raw. Scrub the potatoes, peel them, and cut out any dark spots or green areas. If a potato has a great deal of greening that cannot be removed, dispose of the potato. (According to the National Institutes of Health, solanine, a toxic substance, is found in green potatoes; this substance can cause *Solanum tuberosum* poisoning. If you or someone you know has become ill after eating green potatoes, call The National Poison Control Center at 1-800-222-1222.)

Your potatoes are as white as the driven snow and are ready for the next step. Put them in a saucepan, add hot water, and bring them to a boil. Cook whole potatoes for 10 minutes and cubes for 2 minutes. Remove them from the heat and drain them.

Pack them into jars and cover with boiling water, leaving 1 inch of headroom. Wipe rims, adjust lids, and process in a pressure canner. See Appendix D for times.

Sweet Potatoes

Scrub sweet potatoes and place them in a saucepan. Add hot water and turn the heat on high. Bring them to a boil, reduce heat, and cook for 15 to 20 minutes, until the potatoes have begun to soften. Remove them from the heat and remove their skins.

Cut the potatoes into cubes. Do not purée or mash, as this makes them too dense to be processed safely. Pack them into jars and add boiling water to cover, leaving 1 inch of headspace. Some people prefer to can these in a light syrup instead of water. See Appendix C for syrup directions. Wipe rims, adjust lids, and process in a pressure canner. See Appendix D for times.

Winter Squash (Including Pumpkin)

Pumpkin is handy to put up in cubes for later service in pies, but early recipes that recommended mashing the pumpkin or puréeing it before canning have been replaced by a safety caution. Pumpkin is very dense, and it's difficult for the heat to penetrate the entire contents of the jar to a sufficient degree to protect against spoilage and botulism. Therefore, can it in cubes and mash it when you're ready to use it.

Smaller pumpkins make better pies and are also easier to work with than bigger ones. Wash the pumpkin and then dry it so it won't be slippery when you cut it. Use a sharp knife, just as if you were going to carve a jack o'lantern. Cut a circle a few inches out from the stem and remove the lid.

Now that you've got a hole to grab onto, you can make cuts down the pumpkin to cut it into sections. Remove the seeds and stringy fibers. Peel the sections and cut them into 1-inch cubes.

Boil the cubes for 2 minutes and then drain. Pack them into jars and add boiling water to cover, leaving 1 inch of headspace. Wipe rims, adjust lids, and process in a pressure canner. See Appendix D for times.

Mixed Vegetables

You can make up a canner load of pints to have ready to add to soups or stews or to serve as the main vegetable for dinner. Process the load according to the longest time required for an individual vegetable. For example, for the following suggested vegetables, you'd process pints for 55 minutes and quarts for 85 minutes because corn is the vegetable requiring the longest processing time. Suggested ingredients include sliced carrots, whole-kernel corn, green beans, lima beans, zucchini, and tomatoes. The USDA Extension Service notes you can substitute other vegetables or change proportions of those listed above. However, don't use winter squash, creamed corn, leafy greens, dried beans, or sweet potatoes.

This recipe works best if all vegetables are approximately the same size or are cut to size. Place all vegetables in a large saucepan and add hot water. Bring them to a boil and cook for 5 minutes. Turn off the heat and ladle the vegetables into jars, adding the boiling water from the saucepan to cover. Leave 1 inch of headspace. Wipe rims, adjust lids, and process in a pressure canner. See Appendix D for times.

Recipes

Here are a couple of recipes that make the most of canned vegetables. Both are familiar, traditional recipes with a modern flavor.

Stewed Tomatoes

Commercially canned stewed tomatoes are often little more than tomatoes with a kiss of onion and a hint of green pepper. If you like stewed tomatoes with some substance—with pieces of green peppers and onions that you can actually see—why not make your own? Stewed tomatoes are a good side dish for homemade macaroni and cheese.

Serves 4
Prep time: 20 minutes
Cook time: 10 minutes

1 TB. olive oil

1 clove garlic, minced

1 medium to large onion, sliced

1 cup sliced green or yellow peppers

1 qt. canned tomatoes (wholes or pieces)

Heat olive oil in a skillet. Add garlic, onion, and peppers and sauté until onion is translucent. Add tomatoes, breaking large pieces. Mix gently and simmer 20 minutes.

Mel's Borscht

This traditional beet soup comes to America via Eastern Europe and Russia.

Serves 4
Prep time: 20 minutes
Cook time: None

1 qt. canned beets

4 cups water

2 tsp. sugar (or to taste)

4 TB. vinegar

¾ to 1 cup sour cream

Mix beets, water, sugar, and vinegar. Process in a blender until smooth. Gradually add sour cream and blend again. (Do not overfill the blender! Prepare in batches and then mix together.) Store in the refrigerator. Shake well when ready to serve. Garnish with a dollop of sour cream.

Chapter 12

Canning Meat, Poultry, Seafood, and Game

In This Chapter

◆ Pressure canning is required

◆ Canning whole cuts, ground meat, or sausages

◆ Working with chicken and turkey

◆ Putting up fatty fish

◆ Working safely with game

Now that you've mastered the boiling water canner and conquered the pressure canner, it's time to get serious about putting up entire meals! Preserving meats and fish that you buy in bulk or that you harvest yourself is economical and allows you to stock up on what your family enjoys most. You can also create combination dishes to have on hand for any occasion.

A major advantage of canning meat, poultry, seafood, and game is lengthened storage life. Freezer life varies widely among these foods, but canned life is easily a year or more. Technically speaking, as long as the seal holds and the foods were prepared and processed properly, they'll keep almost indefinitely. True, quality may lessen over time, but not anywhere near as rapidly as in the freezer.

General Procedures

Just as you preserved only the best-quality fruits and vegetables, you'll do the same with meat, poultry, seafood, and game. The same basic rules of cleanliness apply here and so do safety procedures. These are low-acid foods and must be processed in the pressure canner.

Generally you'll freeze larger cuts of meat or poultry. If you don't have room in the freezer or if electricity isn't reliable at the mountain cabin, however, you can put up pints or quarts and have plenty of healthful, good-quality food ready for use.

Keep Your Cool

This ranks right up there with keeping a clean work area. Keep everything refrigerated until you're ready to use it. If you can't get to the processing within two days, freeze the food until you can. Ice fish as soon as possible after catching them and cool harvested game or home-produced meat after slaughter to 40°F or below.

Keep Trim

Lean meat is best for canning. Trim away fat from the outside of the meat and cut away any gristle. Extra fat can prevent jars from sealing. The globules work themselves loose and can lodge between the jar rim and the lid. Also cut away any bruising you see. Remove any large bones from meat before canning. The bones take up space, and you don't eat them anyway.

Keep Moving

If you're going to be canning whole meats, assemble all your supplies before you take the meat out of the refrigerator. This will help you keep both your work area and your hands free and clean. Decide if you'll can the meat in pints or quarts and whether you'll raw pack or hot pack. Once you begin, you'll want to keep at it until the canner is filled so the meat doesn't sit overly long at room temperature.

Canning Beef, Pork, or Lamb

Having pint or quart jars at the ready filled with tender chunks of meat in a rich broth makes meal planning a cinch. Want to make a stew but time is short? You've got all the ingredients at hand if you're a home food preserver. How about roast beef with gravy, mashed potatoes, and canned corn for a comfort meal on a cold winter night? Again, check. You've got it covered.

Don't shy away from canning meat because it sounds tough. It's not, and neither is the meat! When you've rounded out the contents of your pantry with ready-to-use meats, you'll be sitting in the catbird seat.

You have two methods for putting up meats—raw pack or hot pack. Raw pack is definitely quicker, but hot pack eliminates shrinkage and gives a better quality product.

Safety Check _____

Always follow approved procedures for slaughtering, chilling, and aging if you're going to harvest your own meat. The Extension Service has informational bulletins for beef, pork, and lamb. The number is in your telephone book.

Raw Pack

This method is straightforward. Wipe the meat with a clean, damp cloth. Meat shouldn't need to be washed. If canning a solid cut, cut the meat to fit the jar you'll be using. You can also use cut-up pieces such as chunks or cubes.

Fill the jar with the meat, leaving 1 inch of headspace. Add salt if you wish—½ teaspoon per pint and 1 teaspoon per quart. The salt is strictly for flavoring and doesn't work as a preservative, so feel free to leave it out. Do not add any liquid to the jar. The meat will create its own juices as it processes. Wipe rims, adjust lids, and process in a pressure canner. See Appendix D for times.

Hot Pack

There are three steps for this method:

1. Make stock to use in filling the jars after you've packed the meat. You can also use boiling water, but stock will give the meat more flavor.

2. Precook the meat to be packed.

3. Pack the meat, add the liquid, and process.

If you've made meat stock, this is an excellent use for it. Otherwise, gather up the meat scraps and bones and place them in a large saucepan to make broth. Add water to cover. Turn the heat on high and bring the broth to a boil. Reduce heat and simmer 2 to 4 hours. Then drain the broth from the saucepan and place it in the

Safety Check

Don't dredge the meat in flour, brown the meat in flour, or use flour in the stock to make gravy. The flour can gum up the process by preventing even heating of the meat during processing.

refrigerator. When the broth has cooled, remove any fat that has congealed at the surface. Return the broth to the saucepan and bring it to a boil.

Next cook the meat. You're aiming for rare since the meat will cook further during processing. You can boil it, broil it, or fry it. Cut the meat to fit the jars and pack hot meat loosely into the jars. Add liquid to cover, leaving 1 inch of headspace. Insert a spatula to remove air bubbles, wipe rims, adjust lids, and process in a pressure canner. See Appendix D for times.

Ground Meats

Ground beef, pork, and lamb can well. Brown the meat first, breaking up any clumps that form. You want the meat loose. Pack the meat loosely into jars and add broth or boiling water to cover. Leave 1 inch of headspace. Insert a spatula to remove air bubbles, wipe rims, adjust lids, and process in a pressure canner. See Appendix D for times.

Lamb and Pork Sausage

Yes, you *can* can sausage. Lamb and pork sausage make wonderful patties for breakfast. If you're using bulk sausage, make the patties bigger because they'll shrink a bit as they cook. If you're planning on making your own sausage, go easy on the spices. Some get stronger or even change flavor during processing. Brown them on both sides and then transfer them to the canning jar, adding boiling hot broth to cover. Leave 1 inch of headspace. Insert a spatula to remove air bubbles, wipe rims, adjust lids, and process in a pressure canner. See Appendix D for times.

Hard Sausages

If you find a great deal at the grocery store on hard sausages such as salami or pepperoni, take advantage even if you don't need them for dinner. Hard sausages have been dried, but they will spoil if not refrigerated, and even then their shelf life is limited.

All you have to do with these is either slice them or cut larger pieces to fit in the jar. Leave 1 inch of headspace. Don't add liquid. Adjust the lids and process in the pressure canner. See Appendix D for times. When you want to make pizza or whip up a batch of salami and cheese sandwiches, you're ready.

Canning Poultry

Poultry refers to domesticated birds: chicken, turkey, duck, goose, guinea hens, and pigeon. Fresh chicken is available year round, and frequently there are good sales where you can stock up. Consider canning some of this along with freezing some.

Fresh turkey is generally found around Thanksgiving; the rest of the year you'll likely find it in the frozen meats section of the grocery store. Fresh duck or goose is difficult to find commercially and generally comes to you courtesy of a successful hunter. In addition to smoking, canning is a good way to put some up.

Cutting Up

Obviously, you're not going to be able to put the whole bird into the canning jar. You're going to need to cut it up. Fortunately, all birds are built along the same lines, so if you know how to cut one up, you can deal with them all. There are four basic cuts to turn a whole bird into parts:

1. Cut through the wing and remove the *drumette.*

2. Make a cut where the leg attaches to the body. Then disjoint the leg. Hold the bird down with one hand while you take the leg in your other hand and bend the leg backward until you've exposed the joint. Cut through the joint and remove the leg.

def•i•ni•tion

> The **drumette** is the fleshy part of the wing and is what you'll be served if you order wings at a restaurant. Many people discard the wings, not realizing there's some good meat there.

3. Separate the thigh from the leg. Make a cut over the joint where the thigh attaches to the leg. Hold the meaty portion of the leg in one hand and the bottom portion of the leg in the other and bend the leg backward until the joint is exposed. Then cut through the joint.

4. Cut along the breastbone—the ridge along the top of the bird. Then pull the two sections apart and cut through the bones holding the parts together.

Removing the drumette.

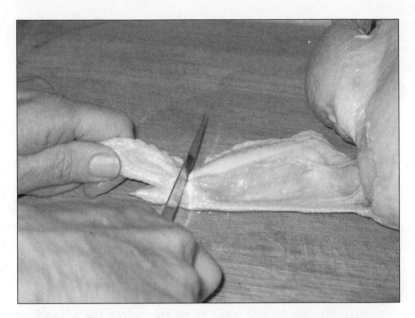

Removing the legs.

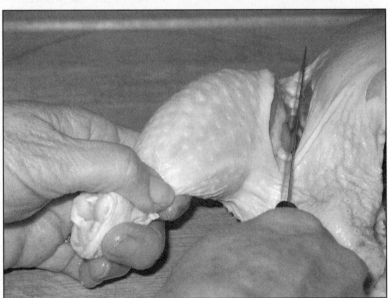

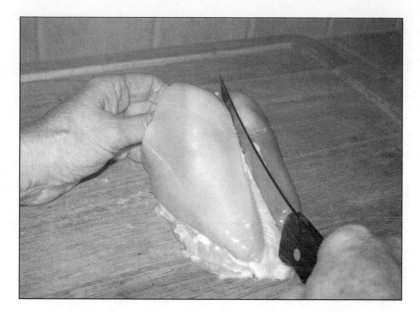

Cutting the breast in half.

At this point, you'll decide if you want to bone the bird or can it with bones. This decision is strictly a personal preference and will depend upon your intended use later on. Removing the leg bone is probably the best choice since it's big and will take up quite a bit of room in the jar. To do this, make a cut along the length of the leg, exposing the bone. Then carefully peel the flesh from the bone.

Boning the breasts is also easy to do. Use a small, sharp knife to make a cut between the ribs and the flesh along the length of the breast. Then continue on, cutting and separating the ribs as you go. When you reach the bottom, the ribs will lift away, and you'll have a boneless chicken breast. Considering the cost of boneless poultry, knowing how to bone it yourself makes good sense. Now you're ready to cut the poultry into pieces that will fit in the canning jars.

For raw pack, pack pieces into jars, leaving 1¼ inch of headspace. Do not add liquid. Wipe rims, adjust lids, and process in a pressure canner. See Appendix D for times.

For hot pack, precook the poultry in stock or broth until it is medium-done. Pack hot poultry loosely into jars and add boiling broth or water to cover, leaving 1¼ inch of headspace. Wipe rims, adjust lids, and process in a pressure canner. See Appendix D for times.

Rabbit or Squirrel: Neither Fish nor Fowl

These don't have wings, but they are handled the same as poultry for canning purposes. These can be dry, so the recommendation is to dress the rabbit or squirrel and then soak it for 1 hour in water containing 1 tablespoon of salt per quart of water. If you're working with wild rabbit, the saltwater helps take away some of the "gaminess." Drain and rinse. Remove all excess fat. Then treat it the same as poultry. See Appendix D for processing times.

Canning Seafood

Fish should be fresh and iced as soon as possible after the catch. Fish are highly perishable and bruise easily. Be careful not to crush them by stacking them several deep during transport. Shellfish should be live when you begin to work with them. Keep them cool and moist.

Fish

Fatty fish such as mackerel, trout, and bluefish (but not tuna) can best. Clean and gut the fish as soon as possible after catching. When ready to can, scale the fish and then remove the heads, tails, and fins. Wash the fish thoroughly and remove bones. Cut the fish in half lengthwise and then cut to fit the jars.

Safety Check

Safe processing times have not been developed for using quart jars for fish. Use half-pints or pints.

You can either soak the fish in a salt brine (1 cup of salt per gallon of water) for 1 hour or add 1 teaspoon of salt to each pint. Pack raw fish tightly into half-pint or pint jars, leaving 1 inch of headspace. Wipe rims, adjust lids, and process in a pressure canner. See Appendix D for times.

Preserving Pointers

Sometimes you'll find crystals in home-canned salmon. These are magnesium ammonium phosphate crystals, they occur naturally, and they're not harmful. When you heat the salmon, the crystals usually dissolve. There's nothing you can do to prevent them, and you don't need to worry about them.

Smoked Fish

Smoked fish have a wonderful flavor and aroma but a short shelf life—even refrigerated, it's not going to keep longer than 7 to 14 days. To be sure you have enough on hand, try canning some. You'll keep that smoked goodness, and the fish will keep much longer.

The first rule is to smoke only the amount of fish you'll be able to can in a day. Since smoked fish can dry out during canning processing times, new recommendations advise you to do a light smoke with them. This means smoking the fish for up to 2 hours in a home smoker at 140°F to 160°F. Then use pint jars—not quarts.

The method for processing smoked fish is a bit different from that of other seafood. Pack the fish vertically into the jars, leaving 1 inch of headspace. You can loose pack or tight pack. Wipe rims and adjust lids. Pour 4 quarts (16 cups) of cool—not hot—water into the pressure canner. Then add the jars to the canner. The water will come up to the jar rims, and this is what you want. See Appendix D for processing times.

Shellfish

It's handy having canned oysters, clams, and other types of shellfish in the cupboard. You've got the major ingredient for chowders and other dishes at your fingertips. Methods for shucking, shelling, and cleaning shellfish are covered in Chapter 6. See Appendix D for processing times.

Here's the preparation for clams:

1. Save the juice when you cut out the meat. Heat the juice to boiling in a small saucepan.

2. Wash the meat in a weak brine made from 1 to 3 tablespoons of salt to a gallon of water.

3. Then place 2 tablespoons of vinegar or lemon juice or ½ teaspoon of citric acid in a medium-size saucepan. Add 1 gallon of water. Heat to a boil. Blanch the meat for 1 to 2 minutes in the boiling solution.

4. Remove from the heat, drain, and pack into jars, leaving 1 inch of headspace.

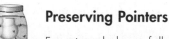

Preserving Pointers

For minced clams, follow step 3 for preparing clams with a session in the meat grinder. Then continue with the remaining steps for preparing whole clams.

5. Add boiling juice and additional boiling water as needed to cover the clams, leaving 1 inch of headspace.

6. Wipe rims, adjust lids, and process in a pressure canner. See Appendix D for times.

Here's the preparation for crabs:

1. After cleaning the crab, cook for 20 minutes in a brine made from 2 tablespoons to 1 cup of salt and ¼ cup of white vinegar or lemon juice to a gallon of water. Remove from heat, drain, and cool.

2. Pick the crab. This means separating the crab meat from the shell. It can be a tedious process and you may find it easier to pull up a chair and get comfortable while you're stacking up the shells.

3. Rinse in a cool brine made from 2 tablespoons to 1 cup of salt and 1 to 2 cups of white vinegar or lemon juice to a gallon of water.

4. Remove excess moisture from the crab by squeezing gently.

5. Pack into pint jars, leaving 1 inch of headspace.

6. Add 2 tablespoons of white vinegar or lemon juice or 1 teaspoon of citric acid to each pint and add boiling water to cover, leaving 1 inch of headspace.

7. Wipe rims, adjust lids, and process in a pressure canner. See Appendix D for times.

Here's the preparation for oysters:

1. After cleaning, wash the meat in a weak brine solution made from ½ cup of salt to a gallon of water. Drain the moisture from the meat and pack it into jars, leaving 1 inch of headspace.

2. Cover with a weak brine solution (1 tablespoon of salt to a quart of water), leaving 1 inch of headspace.

3. Wipe rims, adjust lids, and process in a pressure canner. See Appendix D for times.

Here's the preparation for shrimp:

1. After cleaning, cook the shrimp 8 to 10 minutes in boiling brine made from ¼ to 1 cup of salt and 1 cup of vinegar to a gallon of water. Remove from heat, drain, and rinse in cold water.

2. Pack into jars, leaving 1 inch of headspace. Cover with boiling salt brine made from 1 to 3 tablespoons of salt to a gallon of water.

3. Wipe rims, adjust lids, and process in a pressure canner. See Appendix D for times.

Canning Game

Wild game is different from domestic meat. That seems obvious, but it bears some explanation. What are the differences? Domestic animals live in a controlled environment. They're fenced in and fed or allowed to graze on specific pastures. They don't have to (or shouldn't have to) struggle to find sustenance. With their dietary needs more than satisfied, they put on weight. This means they have enough food to enable them to store the excess as fat. Fat makes meat tender and flavorful.

Wild game animals have a tougher life. They are constantly on the search for food. They tend to be leaner, and as a result tougher, than their domestic cousins. Pressure canning their meat solves the toughness problem, but not the gaminess that some people find distasteful. So what is that gamey taste?

Not to put too fine a point on it, but after all, it's game. It has its own particular flavor and aroma, and if you're expecting venison to taste like beef, you're going to be disappointed. If you're expecting venison to taste like venison, however, you're going to be satisfied. If you're an aficionado of game, you enjoy its distinctive taste and aroma. That said, there are a couple factors that contribute to a gamey taste, and you can do something about both of them.

First of all, be sure the game is kept properly chilled after harvesting. Once the animal becomes warm, there's not much you can do to reverse the natural processes that led to a disagreeable taste.

Second, be sure to remove all the fat. Especially with deer meat, fat can contribute to gaminess. It may seem contradictory, since the fat on domestic animals doesn't make them taste gamey, but that's just the way it works.

Some people add a teaspoon or two of vinegar while they're cooking venison, and some people insist that soaking the meat in milk before cooking it works fine. Neither of these methods will cause any harm. Salt and tomato juice are also used, and they're discussed in a moment.

Before preparing game for canning, soak it for 60 minutes in a brine made from 1 tablespoon of salt to a quart of water. This reduces the gamey taste. Then rinse and remove the large bones. Cut meat into strips, chunks, or cubes.

For raw pack, pack meat into jars, leaving 1 inch of headspace. Do not add liquid. You can add 1 teaspoon of salt to each jar if you wish for flavor, but it's not necessary. Wipe rims, adjust lids, and process in a pressure canner. See Appendix D for times.

For hot pack, precook the meat until rare. You can stew it, roast it, or simply brown it in olive oil or fat. Then pack it into jars and cover it with boiling broth, water, or tomato juice, leaving 1 inch of headspace. Tomato juice is often used to deal with the gamey nature of game. Then wipe rims, adjust lids, and process in a pressure canner. See Appendix D for times.

Determining Proper Processing Times

If you'd like to put up some soup, stew, or chili to have ready for a quick supper on a cold night, there are a few things to keep in mind to make sure your meal is nutritious and safe. It's as easy as 1-2-3:

1. You'll pressure process it, of course, since you're dealing with vegetables and meats.

2. The amount of time in the pressure canner will be determined by the vegetable or meat that takes the longest amount of time. It's in charge!

3. Hold off on the flour as a thickening agent until you're ready to heat the stew for serving. Flour thickens the liquid and can keep it from heating to the required temperatures necessary to ensure a safe product.

Recipes

Hams are generally quite big, and even if you have them cut in half, you're probably going to have more than you can use before the freezer life is up. Can some of these smaller pieces, and you'll have some spectacular pea soup on short notice.

The second recipe gives you some choices: beef, elk, or venison. You pick the meat and get ready for rave reviews.

Split Pea with Ham Soup

"Peas porridge hot, peas porridge cold. Peas porridge in the pot nine days old." Nine days may be pushing it, but this hearty soup is always best on the second and third days. Serve with crusty rolls.

2 cups split peas

1 ham hock

1 stalk celery, chopped

2 carrots, chopped

1 medium onion, chopped

Salt and pepper to taste

3 qt. cold water

Makes 5 to 6 pints
Prep time: 25 minutes
Cook time: 4 to 6 hours (does not include processing time)

If peas require soaking: Place them in a large cooking pot and cover with cold water. Allow to sit overnight. In the morning, add ham hock, celery, carrots, onion, salt and pepper to taste, and 3 quarts cold water. Bring to a boil, then reduce heat and simmer 4 to 6 hours.

If peas do not require soaking: Combine the peas, ham hock, celery, carrots, onion, salt and pepper to taste, and 3 quarts cold water. Bring to a boil, then reduce heat and simmer 4 to 6 hours.

Pour soup into pint or quart canning jars, leaving 1 inch of headspace. Wipe rims, adjust lids, and process in a pressure canner at 10 pounds of pressure for 75 minutes for pints and 90 minutes for quarts.

Chili con Carne

Con carne means "with meat," but there's no reason to stick to beef all the time. Expand your options and try venison or elk.

Makes 6 pints
Prep time: 25 minutes
Cook time: 45 minutes (does not include processing time)

2 medium onions, chopped

2 cloves garlic, minced

3 lb. ground beef or venison (about 1½ qt.)

3 TB. olive oil

6 cups crushed tomatoes

1 tsp. paprika

1 chili pepper, chopped

Salt and pepper to taste

1. Sauté onions, garlic, and ground beef in olive oil in a large cooking pot. Add tomatoes, paprika, chili pepper, and salt and pepper to taste. Simmer for 30 to 45 minutes.

2. Ladle into pint or quart canning jars, wipe rims, adjust lids, and process in a pressure canner for 75 minutes for pints and 90 minutes for quarts.

3. When ready to serve, add one or two 14.5-oz. cans of red beans or kidney beans and simmer 30 minutes.

Clam Chowder by the 4's

This recipe can be doubled or tripled to make a full canner load.

Makes 4 pints
Prep time: 25 minutes
Cook time: 25 minutes (does not include processing time)

4 cups clams with liquor

4 tsp. butter

4 inch square salt pork

1 medium onion, diced

4 cups milk

4 cups diced potatoes

Salt and pepper to taste

Drain clams, reserving liquor. In a skillet, combine butter, salt pork, and onion and sauté until onion is translucent. Add milk, potatoes, and clams; season to taste with salt and pepper. Cook over low heat 10 to 15 minutes. Pour into pint canning jars, wipe rims, adjust lids, and process in a pressure canner for 100 minutes for pints.

Part 4

Pickles, Relishes, and Fermented Foods

Pickles and relishes provide color, crunch, and a variety of flavors, and they work well as accompaniments to all kinds of main courses. The basic difference between pickles and relishes is that, in pickles, the fruits or vegetables are either whole or cut in slices; in relishes, they are chopped. There's not much you can't pickle, and in Part 4 you'll learn how!

Chapter 13

Introduction to Making Pickles, Relishes, and Fermented Foods

In This Chapter

- The pickling process
- Sweet, tart, and spicy
- What you need to get started
- Checking the seal and storing your pickles
- Pickle problem-solving

Pickles are found in cultures all over the world, and each country seems to have its own specialty. Pickling is the term used for preserving a food with acid and salt. There are two ways to approach pickling: the long way and the short way. Quick- or fresh-pack pickles use vinegar and sugar to create a crisp crunch, while fermented pickles sit in a brine for several weeks while flavor develops. Whichever method you choose, you'll have some fun.

The Science Behind Pickling

Pickling is closely tied to the fermentation process, and it's an ancient way of preserving foods. The early methods of pickling involved soaking in a salt brine and allowing fermenting to take place. In this process, certain types of bacterial growth are encouraged (lactic acid bacteria), and others (the ones that cause food to spoil) are discouraged. It's a selective process.

During the fermenting process, there's a delicate balance among the ingredients in the pickling crock, and keeping everything in balance is the key to producing an excellent pickle. Two important players in this production are lactic acid bacteria and salt.

Lactic acid bacteria feed on the sugar contained in cucumbers. This allows the bacteria to grow and multiply and also imparts the familiar "bite" of fermented pickles.

Salt is very important in keeping the balance. It's like Goldilocks and the three bears. If there's too much salt, lactic acid can't survive let alone thrive. Too little, and the spoilage bacteria get the fighting edge. With just the right amount, though, your pickles are perfect.

Preserving Pointers

Oxygen is also a spoiler for fermenting pickles, so making sure you're keeping out the air is essential. Keep the crock tightly covered.

Finally, the temperature needs to stay a fairly constant 70°F to 75°F to help the lactic acid bacteria stay alive, healthy, and on the job. By keeping the temperature at the low range of what's optimal, you'll regulate the speed of fermentation. Slow is best here for getting the best product.

The Wonderful World of Pickles

There's not much you *can't* do when you want to make pickles. Generally speaking, there are brined or fermented pickles, quick-pack pickles, relishes, and pickled fruits and vegetables. So many choices! Such wonderful flavor and texture—and it's all yours if you're a home food preserver.

Brined or Fermented Pickles

These take the longest to make—a week or longer—but if you love pickles, they're the best. It's a curing process done in a crock. Brining and fermenting are two different processes. Brining uses a saltwater solution in a specific strength to cure the pickles. Afterward, acid must be added (vinegar) as a preservative. Fermenting causes lactic acid bacteria to grow and act as a preservative.

Kosher dill pickles have just enough garlic added to the brine to give them their characteristic texture and flavor. These pickles aren't necessarily kosher, however. It's become a commonly applied name to this particular kind of pickle. If you're buying them ready made, you'll need to check the label to see if they were made under rabbinical supervision.

In Other Words

The best pickles in the world came from Glick's Delicatessen in New Haven, Connecticut. ("No one kicks who comes to Glick's.") For one nickel, you chose the best kosher dill from the pickle barrel, had it wrapped in deli paper, and walked out the door happily munching away.

—Karen, writer

Quick-Pack Pickles

These are quick, as the name says. No crock is needed, just a large kettle or cooking pot on the stove. You can cure these pickles for a few hours first or move directly to the cooking phase with vinegar and a mix of fresh spices. Vinegar is the pickling and preserving agent, and to ensure a safe product, it needs to contain 5 percent acetic acid. These pickles are finished in the boiling water bath.

Safety Check

To be safe, always use tested, approved recipes when making pickles. Don't alter the proportions of ingredients in the recipe, and you'll help prevent the growth of harmful bacteria such as *Clostridium botulinum*, the bacteria that causes botulism.

Relishes

Relishes are pickles gone bite size. Fresh fruits or vegetables are chopped into small pieces, added to a spicy vinegar solution, and cooked for a short period of time on the stove. Relishes are finished in the boiling water bath. See Chapter 16 for complete directions and recipes.

Pickling Fruits and Vegetables

Think sweet/sour for these pickles. They can be created from one variety of fruit or vegetable or a mix of several. The right proportions of sugar and 5 percent vinegar are combined with fresh spices to make a safe product that is finished in the boiling water bath. See Chapter 14 for complete directions and recipes.

Equipment and Supplies

The first ingredients to consider are the fruits or vegetables you'll be pickling. If you start with firm, ripe, fresh produce, you'll be well on your way to a fine pickle. Don't be seduced by the bargain bin. Moldy, overripe, or shriveled produce is not a good deal. If you wouldn't eat it, you shouldn't pickle it. You'll need about 14 pounds of cucumbers to make a full canner load of 7 quarts of pickles.

Cucumbers come in two basic types: slicing and pickling. Choose pickling cucumbers! The slicing varieties don't hold up to the pickling process. They're meant to be eaten fresh. Pickling cucumbers are generally smaller than slicing cucumbers. They also have wartier skins—a real knobby texture. You'll probably have an easier time finding these at a pick-your-own farm or at a farmers' market. Supermarkets generally carry only slicing cukes.

Cucumbers shouldn't be waxed since the wax is a barrier that keeps the brining solution from entering.

Don't delay after you've gotten your produce picked or purchased. Pick and process the same day if you can. If you must wait until the following morning, keep the produce refrigerated.

Preserving Pointers

Lime or alum appears frequently as an ingredient in older recipes. They were used as firming agents. Just give your cucumbers a good ice water soak for 4 to 5 hours before you begin the pickling process, and you'll get crisp pickles without these additives.

For fermented pickles, you'll need pickling or kosher salt, a stoneware crock, and a weight (such as a dinner plate) to keep the pickles under the brine. Be sure the crock is large enough to hold the pickles and salt with a few inches to spare at the top to accommodate the brine that forms during the fermenting process. A general rule is 1 gallon of space for each 5 pounds of fresh produce.

For quick-pack pickles, you'll need pickling or kosher salt, 5 percent vinegar, sugar, and spices, according to the recipe you'll be following.

The salt you use is important. For pickling, choose either kosher or pickling salt. Both are pure, which means they have no additives such as iodine that can turn pickles dark and the pickling liquid cloudy, or anticaking ingredients that keep the salt free-flowing. Kosher salt tends to be coarser than pickling salt.

Kitchen scales are not a luxury item. If the recipe specifies a certain weight of produce, you'll need to get an exact measure. Especially in fermented pickles, guesswork is almost certainly an invitation to failure. You've got a considerable investment in produce as well as in your time and effort. Don't sabotage it!

General Procedures

Have a plan for your produce. Everything big or small has a place in pickle making. If you'll be making gherkins, use the smallest cucumbers—about 1½ inches in length. Dills use the larger sized cukes—about 4 inches long. Produce that's overly large can be sliced or chopped to make relishes or pickled fruits or vegetables.

Wash the produce thoroughly. You don't want any soil remaining to potentially cause softening of the pickles. For the same reason, slice off the blossom end that contains enzymes that can cause softening. You don't have to hack a huge portion from the cucumber, just a tiny slice will suffice.

Assemble all the ingredients before you plunge into processing. It's aggravating to have to stop and search for something when you're in the middle of something important. Preparation prevents pickle problems.

Follow the recipe exactly. Don't change the amounts of salt, sugar, or vinegar. You can exchange or omit certain spices if you wish. If you don't like turmeric, leave it out. Love cinnamon? Add an extra stick to your pickled fruits.

Always finish with the proper time in the boiling water canner. This inactivates certain enzymes that can cause changes in color, texture, and flavor, destroys spoilage microorganisms, and ensures the seal. If you'll be processing your jars for less than 10 minutes, sterilize the jars by boiling them for 10 minutes before packing them with pickles.

Safety Check

Wash all jars in hot soapy water, rinse them thoroughly, and keep them hot until you're ready to fill them. Just because a jar looks clean doesn't mean it is clean. Be scrupulous!

Some pickle recipes call for pasteurization instead of processing in a boiling water bath. This method uses lower temperatures (180°F to 185°F) and can give you a higher-quality product. If your recipe indicates this method can be used, follow this procedure:

1. Set jars in a boiling water canner that's been filled halfway with warm water (120°F to 140°F). Add additional warm water to cover the jars to a level 1 inch above their tops.

2. Turn on heat under the canner. When the water reaches 180°F to 185°F, begin timing. Process for 30 minutes at this temperature. Use a thermometer to ensure the water remains in this range. If the temperature increases, pickles may soften.

3. After 30 minutes, remove the jars immediately from the canner and set them on a clean, dry surface.

Again, a reminder: this process should only be used in recipes that indicate it is safe.

Storing

The first step in storing is testing the seals within 12 to 24 hours of processing. To do this, you'll remove the screw band. Your jar is sealed if the lid is concave in the center. (Compare it to an unused lid, and you should see a difference. The unused lid is raised in the center.) The lid shouldn't move when you press on it. One old-time way of checking a seal was to hit the lid with a spoon and listen for a pure ring (as opposed to a dull thud). However, this method isn't all that reliable.

If your lids have sealed, you're ready to move on to step two: washing the outside of the jars. Many jars are sticky after processing, and rinsing them in warm water will remove that sticky residue. Wipe with a clean, dry towel.

Next, use an indelible pen to label each lid with the jar's contents and the date. Leave the screw band off. Leaving the band on can make a jar that's come unsealed appear to still have a tight seal. Also, rust can form between the band and the jar, and that can make unscrewing the band later quite difficult. It also looks nasty.

> **Preserving Pointers**
>
> Rotate your stock! Just as stores rotate their stock, putting older items out front and placing new items behind them, so should you. First in, first out is the home food preserver's motto.

Finally, store jars away from sunlight in a cool, dry location. Shelf life of home-canned pickles is about a year. As long as they were properly prepared, processed, and stored and the lids are still sealed, the food should be fine. Quality decreases over time, however, so eat up!

Before using your pickled products, check to be sure the lid is still sealed. If it's bulging or any liquid has seeped out (indicating a poor seal), or if after opening the jar you notice an off odor, mold, foam, questionable texture to the pickles, or any kind of movement of the liquid in the jar, dispose of the product without tasting it. Boil it for 10 minutes and dispose of the contents in the garbage.

You can reuse the canning jars, of course, even if the pickles have spoiled. The Extension Service recommends cleaning them with a solution made from one part chlorine bleach to five parts water. Allow the solution to remain on the glass surfaces for 5 minutes, then rinse. You can then wash them in the regular cycle of your dishwasher.

Safety Check

This message bears repeating often: *never* taste food that you suspect has spoiled.

Troubleshooting

In a pickle about your pickles? When pickles go wrong, it can be frustrating. Generally, there are some simple explanations for what happened, and knowing the cause gives you a chance to find a remedy for the problem. Here are some of the most common pickle problems and what to do about them.

Hollow Pickles

A hollow pickle can start out as a hollow cucumber. This can happen if the cuke didn't mature properly, was on the vine too long, or sat around on the counter or in the refrigerator waiting to become a pickle.

You can usually spot these when you're giving them their initial scrub in the sink. They're floaters. That doesn't mean they're not useful in relishes, where they're cut up into small pieces, but they're definitely not whole pickle timber.

If you're fermenting pickles and end up with some hollow ones, the fermenting process might have been too quick, or the temperature during fermenting might have been too high.

Soft Pickles

Nobody likes soft pickles. Sometimes soft is coupled with slippery, and it's just not a good thing at all. You can't turn a soft pickle crunchy again, so it's best to prevent it in the first place. Depending on what caused the softening, the pickle is either safe to eat or it's not.

Did you remove the blossom at the tip? Enzymes responsible for softening are located there, so be sure to slice off the end. If this is the cause, the pickles are safe to eat but unappetizing.

If harmful bacteria got a chance to grow during the fermenting process because the salt concentration was too light, toss the pickles. They are not safe to eat. It's essential to follow the recipe exactly regarding amount of ingredients and proper procedures. Don't cut back on the salt or the acid and be sure the cukes remain covered with brine throughout the fermenting process. Skim off any scum that forms during fermenting as well.

Finally, observe proper processing procedures. Follow the fermenting process with the correct amount of time in the boiling water bath to ensure a proper seal. If the seal fails, the pickles are not safe to eat and must be disposed of.

Splotches and Blotches

Both of these problems are cosmetic. The pickles are safe to eat but won't win any prizes for beauty. Too much sun can cause skin scalding, and too much time on the vine can make cukes old. In that case, you're probably really dealing with age spots. Also, keeping the cucumbers in the fridge too long before processing them can cause browning. Cucumbers should be fresh, firm, not overripe, and a uniform green color if they're going to make a pickle worth its salt.

Weird Colors

Pickles that turn out an alarming shade of green or garlic that becomes blue or purple usually means that copper is to blame. If that's the case, the pickles should be discarded. Where does the copper come from?

You may have some expensive copper cookware that works beautifully for most kinds of cooking, but it's not the right choice for making pickles, and neither is brass or iron. Also avoid using galvanized utensils. Copper reacts with acid and salt to make copper sulfate and creates these changes. If you use stainless steel, enamelware, or stoneware, you won't have this problem.

Dark Pickles

Dark pickles are another unattractive feature, but the pickles are still safe to eat. It could be a spice problem. If you've used ground spices instead of whole, used too much (didn't follow the recipe), or left the whole spices in the pickling solution when you packed the jars, you may end up with dark pickles (sounds rather like a title for a bad novel).

It could also be a salt problem. Use pickling or kosher salt—never iodized table salt for your pickles. Finally, it could be a water problem. Soft water—not hard—is best for pickling.

Shriveled Pickles

These pickles are screaming, "Too much! Too much!" Follow the recipe ingredients instructions carefully. If you use too much sugar, too much salt, or too much vinegar at the outset and then cook the pickles too much or process them too long, they'll just shrivel up. Be sure to follow the directions exactly! The pickles are safe to eat but won't impress the judges.

Safety Check

You wouldn't eat purchased food that smelled or tasted "off." Don't eat food you've made that has the same problems. It's a false economy. Illness is expensive and not worth the price of a batch of bad pickles.

The Least You Need to Know

- Pickling is the term for preserving foods with both acid and salt.
- Quick-pack pickles can be done in a day; brining and fermenting are longer processes that produce great pickles.
- Relishes are pickles gone micro—use fresh chopped veggies or fruits to make these products.
- Always check the seal before using a jar of home-preserved pickles. Check for proper aroma and texture. If at all in doubt, dispose of the product in a safe manner.
- Following tested recipes exactly is the key to success.

Pickling Fruits and Vegetables

In This Chapter

- ◆ Thinking beyond cucumbers
- ◆ No need to brine or ferment
- ◆ Simple ingredients and simple procedures
- ◆ Creating your own combinations

Think pickles and your brain conjures up all kinds of cucumber products. What you may not know is that you can pickle almost any kind of fruit and a great many vegetables as well. This chapter will cover quick-pack pickles. Quick-pack pickles don't require a brining process. They're quick to make and add interest, texture, color, and flavor to every main course. You assemble the ingredients, simmer the pickling solution, add the fruit or vegetables, pack the jars, process, and you're done.

Pickling Fruits

Whether sweet/spicy or sweet/sour, fruit pickles are easy to make and are excellent gift items. Get started early since pickles take time to develop flavor. If you make a batch as each fruit comes into season, you'll have a nice selection when the holidays roll around.

Small-sized fruits are the best sizes for pickling whole. These make a prettier product, and you can usually find small fruit at roadside orchards. You can sometimes get good bargains on small fruit because it's ... well, small, and people like big fruit for eating. Check out peaches, nectarines, and pears.

For other fruits, such as cantaloupe and watermelon, size doesn't matter since you'll cut cubes in uniform sizes for an attractive presentation. In the case of watermelon, you can even make a delicious pickle from the rind! More on this later in the chapter.

General Procedures and Supplies

For starters, you'll want fruit that hasn't been waxed. Waxing is a pain to deal with and, if you're working with whole fruit, makes it just about impossible for the pickling agents to penetrate the skin.

How do you spot a piece of waxed fruit? Easy! It's very shiny and glows about as brightly as your furniture after you've finished your spring cleaning.

Preserving Pointers

Go organic when you can. The fruit isn't gassed or waxed. We've gotten so used to demanding perfect *looking* fruit that we forget what fruit is all about—good taste!

Mixing fruits results in some wonderful combinations of pickles. Try mixing cantaloupe and peaches or pears and cherries. Or pickle a fruit salad. Don't be afraid to experiment. Fruit is acidic, and the addition of sugar and vinegar makes any experimentation on your part perfectly safe.

The process and the ingredients for making all kinds of pickled fruits are essentially the same. You'll need vinegar, sugar, water, spices, and of course, fruit.

◆ Vinegar can be either white or apple cider. Some recipes call for white, some for apple cider, and some don't specify so you can use either kind. Keep in mind that white vinegar is clear and apple cider vinegar is brown. If color matters, use white. Vinegar is what adds the acidity to pickles and is important in producing a safe as well as tasty product. Cider vinegar is generally used more for fruits since it's milder than white vinegar.

◆ Sugar in fairly large amounts is necessary, although not nearly as much as is needed in jams and jellies. You can use white or brown, although brown will darken the syrup a bit. Unless corn syrup is specifically called for, it's best to avoid it as well as honey. They can change the flavor of the pickles, and not for the better.

◆ You'll get a better pickle if you use soft water as opposed to hard. If you don't know if your water is hard, boil a quart of it and then let it sit for 24 hours. If there's any scum on top or sediment on the bottom, you've got hard water. If your water is hard, skim off any scum on the top and dip out the water you need without stirring up the sediment on the bottom.

◆ You're using fresh fruits, and your spices should be fresh as well. Generally you'll need whole cloves, cinnamon, and nutmeg. Unless a recipe specifically calls for ground spice, stick with the whole variety. Ground spices can make your pickles dark and cloudy.

You'll see that many of these recipes recommend using a spice bag to keep the spices from making the pickle too strong during storage. This is a matter of taste, however, and a spiced peach with a small clove embedded in it is scrumptious. If you decide to go with the spice bag, you can't reuse the spices in it.

Spice bags are easily made from materials you have around the house. You can use cheesecloth, a foot cut from a clean pair of hosiery, or any other porous fabric that will allow the spices to transmit their flavor to the syrup.

> **In Other Words**
>
> And the sweet-sour pickles of peach and pear, / With cinnamon in 'em, and all things rare!
>
> —James Whitcomb Riley, nineteenth-century American poet (he loved his fruit pickles!)

Pickling Vegetables

Vegetables are low-acid foods, which means you must add the right amount of vinegar to make them not only tangy but safe to eat. It's the single most important part of the pickle, apart from the food, of course.

Just as with fruits, feel free to create your own combinations of vegetable pickles. Mix cauliflower florets and green bean slices or carrots and pearl onions. The sky's the limit! The vinegar makes these low-acid foods safe.

Chapter 13 gives the general procedures for making pickles, so let's get started right away with some recipes to fill your pantry and provide you with gifts galore for your friends and family.

Preserving Pointers

Slice off the blossom end of cucumbers. It can contain enzymes that work to cause softening. The next step is to sort the veggies, keeping similar sizes together. If you're making pints and want the cucumbers whole, measure them against the side of the jar to get the right size. Gherkins use shorter cucumbers, while dills are traditionally longer.

Recipes

Never change the amount of vinegar specified in the recipes. Bottled vinegar in 5 percent strength is a preservative for quick-pack pickles and, in the case of vegetables, lowers their pH below 4.0, making them safe as well as delightfully tart.

Pickled Grapes

This is something quite fun! The flavor develops over several days and the skins will shrivel a bit, but the taste is something special.

Makes 4 pints

4 lb. seedless grapes

1 TB. broken ginger root

1½ TB. whole cloves

2 pieces stick cinnamon

1 cup sugar

2 cups water

1 cup vinegar

Wash grapes and remove stems. Add ginger root, cloves, and cinnamon pieces to spice bag. Add spice bag, sugar, water, and vinegar to a large saucepan and heat until sugar is dissolved. Add grapes and cook slowly until tender. Pack boiling hot into hot, sterilized jars. Seal. Process in a boiling water bath for 5 minutes for pints.

Pickled Peaches, Apricots, or Pears

Seckel peaches make excellent pickles. They're firm enough to take the processing and yet just the right texture for good eating. For the following recipe, you may combine fruits for added interest.

4 qt. small peaches, apricots, or pears

Whole cloves

6 (3-inch) pieces stick cinnamon

8 cups sugar (white or brown or combination of the two)

1 qt. vinegar

Makes 8 pints

If using peaches, remove the skins (see Chapter 4). Pears may be peeled, if desired. Apricots require no special preparation. These fruits are pickled whole, so you don't remove pits or core them.

Stick 4 cloves into each piece of fruit. Boil sugar and vinegar together in a large saucepan for 2 minutes. Add fruit to syrup (one variety at a time) and cook gently until soft. Pack into hot, sterilized jars. Add a small piece of cinnamon to each jar and syrup to cover, leaving $\frac{1}{2}$ inch headroom. Wipe rims, adjust lids, and process in a boiling water bath for 5 minutes for pints, 10 minutes for quarts.

Pickled Watermelon Rind

Sometimes you run across a watermelon with a really thick rind. While this isn't what you want for eating purposes, it's terrific for making pickles. If you've got one of these treasures with an average rind width of $\frac{1}{2}$ inch or more, read on! A 16-pound watermelon will give from 5 to 6 pounds of rind. One pound of rind will make about a pint of pickles.

Makes 4 to 5 pints

4 qt. rind

Boiling water to cover

2 TB. salt

1 qt. vinegar

8 cups sugar

$\frac{1}{4}$ cup broken stick cinnamon

1 TB. whole cloves

1. Cut away green outside skin and also all pink inside flesh of the rind. (It won't crisp up.) You want pure white rind—or as pure as you can get it. Cut rind into cubes. Size will vary according to how thick the rind is, of course.

2. Place cubes in a large saucepan and add boiling water to cover. Add salt. Simmer until rind is tender. Drain and chill rind in very cold water at least 1 hour or overnight.

3. In the morning or after rind has chilled, prepare syrup by boiling vinegar and sugar together. Add cinnamon and cloves to spice bag and add bag to syrup. Drain rind and place in syrup. Simmer mixture until rind becomes somewhat translucent. Remove spice bag. Pack rind into hot, sterilized jars and add syrup, leaving $\frac{1}{2}$ inch of headspace. Process in a boiling water bath for 5 minutes for pints.

Pickled Cantaloupe

A melon that is slightly underripe works best for pickles. You can double this recipe if you want to end up with pints instead of half-pint jars.

1 medium cantaloupe	**2 pieces stick cinnamon**
2 cups water	**2 TB. ground cloves**
1 qt. vinegar	**4 cups sugar**
1 tsp. mace	

> *Makes 2 pints*

1. Cut away all outside skin and scoop out all seeds and pulpy inner fiber of cantaloupe. That will leave you with firm orange flesh. Cut this into cubes or scoop into balls. Aim for uniform sizes.

2. Combine water and vinegar in a large saucepan and bring to a boil. Add spice bag filled with mace, cinnamon, and cloves. Place melon pieces in a glass or ceramic bowl and pour boiling vinegar solution over them. Let stand overnight on the counter.

3. The next day, pour off vinegar into a saucepan and bring to a boil. Add sugar and melon. Simmer until clear, about 1 hour. Pack into hot, sterilized jars. Bring vinegar mixture to a boil and cook to make a medium syrup. To prevent cantaloupe from cooling down, place jars in hot water while you are waiting. Pour boiling syrup over cantaloupe and seal at once. Process in a boiling water bath for 5 minutes for pints, 10 minutes for quarts.

Wilma's Bread and Butter Pickles

These are probably the best bread and butter pickles you will ever find. They're both sweet and tart and definitely crunchy.

Makes 9 pints

4 qt. sliced medium cucumbers

6 medium white onions, sliced

2 green peppers

3 cloves garlic, sliced

1 small jar pimientos

⅓ cup salt

Cracked ice to cover

3½ cups sugar

1½ tsp. celery seed

1½ tsp. turmeric

2 TB. mustard seed

6 cups cider vinegar

Do not pare cucumbers. Slice them thin. Add onions, peppers, garlic, pimientos, and salt. Mix well. Cover with cracked ice and let stand 3 hours. Drain thoroughly. Combine sugar, celery seed, turmeric, mustard seed, and vinegar and pour over cucumber mixture. Heat just to a boil. Process 10 minutes for quarts, 5 minutes for pints.

Quick Kosher Dill Pickles

The old-fashioned kosher dills are fermented and take time to develop flavor. These are the quick-pack variety, very crunchy and very tasty.

4 lb. pickling cucumbers
(4 inches long)

14 garlic cloves, split

¼ cup pickling salt

2¾ cups distilled white vinegar (5 percent)

3 cups water

14 heads fresh dill

28 peppercorns

> *Makes 6 to 7 pints*

1. Wash cucumbers and cut in half lengthwise. Heat garlic, salt, vinegar, and water to boiling. Remove garlic and place 4 halves into each pint or quart jar. Pack cucumbers into jars, adding 2 heads dill and 4 peppercorns to each jar.

2. Pour hot vinegar solution over cucumbers to within ½ inch of top. Adjust lids and process in a boiling water bath for 10 minutes for pints and 15 minutes for quarts.

Pickled Beets

If you're looking for easy, this is easy. All you need are beets, vinegar, sugar, and whole cloves.

3 qt. small beets, peeled

4 cups vinegar

1½ cups sugar

½ tsp. whole cloves

> *Makes 6 pints*

1. Cook beets until tender. Plunge into cold water and slip skins.

2. Mix vinegar, sugar, and cloves. Simmer 10 minutes. Add beets and simmer 10 more minutes. Pack into hot, sterilized jars and fill with pickling solution. Leave ½ inch headroom. Process in boiling water bath for 20 minutes.

Reduced-Sodium Pickles

You can't reduce the amount of salt in fermented pickles, but you can with quick-pack pickles. This recipe gives you the best of both worlds.

> *Makes 4 to 5 pints*

3 lb. pickling cucumbers (4 inches long)

1²/₃ cups distilled white vinegar (5 percent)

3 cups sugar

1 TB. whole allspice

2¹/₄ tsp. celery seed

1 qt. distilled white vinegar (5 percent)

1 TB. canning or pickling salt

1 TB. mustard seed

¹/₂ cup sugar

1. Wash cucumbers. Cut ¹/₁₆ inch off blossom end and discard. Cut cucumbers into ¹/₄ inch slices. Combine 1²/₃ cups white vinegar, 3 cups sugar, allspice, and celery seed in a saucepan and bring to a boil. Keep syrup hot until used.

2. In a large kettle, combine 1 quart white vinegar, salt, mustard seed, and ¹/₂ cup sugar. Add cut cucumbers, cover, and simmer until cucumbers change color from bright to dull green (5 to 7 minutes). Drain cucumber slices. Fill the pint jars and cover with hot canning syrup, leaving ¹/₂ inch of headspace. Adjust lids and process in a boiling water bath for 10 minutes.

4-Day Sweet Gherkins

Four days may not seem all that quick, but it's still quicker than brining. Gherkins are distinctive little pickles. They're crooked and knobby and very tasty.

7 lb. cucumbers (1½ inch in length or shorter)

6 qt. boiling water to cover

½ cup canning or pickling salt

6 cups distilled white vinegar (5 percent), divided

8 cups sugar, divided

¾ tsp. turmeric

2 tsp. celery seeds

2 tsp. whole mixed pickling spice (optional)

2 cinnamon sticks

½ tsp. fennel (optional)

2 tsp. vanilla (optional)

Makes 6 to 7 pints

1. Wash cucumbers. Cut ¹⁄₁₆ inch slice off blossom end and discard, but leave ¼ inch of stem attached. Place cucumbers in a large container and cover with boiling water. Let the bowl sit on the counter. Six to eight hours later, drain and cover with 6 quarts fresh boiling water containing ¼ cup salt. Repeat on the second day.

2. On the third day, drain and prick cucumbers with a table fork. Combine and bring to boil 3 cups vinegar, 3 cups sugar, turmeric, celery seeds, pickling spice (if using), cinnamon sticks, and fennel. Pour over cucumbers. Six to eight hours later, drain and save the pickling syrup. Add another 2 cups each of sugar and vinegar to the syrup and reheat to boiling. Pour over pickles. On the fourth day, drain and save syrup.

3. Add another 2 cups sugar and 1 cup vinegar. Heat syrup to boiling and pour over pickles. Let sit and then drain 6 to 8 hours later, saving the pickling syrup. Add 1 cup sugar and 2 teaspoons vanilla and heat to boiling. Fill the pint jars with pickles and cover with hot syrup, leaving ½ inch of headspace. Adjust lids and process in a boiling water bath for 5 minutes.

Pickled Mixed Vegetables

This makes an attractive side dish for any meal. It's colorful and has different textures and shapes.

Makes about 10 pints

4 lb. pickling cucumbers, washed and cut into 1-inch slices

2 lb. small onions, peeled and quartered

4 cups cut celery, cut into 1-inch pieces

2 cups carrots, peeled and cut into ½-inch pieces

2 cups sweet red peppers, cut into ½-inch pieces

2 cups cauliflower flowerets

Cubed or crushed ice to cover

5 cups distilled white vinegar (5 percent)

¼ cup prepared mustard

½ cup canning or pickling salt

3½ cups sugar

3 TB. celery seed

2 TB. mustard seed

½ tsp. whole cloves

½ tsp. ground turmeric

Combine cucumbers, onions, celery, carrots, red peppers, and cauliflower and cover with 2 inches cubed or crushed ice. Refrigerate 3 to 4 hours. In 8-quart kettle, combine vinegar and mustard and mix well. Add salt, sugar, celery seed, mustard seed, cloves, and turmeric. Bring to a boil. Drain vegetables and add to hot pickling solution. Cover and slowly bring to a boil. Drain vegetables but save pickling solution. Fill vegetables in sterile pint jars or quarts, leaving ½ inch of headspace. Process in a boiling water bath for 5 minutes for pints and 10 minutes for quarts.

Chapter 15

Pickling Meats, Fish, and Eggs

In This Chapter

- ◆ Pickling without preservatives
- ◆ Gotta have salt
- ◆ Fatty fish and your health
- ◆ Brine time

Pickling as a means of preserving was developed long before refrigeration and was a way of making sure there would be enough meat to last through the long winter. Meats, fish, and eggs are often overlooked when it comes to pickling, but they make great pickles! Expand your food preserving skills by trying something new. Whether you prefer sweet, hot, or spicy, there's a pickling recipe to suit your taste buds.

Pickling Meats

Older methods for pickling meats called for saltpeter (potassium nitrate). Saltpeter enhances taste, gives meat its characteristic red color, has some ability to inhibit botulism, and is also used as a preservative. Saltpeter isn't necessary, however, and you can make a very acceptable pickling solution without it.

Both potassium and sodium belong to the same family of elements. Potassium nitrate and potassium nitrite, and sodium nitrate and sodium nitrite, are different compounds but have similar properties. The health concern that has been raised is with nitrates and nitrites, but current research indicates that the sodium nitrate and sodium nitrite contained in pickling salts and processed meats do not pose a health risk.

The choice of whether or not to use nitrates and nitrites is up to you. You can use Kosher or any other noniodized table salt instead. Table salt is sodium chloride (NaCl).

Beef

Corned beef is a type of pickled beef that's familiar to most of us. Beef lends itself quite well to pickling, and the brisket (taken from the chest just ahead of the fore-shank) and tongue, as well as roasts (including boneless round or chuck roast), work well. The *corning* process isn't difficult, and if you'd like to try it yourself, you'll save some money over the corned beef you'll find at the grocery store.

def•i•ni•tion

Corning is a means of preserving meat that gets its name from the large salt crystals, or "corns," that were once used to rub into the meat to cure it.

Ingredients

You'll need salt. It's the essential ingredient. Kosher salt is excellent for pickling and brining, although you can use noniodized table salt as well. For a 5-pound roast, you'll need about ¾ cup of salt.

Then come the spices. Here you have considerable leeway, and it's all right to experiment with different combinations and amounts of spices. If you want a sweeter corned beef, add brown sugar. If you prefer it a bit tangier, omit it. Here's a general list of ingredients:

- Bay leaves: 2
- Cracked peppercorns: 1 to 2 tablespoons
- Sage: ½ teaspoon
- Paprika: ½ teaspoon

- Garlic: 1 clove diced

- Ginger: $\frac{1}{2}$ teaspoon

- Brown sugar: 1 tablespoon

- Nutmeg: $\frac{1}{4}$ teaspoon

- Thyme: $\frac{1}{2}$ teaspoon

Vary these amounts and ingredients to suit your own taste.

Method

In a medium-size bowl, mix together the spices, garlic, and salt. Wash and dry the cut of meat. Place it on a cookie sheet. Rub the meat on both sides with the salt/spice mixture.

If you have a medium-size stone crock, you can then put the meat inside, cover it with water, and weight it down with a plate to keep the meat under the water. The salt will work into the meat, releasing juices and creating the brine that will corn (pickle) the meat. Keep the crock in a cool location and turn the meat once a week for 4 weeks. Check to see if the brine is salty enough for your taste, and if it isn't, you can add more salt.

Another way that's definitely more modern and less messy than loose meat in the crock is to use a gallon freezer bag. Put the meat in the bag, burp out as much air as you can, zip it closed, and then put it in the crock. Weight the bag down with a plate. Keep the crock in a cool location. Turn the freezer bag over every day for 4 weeks. Make sure the meat is totally covered with brine at all times.

When you're ready to use the corned beef, remove the meat from the crock and rinse it in cool water to remove the brine. If you find that the brine is very salty, you may want to soak the meat in cool water for about half an hour. Then rinse and pat it dry. It will keep about 1 month in the fridge. To make Corned Beef and Cabbage, see the Recipes section at the end of this chapter.

Pig Hocks and Pigs Feet

These pickled products are interesting to try. The following method was taken from the Cooperative Extension Service, Bulletin 865, University of Georgia at Athens.

Ingredients

Your butcher should have some pigs feet or pigs hocks, but they're not a common item in the meat case, so you'll probably need to ask. Then you'll need the following:

- Vinegar (2 quarts)
- Red pepper (1 small)
- Horseradish (2 tablespoons grated)
- Peppercorns (1 teaspoon whole black)
- Allspice (1 teaspoon whole)
- Bay leaf (1)

Method

Using a scrub brush, scrub the feet or hocks thoroughly in cool water. Then scald, scrape, and clean them thoroughly. Place in a medium-size bowl, sprinkle lightly with salt, and let stand for 4 to 8 hours in the refrigerator. Rinse well. Then place them in a large cooking pot, cover them with water, bring them to a boil, reduce heat, and cook until tender but not until the meat is so tender that it falls off the bones.

Place the remaining ingredients in a medium-size cooking pot and bring to a boil.

Remove the feet from the hot water and pack them into hot glass canning jars, leaving ½ inch headspace. Fill the jars with the pickling solution, leaving ½ inch headroom. Remove air pockets by inserting a spatula into the jar and running it around the inside. Wipe the jar rims and adjust the lids.

Process for 75 minutes in a pressure canner: 10 pounds for a weighted gauge pressure canner and 11 pounds for a dial gauge pressure canner. Follow the directions for altitude adjustment, proper processing, and proper cooling. When the pressure has returned to 0, remove the lid, remove the jars, and allow them to cool on a flat, dry surface. They'll keep at least a year in the pantry. Store them in a cool, dry place.

Pigs hocks or feet are served cold, so be sure to refrigerate a jar for several hours before serving.

Safety Check

Always remove the lid from a pressure canner with the lid turned away from you to prevent scalding yourself. Steam burns can be serious!

Pickling Fish

Pickling fish isn't difficult, and it's an excellent way of preserving the catch. The best product results from using fish with a high oil content, such as herring, shad, striped bass, Chinook salmon, or black cod. It's all a matter of taste, however, and many other varieties of fish and shellfish can be pickled. To be sure your product is safe, always follow approved, research-based recipes that have been extensively tested by experts in food safety. The recipes that pass muster consistently produce a safe product and are recommended for the home food preserver.

The pickling process uses vinegar, also known as acetic acid. The vinegar makes the fish acid, which prevents botulism. Vinegar also adds flavor, softens the fish bones, and stops spoilage caused by certain bacteria. To kill all the bacteria present would take a vinegar with 15 percent acetic acid, but the vinegar you buy at the store is usually 5 to 6 percent acetic acid. Distilled white vinegar is preferred because apple cider vinegar can impart a "fruity" taste to the fish, which of course would not be desirable.

Preserving Pointers

Pickled fish is not a good food for people on sodium-restricted diets. About 5 ounces of pickled herring contains over 1,200 milligrams of sodium! However, fatty fish, such as herring, is also high in omega-3 fatty acids—the good fats. It's also a good source of vitamins A and B_{12}.

Vinegar can't do it all, however. Enzymes are still active, and vinegar can only slow them down to a certain extent. This means that you should only pickle as much fish as you are likely to use within 4 to 5 months, and then be sure to keep it refrigerated.

Salting

Salting is usually an important first step in the pickling process. Salt removes water from the fish, serves to ensure good texture, deactivates certain enzymes, and kills some bacteria. If you won't be pickling the fish right away, salting cures the fish so you can store it without having to refrigerate it. With this method, the fish will keep anywhere from 2 to 3 months. If refrigeration isn't a problem, however, the fish will keep longer (6 to 12 months) if you do refrigerate it.

If the recipe doesn't require salting, you should freeze the fish prior to pickling. Keep it in the freezer for 3 to 4 days to kill parasites that may be present in the fish.

The Pickling Process

The pickling process is spread out over about a week and involves four steps: preparing the fish, preparing the pickling solution, curing, and pickling.

1. **Preparing the fish:** Clean, scale, and gut the fish. Remove the head. Remove the backbone in large fish. This is not necessary for small fish such as herring, but do be sure you've cut away the kidney, which is next to the backbone. It can be difficult to see because it's just a darkish line there.

2. **Preparing the pickling solution:** There are many recipes for pickling solution, but the ingredients will be vinegar, sugar, salt, spices, and onions. To prevent the risk of botulism, never decrease the amount of vinegar needed to make a solution that contains one or more parts of 5 percent vinegar to each part water. If you want a sweeter solution, add more sugar; don't cut back on the vinegar.

Ingredients

The Cooperative Extension Service provides the following basic pickling solution for fish. It makes about 1 gallon of solution:

◆ 3 pints water

◆ 4 pints 5 percent white vinegar

◆ 2 cups granulated sugar

◆ 4 tablespoons salt

◆ ¾ cup pickling spice

◆ 2 small white onions (chopped or sliced)

◆ ¼ teaspoon dry, chopped garlic (or 1 to 2 chopped fresh cloves)

Bring all ingredients to a boil and allow them to cool before using.

3. **Curing the fish:** This involves dry salting or curing with brine for 5 to 8 days.

    If you dry salt, you'll first lay down about ¼ inch of salt in the bottom of a pan suited to the size of the fish you're curing. Alternate layers of fish and salt. Place the top fish skin side up and cover it with a layer of salt. It's best to refrigerate the curing fish, but if you don't have room, keep the fish below 50°F during the curing process.

    If you brine the fish, you'll first make up a brine mixture that's 1 part salt to 3½ parts water. You'll need an equal volume of both fish and brine. Pour the brine into a crock suitable for pickling and then add the fish. Be sure the brine completely covers the fish. You'll need to put a weight on the fish to keep them from rising above the brine. Again, refrigeration is best, but at least keep the fish at 50°F or below during the curing process.

4. **Pickling the fish:** If you've dry salted the fish, first rinse it in cool water to remove excess salt. If you prefer, you can let the fish soak in cool water for up to 24 hours to remove additional salt. This is called freshening. If you've brined the fish, first rinse it in cool water.

    If you prefer the fish without skin, this is the time to remove it. Decide if you want strips or chunks and cut the fish accordingly. Then pack the fish into glass jars, cover with pickling solution, secure the lids, and let the curing process finish under refrigeration. It will take 1 to 2 weeks for the bones to soften.

Pickling Eggs

Pickled eggs are fun to make, and recipes range from sweet and sour (see the recipe at the end of this chapter) to dilled. They're made from adding pickling solution to peeled, hard-boiled eggs.

Eggs are a nutrient-dense food, packed with vitamins and minerals, and they are also an excellent source of protein. Eggs contain all the essential amino acids and are low in fat. However, eggs—or, more specifically, egg yolks—are a significant source of cholesterol. One egg can contain 210 milligrams of cholesterol.

Better Boiling

Eggs that are a few days old before they're cooked peel more easily than fresh eggs, but fresh is always preferable to not-so-fresh.

The Georgia Egg Commission (www.georgiaeggs.org) has the easiest recipe for perfect hard-boiled eggs you'll ever find. Place the eggs in a single layer in a saucepan and add water to cover the eggs by an inch. Cover the saucepan and bring just to a boil, turn off the heat, and remove the pan from the burner to prevent further cooking. With the cover in place, allow the eggs to remain in hot water for 15 to 17 minutes.

> **Safety Check**
>
> There have been reported cases of botulism with regard to improperly stored pickled eggs. Pickled eggs must be stored in the refrigerator, where they'll keep well for several months. Do not leave pickled eggs out of the refrigerator for more than 2 hours.

Drain the water from the pan and then run cold water over the eggs, or you can put the eggs in ice water until the eggs are completely cooled down. Crack the shell all around. Then beginning at the larger end of the egg, peel the shell from the egg. This is where the air cell is located; you'll have an easier time of it if you start here. It's also easier to peel an egg if you keep it under cool running water.

Ingredients

Basic ingredients for pickling eggs include vinegar, water, a mixture of spices, and onion. Water and vinegar are usually in equal proportions. You'll find recipes for two different types of pickled eggs in the Recipes section of this chapter.

Method

You'll want to use a quart glass canning jar for the next step. Fill the jar loosely with peeled eggs. The jar should hold about a dozen. Heat the pickling mixture to a near boil and then let it simmer for 5 minutes. Turn off the heat and pour the mixture over the eggs in the jars, being sure to cover the eggs completely. Set the lid and ring in place and store in the refrigerator.

It will take anywhere from 1 to 4 weeks to season the eggs, depending on their size. Keep them refrigerated during this time. They'll keep for several months.

Recipes

Pickling is the first step, and enjoying what you've pickled is the next and best part! The following recipes will get you started.

Corned Beef and Cabbage

This is a dish more associated with the Irish in America than in Ireland, and it's definitely part of St. Patrick's Day feasting. The ingredients are simple and the dish is satisfyingly filling.

1 corned beef brisket

Carrots (allow one for each person to be served)

White potatoes (allow one for each person to be served)

1 medium to large head of cabbage

Serves 6
Prep time: 25 minutes
Cook time: 2½ hours

1. Place the corned beef brisket in a large cooking pot, along with some of the pickling solution (if you've corned the meat in a gallon bag). The amount is a matter of taste. If you find the solution saltier than you like, just add a little. If it's not too salty, you may wish to add more.

2. Add cool water to cover and bring to a boil. Turn down the heat and simmer gently until meat is tender—about 2½ hours.

3. About 1 hour before serving, peel carrots and potatoes. Cut carrots in half lengthwise and add to the pot. Add potatoes whole. Quarter cabbage and remove core. Add cabbage to the pot and cover with a lid. Cook over low heat until vegetables are done and meat is tender.

Sweet and Sour Eggs

Pickling eggs is fun and quite easy. There are many different recipes for safely producing this food. This recipe is courtesy of the Georgia Egg Commission's undated publication, "Peter Piper Picked a Peck of Pickled Eggs."

Makes 1 dozen eggs

Prep time: 20 minutes

Cook time: 15 minutes (does not include time for hard boiling eggs)

---

1 dozen eggs, hard-boiled and peeled

1½ cup apple cider

½ cup cider vinegar

1 pkg. (12 oz.) red cinnamon candy

1 TB. mixed pickling spice

2 tsp. salt

1 tsp. garlic salt

Follow procedures for hard boiling and peeling 1 dozen eggs given earlier in the chapter. Fill a quart jar loosely with peeled eggs. The jar should hold about a dozen. Combine apple cider, cider vinegar, cinnamon candy, pickling spice, salt, and garlic salt. Heat the pickling mixture to a near boil and then let it simmer for 5 minutes. Turn off the heat and pour the mixture over the eggs in the jars, being sure to cover the eggs completely. Set the lid and ring in place and store in the refrigerator. It will take anywhere from 1 to 4 weeks to season the eggs, depending on their size. Keep them refrigerated during this time. They'll keep for several months.

Dark and Spicy Eggs

Here's another tasty recipe courtesy of the Georgia Egg Commission's undated publication, "Peter Piper Picked a Peck of Pickled Eggs."

1 dozen eggs, hard-boiled and peeled

1½ cup cider vinegar

½ cup water

1 TB. dark brown sugar

2 tsp. granulated sugar

1 tsp. mixed pickling spice

¼ tsp. liquid smoke or hickory smoke salt

2 tsp. salt

Makes 1 dozen eggs
Prep time: 20 minutes
Cook time: 15 minutes (does not include time for hard boiling eggs)

Follow procedures for hard boiling and peeling 1 dozen eggs given earlier in the chapter. Fill a quart jar loosely with peeled eggs. The jar should hold about a dozen. Combine cider vinegar, water, sugars, pickling spice, liquid smoke, and salt. Heat the pickling mixture to a near boil and then let it simmer for 5 minutes. Turn off the heat and pour the mixture over the eggs in the jars, being sure to cover the eggs completely. Set the lid and ring in place and store in the refrigerator. It will take anywhere from 1 to 4 weeks to season the eggs, depending on their size. Keep them refrigerated during this time. They'll keep for several months.

Chapter 16

Relishes

In This Chapter

- ◆ The key ingredient—freshness
- ◆ Some like it hot(ter): salsas
- ◆ A trio of basic ingredients: tomatoes, peppers, and onions
- ◆ Hold the tears

Relishes are quite a bit like pickles except they're in smaller pieces. They're made from chopped fruits or vegetables, assembled in any variety of combinations and simmered in a spicy vinegar solution.

General Procedures

The key word here is "fresh." Fresh vegetables and fruits are not only tastier, they're also more attractive and easier to cut. Young, tender vegetables and fruits make the best relishes, so this is not a place for the tired, the shriveled, and the shopworn. Choose the best ingredients and get started on your relishes without delay.

There are quite a few ways to arrive at a bowl full of nicely chopped fruits or vegetables. You can use a sharp knife and cutting board, a food processor, or a vegetable shredder. The process isn't complicated but can be a bit messy if you're working with juicy fruits and veggies.

Size is a matter of personal taste, and the term "bite-sized" is relative. Some folks dice the veggies and fruits to get them super small, while others like bigger chunks. There's no gold standard here. Let whatever you like to eat guide your hand.

Preserving Pointers

Tip the cutting board every so often and pour the liquid that accumulates from cutting fresh vegetables and fruits into a small bowl. You'll want to capture that juice and not watch it spill off onto the counter.

Making Salsas

Salsas are bright, colorful, crunchy, and essential parts of Tex-Mex cuisine. The word "salsa" simply means "sauce" in Spanish, but there's nothing simple about the wide variety of ingredients you can choose to put in your own salsas. The basics include tomatoes, peppers, and onions.

You can use bottled lemon or lime juice instead of vinegar as long as you keep the proportions the same. Bottled lemon or lime juice is more acidic than vinegar, so you can substitute them for the vinegar but not the other way around. The percentage of acidity is constant in bottled lemon or lime juice, but it can vary widely in fresh juice. For safety, always use bottled juice.

Safety Check

The main caveat in making salsas is not to reduce the proportions of vegetables (low-acid foods) to the tomatoes and acid components. It's the acidity that makes the salsas safe to eat.

The proportions given in the recipes at the end of this chapter follow the recommendations of the Extension Service for safe products. For more salsa recipes, request the brochure "Salsa Recipes for Canning" from your local Cooperative Extension Office.

A Tomato Primer

There are many different types of tomatoes, and they come in a wide range of sizes and colors. For salsas, Romas are probably your best bet, and *tomatillos* are excellent as well. One's red and one's green. Together they make a fiesta!

If you're not familiar with tomatillos, they're an interesting fruit. Like tomatoes, they belong to the nightshade family, even though they look a bit strange on the outside. After you remove the dry outer skin or husk, however, you're looking at a nice, round, green, almost tomato-type item. Peeling and seeding aren't necessary for tomatillos.

def•i•ni•tion

The **tomatillo** (*Physalis philadelphica*) is a relative of the tomato. It originates in Central America and has been cultivated in Mexico and Guatemala since pre-Columbian times. It's also referred to as the "husk tomato," "jamberry," or "groundcherry."

Roma tomatoes.

Tomatillo in the husk (left), and a husked tomatillo (right).

For salsas, you want tomatoes with thick walls and firm flesh that hold up well during the chopping and the processing. It's true you can use regular eating or salad tomatoes, but you're likely to end up with a more watery product that lacks shape. The difference is obvious when you slice into a Roma. You'll notice a distinct lack of juice spilling off the cutting board. You'll also see less mush accumulating as you chop and slice away.

A Pepper Primer

Tomatoes give salsa substance, and peppers give it texture and heat. Actually, not all peppers turn on the heat, and if you prefer a mild salsa, you've got plenty of varieties of peppers to choose from. Peppers run the gamut from mild to hotter than Hades. If the recipe you're using calls for long green chiles, choose a mild variety.

There's actually a rating scale for heat in peppers—it's called the Scoville Heat Unit Scale, named for Wilbur Scoville, the man who created the system back in 1912. The bell pepper, a staple of salads, salad bars, and stuffed pepper dishes, rates a mere zero on the Scoville scale. Blocky and firm, bell peppers are green but turn red when mature and also come in shades of yellow or gold. The hottest peppers score in the thousands on the Scoville scale. For the purposes of making salsa, you may want to mix some bells with an Anaheim (a bit hotter with a Scoville index around 1,000) or a jalapeno (around 5,000 on the index!).

The shapes of hot peppers are different from the milder varieties, and many are elongated and wrinkled. Anaheims can be deep green at the red end of the color spectrum, so they may appear almost burgundy. They're usually around 4 to 5 inches long with a flattened pod. Jalapenos are most often red or green and from 2 to 3 inches in length. Whatever peppers you enjoy eating will be good additions to your salsa.

Safety Check

Be careful when handling hot peppers. You can seriously irritate your eyes if you happen to rub them while working with the hot varieties. The seeds are hot as well. Wear gloves when handling hot peppers and wash up thoroughly afterward.

If you want to peel them (and you don't need to), first slice along each side of the pepper. This makes an escape vent for the steam you'll be generating. Then place the peppers on a cookie sheet and put them in an oven that's been preheated to 400°F for 6 to 8 minutes or under the broiler until the skins blister.

Remove the peppers from the oven and cover them with a damp cloth. After they've cooled for a few minutes, you'll be able to slip the skins, and they'll be ready to chop.

You can remove the seeds from the hotter varieties of peppers, if you wish. Also, the white membranes that extend from the seeds to the walls of the pepper have the highest concentration of capsaicin, the substance that gives peppers their heat. Remove that membrane and the seeds and you'll turn down the thermostat a little.

An Onion Primer

Onions are the third main ingredient in salsa. Just as with peppers, you have a choice of colors and intensity of flavors. Yellow onions have the strongest flavor, and that lets them compete favorably when mixed with a slightly hot pepper such as an Anaheim.

White onions are milder, and red onions are sweeter.

Sometimes onions do bring tears to your eyes, and there are as many recommendations for dealing with this as there are cures for hiccups:

♦ Peel onions under cool, running water. That will work, although it's tough to dice and chop that way.

Preserving Pointers _____

The irritant in onions is actually caused by an enzyme reaction. What you're smelling is sulfuric acid.

♦ Breathe through your mouth. It's worth a try, although it's the compounds stinging your eyes that cause the watering, not your nose.

♦ Eat a piece of bread while you're peeling. This is probably a variation on the "breathe through your mouth" advice. Your mouth will be open while you're biting into the bread, and you'll most likely take a breath then as well.

♦ Work quickly and use a sharp knife. Be careful around sharp knives, although if the knife is well honed, your work will go faster, and you'll spend less time on close terms with the onion irritant.

♦ Try using a small fan to blow the fumes away from you.

♦ Cut off the root end first and toss it in the garbage. This operates on the theory that the problem is located in this part of the onion only.

In Other Words _____

An onion can make people cry, but there's never been a vegetable that can make people laugh.

—Will Rogers, Cherokee-American cowboy and humorist

♦ Wear a pair of swimming goggles. This has to work, but if you chop a great many onions, a major topic of conversation at dinner will be the circles around your eyes.

Keep in mind that onions get stronger as they age, but their flavor actually decreases, so it's best to use them promptly.

Keeping Your Produce Fresh

The nice thing about ingredients for making salsa is that they all come ripe around the same time, toward the end of the garden year. Whether you've grown your own produce or have made your purchases at the farmers' market or grocery store, it's important to store these items under optimal conditions until you're ready to create your salsas. You'll need fresh produce for your salsas, but for short-term storage, each item has different requirements.

For tomatoes, this means keeping them at room temperature and out of direct sunlight until they've fully ripened. Stored in the fridge, tomatoes get soft and lose their flavor. Always store them stems up, since the shoulders are the most vulnerable spots on this fruit for bruising.

Green peppers keep well in the vegetable compartment of your refrigerator. If there is a humidity regulator, take advantage of it and increase the humidity as much as possible. Take the peppers out of any plastic bag you transported them in. This helps the air circulate and keeps the peppers from softening quickly. Plan on using them within a few days.

Onions like it cool and dry. Keep them out of direct sunlight and they'll keep for months.

Spices

Here you can use whatever you like. Black pepper, oregano, cilantro, and cumin are often used. If you prefer to use fresh cilantro for its aroma and flavor, add it to the salsa just before you serve it.

Recipes

After so much talk about salsa, it's time for a couple of recipes! I also include some fruit and vegetable relishes to round out the chapter.

Tomatillo Green Salsa

Go totally green with this classic mild salsa. You can use either green tomatoes or tomatillos. If you are looking for salsa with a bit more zip, you can replace an equal amount of mild chiles with hotter ones. Just keep the proportions the same. The following recipe is adapted from "Salsa Recipes for Canning" (PNW0395), a publication of Pacific Northwest Extension Publications.

5 cups chopped tomatillos (or green tomatoes)

2 cups long green chiles, seeded and chopped

4 cups chopped onions

1 cup bottled lemon or lime juice

6 cloves garlic, finely chopped

Salt and pepper to taste

Makes 4 to 5 pints
Prep time: 30 minutes
Cook time: 20 minutes (does not include processing time)

Combine tomatillos, chiles, onions, lemon or lime juice, garlic, and salt and pepper to taste in a large cooking pot. Turn heat on high and bring ingredients to a boil. Then reduce heat and simmer for 20 minutes, stirring occasionally. Pack into hot, sterilized glass pint canning jars, leaving ½ inch of headspace. Wipe rims, adjust lids, and process in a boiling water bath for 15 minutes.

Serving suggestion: Before serving, blend in 1 tablespoon fresh chopped cilantro leaves to each pint. Chill before serving.

Roma Salsa

This is a good, chunky salsa with enough color to liven up a bowl of tortilla chips. The following recipe is adapted from "Salsa Recipes for Canning" (PNW0395), a publication of Pacific Northwest Extension Publications.

Makes 14 to 16 pints

Prep time: 30 minutes

Cook time: 25 minutes (does not include processing time)

---

7 qt. Roma tomatoes, peeled, cored, and chopped

4½ cups long green chiles, seeded and chopped

5 cups chopped onion

½ cup jalapenos, seeded and finely chopped

6 cloves garlic, finely chopped

2 cups bottled lemon or lime juice

Salt and pepper to taste

Combine tomatoes, chiles, onions, jalapenos, garlic, lemon or lime juice, and salt and pepper to taste in a large saucepan and bring to a boil, stirring frequently. Then reduce heat and simmer another 20 minutes, stirring occasionally. Pack into hot, sterilized glass pint canning jars, leaving ½ inch of headspace, wipe rims, adjust lids, and process in a boiling water bath for 15 minutes.

Serving suggestion: Before serving, blend in 1 tablespoon fresh chopped cilantro leaves to each pint. Chill before serving.

Cranberry Orange Relish

Just when the winter blahs have descended and there doesn't seem to be a bit of color anywhere, along comes this vibrant, zesty relish to brighten your main course. This recipe is courtesy of Ocean Spray Cranberries, Inc.

1 bag cranberries

4 to 5 medium apples, cored and finely chopped

2 oranges, peeled, seeded, and chopped

¼ cup orange peel

2 cups sugar

Makes about 8 cups
Prep time: 30 minutes
Cook time: None

Mix together cranberries, apples, oranges, orange peel, and sugar. Chill before serving.

Beet Relish

Beet skins will slip easily if you plunge the beets into very cold water after cooking. Always leave some root and crown attached to keep the beets from bleeding while they're cooking. You want your relish to be beet red!

12 medium-size beets, cooked, skins slipped, and diced

1 medium onion, chopped

2 cups cabbage, finely chopped

1 sweet red pepper, diced

1½ tsp. salt

¾ cup sugar

1½ cups vinegar

Makes 3 pints
Prep time: 45 minutes
Cook time: 1 hour (does not include processing time)

Combine cooked beets, onion, cabbage, red pepper, salt, sugar, and vinegar in an 8- to 12-quart saucepan. Bring to a boil, then reduce heat and simmer an additional 15 minutes. Pack into hot, sterilized glass canning jars, adjust lids, and process in a boiling water bath 5 minutes for pints.

Corn Relish

Fresh corn on the cob is one of the true delights of summer, but as the season winds down, you may find some of the corn you're either picking or buying isn't quite as young and tender as you'd like. Enter corn relish to solve that problem. You want the kernels to be a bit chewy for this relish.

Makes 4 to 5 pints
Prep time: 1 hour
Cook time: 25 minutes (does not include processing time)

12 medium ears fresh corn

1 cup diced sweet red peppers

1 cup chopped celery

½ cup minced onion

1½ cups apple cider vinegar

¾ cup sugar

2 tsp. salt

1½ tsp. dry mustard

1 tsp. celery seed

½ tsp. turmeric

1. Husk corn and remove all silk. Place ears in boiling water and cook for 5 minutes. Remove from heat and allow to cool. Using a sharp knife or corn slicer, remove kernels from cobs, being careful not to scrape the cobs. (That would give your corn a "cobby" taste.)

2. In an 8- to 12-quart cooking pot, combine red peppers, celery, onions, vinegar, sugar, salt, dry mustard, celery seed, and turmeric and bring to a boil, stirring frequently. When mixture reaches a boil, add the corn and mix thoroughly. Boil an additional 5 minutes and then pack into hot, sterilized glass canning jars, leaving ½ inch of headspace. Wipe rims, adjust lids, and process in a boiling water bath for 5 minutes for pints.

Pear Relish

This is a big recipe and it makes wonderful gifts, so when pears come into season, get ready to chop away. It's sweet and tangy at the same time.

2 gal. pears, cored (about 60 pears)

6 red bell peppers, seeds removed

6 bell peppers, seeds removed

6 Anaheim chiles, seeds removed

4 jalapenos, seeds removed

1 dozen medium yellow onions

2 cups prepared mustard

3 cups sugar

1 TB. salt

> *Makes 16 to 18 pints*
>
> **Prep time:** 45 minutes
> **Cook time:** 30 minutes
> (does not include processing time)

Finely chop pears, peppers, chiles, jalapenos, and onions. Place in a large cooking pot and add mustard, sugar, and salt. Bring to a boil over medium heat. Reduce heat and cook for 20 minutes, stirring occasionally. Pack into pint glass canning jars, leaving ½ inch of headspace, wipe rims, seal, and process in a boiling water bath for 5 minutes.

Piccalilli

This is a very old favorite, dating back to the eighteenth century and probably Revolutionary War days. The origin of the term is lost in the mists of time, but you can almost see the word "pickle" in it. Maybe it means "little pickle pieces?" Hard to tell, but this is a very good relish. Piccalilli is also a good way to use up odds and ends from the garden at the end of the season and expand your home food preserving pantry.

Makes about 4 pints

Prep time: 1 hour
(does not count mixture standing overnight)

Cook time: 40 minutes
(does not include processing time)

---

6 medium green tomatoes, coarsely chopped

6 sweet red peppers, coarsely chopped

6 medium onions, coarsely chopped

1 small cabbage, coarsely chopped

¼ cup salt

2 cups vinegar

2½ cups light brown sugar

2 TB. pickling spices

1. Place tomatoes, red peppers, onions, and cabbage in a large ceramic or glass bowl. Sprinkle salt on top and let stand overnight on the counter. This draws out the moisture from the cabbage. The next morning drain off water. Then cover vegetables with cool water and drain again.

2. Place in an 8- to 12-quart cooking pot and add vinegar, brown sugar, and pickling spices (put spices in a spice bag) and bring to a boil. Reduce heat and simmer an additional 20 minutes. Remove the spice bag. Pack piccalilli into hot, sterilized glass canning jars, leaving ½ inch headspace, wipe rims, adjust lids, and process in a boiling water bath for 5 minutes for pints.

Fermenting

In This Chapter

- The basics of fermentation
- Brine time
- Making fermented dill pickles and sauerkraut
- Solving problems

Fermentation is a process that preserves foods by making them so acidic that undesirable microorganisms can't grow and spoil the food being fermented. It's a long process, and it's also a good use for those stoneware crocks you've collected over the years.

Origins of Fermentation

Fermentation is a natural process by which fruits, milk, and grains change their chemical composition by converting sugar to carbon dioxide and alcohol in the absence of air.

The discovery of fermentation was probably accidental, at least as far as food was concerned. Somebody somewhere left the grape juice out and it changed. It acidified yet kept a certain tangy sweetness. It had fermented. And thus, wine was born.

The next great leap forward probably happened when someone left the apple juice out. Later, it became apparent that it too had changed. Perhaps someone dropped a piece of food into the vat and left it there for someone else to fish out. When the person did, he or she noticed that it too had changed. It hadn't spoiled and even had a nice crunch.

The beginnings of pickles undoubtedly had an origin something along those lines.

Today we understand a great deal about how fermentation works, and by applying these basic rules of science, we can produce a pickle extravaganza.

General Procedures

To make a good-quality fermented pickle, it's absolutely essential to follow a tested and approved recipe to the letter. If you don't take shortcuts with the process, you'll be well rewarded for your time and effort.

Time is a crucial ingredient with fermented pickles, and they can take from 4 to 6 weeks to arrive at the proper degree of readiness. During that time, you can't ignore them or neglect them, so be sure to start them when you'll be on hand to supervise their progress.

Safety Check

Check to make sure the crock is free of chips and cracks that will allow the liquid to seep through. If you find some damage, you can line the crock with a heavy, food-grade piece of plastic and secure it around the rim.

During that 4- to 6-week time slot, the pickles will be immersed in brine. They're not just hanging around, however. Important bacterial action is taking place just below the water line. The bacteria in question are lactic acid bacteria, and they're found naturally on cucumbers. Fermentation encourages their growth as they work to preserve cucumbers by lowering their pH level to less than 4.0. In addition, they give fermented pickles their characteristic taste.

A stoneware crock is the traditional vessel for fermenting, but if you don't have one, food-grade plastic containers work well. Many fast-food restaurants will let you buy or beg some.

Brine Basics

Each recipe will give you specific directions as to amounts of ingredients to use in making the brine, and this includes water. Hard water can cause the brine to become cloudy, but if you don't have soft water, you can boil hard water and then let it sit for 24 hours. If any scum forms, skim this off. Also, as you take water from the pan to make the brine, don't disturb the sediment on the bottom of the pan.

Brine Maintenance

This includes monitoring the temperature. You want the temperature to remain constant within the ideal range of 65°F to 80°F. If the temperature gets colder or hotter than this, pickles will either spoil or be poor quality.

Removing the scum that forms on top of the crock during fermentation is a daily task. This scum is made up of yeasts and molds that feed on lactic acid and produce enzymes that make the pickles soft. Without sufficient lactic acid, the pickles will spoil, so keep your crock scum free.

Brine Bubbles

It's alive! It truly is. The bubbles that rise to the surface of the brine tell you that fermentation is happening. When the process is complete, the bubbles stop. Check the pickles at this time. Take a cucumber out of the crock and slice it in half. There should be no visible rings or white spots.

You'll probably see that the brine has become cloudy. This is due to bacterial growth that occurs during the fermentation process. Carefully pour the brine through a strainer and into a large cooking pot. Heat the brine to boiling and reserve it to use in covering the pickles after you pack them into jars.

Fermenting by the Numbers

There's a logical sequence to the fermentation process. It takes several days, but the steps are always the same. You should see the following:

1. Clear brine for the first 1 to 3 days

2. Cloudy brine and gas bubbles the next 2 to 3 days

3. Cloudy brine and no gas bubbles for 5 to 6 days

4. Finished! (10 to 12 days from the beginning)

Before packing the pickles, check to be sure they're perfect. They should be firm, crisp, and have good color. If you detect any signs of spoilage—soft, slippery, stinky, strange color—do not eat them. Dispose of them.

Fermented Dill Pickles

The following procedures are from the USDA's *Complete Guide to Home Canning* (see Appendix G). This is an example of using a tested and approved recipe—something the home food preserver should always do!

You'll need the following ingredients to make 4 pounds of pickles:

- 4 pounds of 4-inch pickling cucumbers
- 2 tablespoons dill seed (or use 4 to 5 heads fresh or dry dill weed)
- $\frac{1}{2}$ cup salt
- $\frac{1}{4}$ cup distilled white vinegar (5 percent)
- 8 cups water

Those are the basics. You can then add one or more of the following optional ingredients:

- 2 cloves garlic
- 2 dried red peppers
- 2 teaspoons whole mixed pickling spices

Here's the general method:

1. Wash the cucumbers and cut $\frac{1}{16}$ inch from the blossom end and discard. (This end contains enzymes that can cause soft pickles.) Leave $\frac{1}{4}$ inch of the stem attached.

2. Place half the dill and half the spices in the bottom of a stoneware crock or other suitable container. Then add the cucumbers and the rest of the dill and the spices.

3. Dissolve the salt in the vinegar and water and pour over the cucumbers.

4. Add a weight (such as a dinner plate weighted down with a leak-proof plastic bag filled with water and securely tied) and drape a clean cloth over the top of the crock to keep out dust or insects.

Place the crock where the temperature will remain between 70°F and 75°F for the 3 to 4 weeks it will take for the fermentation process to complete. Cooler temperatures will slow down the fermentation process, and higher temperatures will cause the pickles to become soft.

Check on the pickles every day if you can, but be sure to check on them at least several times a week. Remove any surface scum that forms. If the pickles become soft, slimy, or begin to smell bad, dispose of them and abort the mission.

Preserving Pointers

If possible, have the crock already in the place where you'll be keeping it during fermentation. This saves wear and tear on your back trying to lift it and avoids spills.

When fermentation is complete, you can continue to store the pickles in the original container in the refrigerator, if it will fit. You'll still need to check in on it and remove any mold or scum that develops on the surface. If that seems less than satisfactory, canning the pickles is the way to go.

To process the pickles, pour the brine into a large pan and bring it slowly to a boil. Then turn down the heat and simmer for 5 minutes. Pack the pickles into jars and cover them with hot brine, leaving ½ inch of headspace. Wipe the rims, adjust the lids, and process in a boiling water bath 10 minutes for pints and 15 minutes for quarts.

These pickles may also be processed by low temperature pasteurization. See Chapter 13 for specific instructions for this method. Also see Chapter 13 for troubleshooting fermented pickles.

Sauerkraut

Cabbage originated in Asia but made an early entrance to Europe. If you remember your grade school geography and the list of explorers you needed to memorize, you will remember Jacques Cartier. His significance to the home food preserver is his introduction of cabbage to the new world.

Cabbage grows well in many climates and keeps well over the winter. It's not surprising then, that people decided it would be a good candidate for fermenting. The result is a food that's known and loved in cultures around the world.

Although fermented cabbage has its origins in Asia, the word "sauerkraut" is German: *sauer* meaning sour and *kraut* meaning cabbage. It's a staple in most German households and a favorite of many folks of German descent.

If the farmers' market has a good supply of cabbage, or if you've grown your own cabbage crop and have root cellared all you'll need over the winter and still have some heads to spare, try your hand at making sauerkraut. Select firm, large heads of cabbage.

You'll need the following ingredients:

- 25 pounds of cabbage

- ¾ cup pickling or kosher salt

You'll get about 9 quarts of sauerkraut from 25 pounds of cabbage, but the actual amount depends on how finely you shred the cabbage and how small the core is.

Preserving Pointers

Think late autumn when you think sauerkraut. Cabbage that matures late in the season (mid-August through mid-September) generally produces bigger heads, and this is ideal for making sauerkraut. Don't let the cabbage sit. Get to making the sauerkraut within two days of picking or purchasing.

Wash the cabbage and remove the outer leaves and any other damaged leaves. Cut the cabbage in half and then quarter it. Remove the core. Treat the cabbage gently. It may look like a tough vegetable, but if the leaves get bruised, the sauerkraut will suffer. This starts a chain reaction that will spoil the kraut:

1. Bruised portions tend to pack together.

2. This keeps the brine from being able to penetrate thoroughly.

3. Unbrined cabbage spoils or doesn't ferment evenly, and the sauerkraut is a bust.

How finely should you shred the cabbage? Not too coarse and not too fine. Aim for about ¼ inch thick. This will usually be the coarse blade on your vegetable shredder or food processor.

The traditional vessel for making sauerkraut is a big stoneware crock. You can also use glass, enamel, or food-grade plastic containers. You'll need to do some serious eyeballing to make sure the crock is deep enough to hold all the shredded cabbage and brine and still leave 4 to 5 inches of space below the rim. Why so much space? During fermenting, gas bubbles will rise. If there's not enough room, the brine will bubble over, and you'll have a major science experiment in the kitchen or wherever you've placed the crock.

The procedure for making sauerkraut is called "dry salting." Place the shredded cabbage in the crock and add 3 tablespoons of salt. Mix thoroughly with your hands (clean, of course!) and then pack the cabbage down firmly into the container. This is your first layer. Repeat this procedure with the next 5 pounds of cabbage and continue the layering until all the cabbage and salt is in the crock. A concentrated brine forms when the salt leaches moisture out of the cabbage.

The brine will form fairly quickly. If it hasn't completely covered the cabbage within an hour, add some prepared brine to the crock to deal with the situation. Add 1½ tablespoons of salt to a quart of water, heat to boiling, and cool. Make as many quarts as you need to get the job done.

Place a plate on top of the cabbage to weight it down under the brine. Add a weight to the top of the plate if needed and cover everything with a clean, heavy cloth (a bath towel works well). Check the brine frequently—once a day is recommended—and remove any scum that forms.

Safety Check

Garbage cans or non-food-grade plastic containers may react with the acid produced during fermentation and may make the sauerkraut unsafe to eat or give it a bad flavor.

You can also use a brine-filled bag to weight down the cabbage. If you go this route, don't lift the bag out of the crock until the bubbling has stopped and fermentation has completed. Place one 2-gallon, food-grade plastic bag inside another. Fill with brine made from adding 1½ tablespoons of salt to 1 quart of water. Tie securely. You'll need about 3 quarts of brine for a 5-gallon crock.

Now it's time to have some faith. You'll need it during the first week because frequently the fermenting cabbage produces a horrific odor. Do not despair, as this is normal and will go away as the fermentation process continues. (Although it's probably a good reason not to keep the crock in the kitchen or any other room you need to visit frequently.)

If you keep the temperature between 70°F and 75°F, the sauerkraut will be fermented in 3 to 4 weeks. Then it's ready for eating, canning, or storage in the refrigerator. (It will keep for several months there.)

For canning, you can choose either hot pack or raw pack:

◆ **Hot pack:** Place the kraut and brine in a large cooking pot, turn heat on high, and bring to a boil. Stir frequently to be sure the entire batch is hot throughout. Then pack it firmly into jars and add brine to cover, leaving ½ inch of headspace. Process in a boiling water canner for 10 minutes for pints and 15 minutes for quarts.

◆ **Raw pack:** Pack the kraut firmly into jars and cover with the brine, leaving $\frac{1}{2}$ inch of headspace. Process in a boiling water canner for 20 minutes for pints and 25 minutes for quarts.

Troubleshooting Sauerkraut

You know you did everything by the book. Well, almost everything. Surely there's some leeway in the directions? It shouldn't matter if you changed the ingredients, the temperature, or took some shortcuts. Right?

Wrong, unfortunately. When you're dealing with fermentation, everything has got to be just right, and even then it may seem the fates are conspiring against you. Here are some common problems, along with their possible causes and recommended solutions:

◆ **The sauerkraut is really dark.** This can have several causes: using iodized salt, not mixing the salt into the cabbage thoroughly, having the temperature too high during fermenting or storage, or not cleaning and trimming the cabbage properly as you began. The solutions are found in the causes. Follow the directions carefully.

◆ **The sauerkraut is soft and mushy.** Again, salt is the culprit—too little or not mixed in well enough. The temperature may also be too high. If you didn't pack the cabbage firmly into the crock, air pockets can form and play havoc with the fermentation process. Use the amount of salt called for and mix it in thoroughly as you're preparing the layers in the crock. Pack the cabbage firmly and be sure to store the crock in a location where the temperature won't soar into the danger zone.

◆ **There's a white scummy surface on top of the brine.** Air got in because the weight didn't weigh enough to keep it out. If the plate's not heavy enough, add bags full of brine. You can skim off the scum. The kraut should be fine.

◆ **There's a moldy surface on top of the brine.** The temperature got too warm during the fermentation process, and/or the crock wasn't covered well enough to keep out the air. This one is not a keeper. Discard the sauerkraut. It is potentially unsafe to eat. Next time, keep the crock in the 70°F to 75°F zone and covered to exclude air.

◆ **The kraut is rotten.** The same conditions that cause mold to grow on the surface can cause the kraut to go bad. Keep the temperature in the 70°F to 75°F zone and keep the crock covered to exclude air. Dispose of the kraut. It's bad.

◆ **The kraut is slimy.** This points to too little salt and too high a temperature during the fermenting process. Discard. Next time be scrupulous about the correct amount of salt and the proper temperature range.

As you can see, operator error is usually the culprit. Since you're only dealing with two ingredients (cabbage and salt), the right proportions are essential to get a good result. If you read the directions carefully before you begin and keep tabs on the temperature during fermenting, the sauerkraut should turn out great.

Recipes

Sauerkraut is always great on hot dogs and as an accompaniment to pork chops and roasts. Here are two recipes that will have your mouth watering. The first is especially scrumptious on a cold winter's night, while the second is a staple of Korean cooking—and it's hot!

Kielbasa and Sauerkraut Casserole

Polish sausage and German sauerkraut team up to make a hearty, flavorful casserole. The secret is the little bit of brown sugar that adds just a touch of sweetness. Of course, the beer adds flavor, too!

2 lb. smoked Polish sausage or kielbasa

1 large onion, sliced

2 lb. sauerkraut with liquid

1 can beer

2 TB. brown sugar

2 TB. brown mustard

Serves 6	
Prep time: 30 minutes	
Cook time: 45 minutes	

1. Preheat oven to 350°F. Slice the sausage into $\frac{1}{2}$-inch pieces and place in skillet. Turn heat on medium and cook sausage until browned. Remove from skillet and drain sausage on paper towels. Sauté onion in sausage grease. When translucent, remove onion and drain on paper towels.

2. In a 1-quart casserole dish, combine sauerkraut and liquid, sausage, onion, beer, brown sugar, and brown mustard. Bake for 45 minutes.

Kimchi

Kimchi is indisputably the national food of Korea, with consumption averaging around 40 pounds per person per year. Kimchi began as salted vegetables but over time incorporated some tasty additions. Common ingredients for kimchi include cabbage, ginger, green onions, radishes, garlic, and powdered red pepper. It's a heady mix. There are many ways to make kimchi. Here's one version that uses cabbage. You can substitute ginger powder (1 teaspoon) for the ginger root, but fresh ginger root gives a better flavor. If you have access to an Asian foods store, buy some kimchi sauce and add a tablespoon to the kimchi.

Makes 1½ quarts
Prep time: 6 hours (includes 4 hours of resting time for cabbage)
Cook time: None

2 heads of Chinese (Napa) cabbage

2 carrots, shredded

1 cucumber, diced

3 TB. kosher or sea salt

Large, food-grade plastic bag

Plastic containers with lids

1 bunch green onions (scallions), chopped

4 TB. chili powder

3 cloves garlic, minced

2 TB. sugar

1 small piece ginger, crushed

1. Wash cabbage. Cut off stems. Cut leaves horizontally into four pieces and then cut these into halves lengthwise. Your goal is to arrive at pieces about 2 inches square.

2. Put a handful of the cabbage in the plastic bag and sprinkle with salt. Repeat the layering process, ending with a layer of salt. With clean hands, gently work cabbage inside the bag until all salt has been absorbed and liquid begins to form. Seal the bag and set aside for 4 to 6 hours. After 2 hours, mix cabbage and liquid once more.

3. Remove cabbage from the bag and rinse. Gently squeeze to remove excess water. Pack cabbage into plastic containers and add green onions, carrots, cucumber, chili powder, garlic, sugar, and ginger. Mix thoroughly with your hands, adding more chili powder as needed to get a rich, dark color.

4. Place lids on the containers and store in a cool location for 5 to 6 days. Then place the containers in the refrigerator. It's ready to eat and will keep in the fridge for months.

Part 5

Fruit Spreads

Whether you're partial to jams or jellies, marmalades, or other kinds of fruit spreads, making them can be an activity for the whole family to enjoy. There's nothing more fun than tasting the product as you go along. Here's where you can let your creativity have some space. Follow a few simple principles and you'll get good results.

Jams, Jellies, and Marmalades

In This Chapter

◆ Four essential ingredients

◆ The basic steps

◆ What equipment and supplies you'll need

◆ The quick freeze

◆ Reduced-sugar fruit spreads

◆ Stumped for answers?

Are you a seat-of-your-pants kind of cook? A pinch here and a dab there? Do you like to experiment? Jam and jelly making will put you on the straight and narrow—at least for the amount of time it takes to make a batch. Measurements must be exact, or your jam or jelly just won't come out the way you want.

However, if you've shied away from making jams or jellies because the process seems too involved or because you need to restrict your sugar intake, it's really never been easier, and now you can make delicious jams without sugar. It doesn't take a whole lot of fruit, and you can put up a batch of freezer jam in less time than it takes to cook a roast. In this chapter, you'll find the basics on jams, jellies, and marmalades, along with specific recipes.

The Science Behind Jam, Jellies, and Marmalades

Four ingredients go into making jams and jellies: fruit, pectin, sugar, and acid. Exact measurements are essential, and for this reason, use measuring cups and spoons and follow directions to the letter. Exact boiling times are also essential, so set a timer to help you maintain accuracy.

Fruit

Most beginning home jelly makers begin with crabapple jelly. It's high in acid and pectin, and this generally means it will set up nicely. Nothing breeds confidence like success, so if you're just starting out with jelly, this is a good first fruit. Other good fruits for first ventures include grapes, green apples, and tart plums.

You can make jam from just about any kind of fruit, but strawberries are the hands-down favorite. They make up beautifully with a rich red syrup and plump pieces of berries. There's just something cheerful about a strawberry.

When you're ready to branch out in your jam and jelly making, you'll find that there's almost an infinite number of possibilities. Just about any kind of fruit will work, as long as you add pectin, sugar, and acid in the right proportions and follow the recipes scrupulously.

Pectin

Pectin is a naturally occurring substance found in fruits. It's present in all fruits but is higher in underripe ones. It's responsible for the gelling of jams and jellies. When you're shopping for pectin, you're likely to see several different brands; all will work well.

Sugar

Sugar is a very important player; in fact, it plays several parts in making sure your jams and jellies turn out the way you want. You may be surprised to see just how much sugar you'll need to follow the recipes, but if you cut back, you'll be disappointed.

That said, manufacturers have worked hard to develop recipes that use less sugar, and some fruit spreads can now be made with sugar substitutes. These will tend to be softer than those made with sugar. Think "gelatin desserts" and you'll have an idea of how these set up.

First of all, sugar helps jams and jellies gel. Jams and jellies contain about 65 to 68 percent sugar. If the percentage falls below 65 percent, the end product will be runny and weak. If it's over 68 percent, the sugar won't dissolve, and you'll have sugar crystals throughout your product, which will taste gritty.

If you're making jam, sugar helps the fruit stay firm so that it doesn't turn into mush. It also adds flavor.

Finally, sugar helps preserve your fruit spreads and extends their shelf life.

Substituting honey, corn syrup, or artificial sweeteners on a one-to-one basis with sugar in jam and jelly recipes won't work. You'll need to use recipes developed for these products.

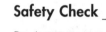

Safety Check

Don't try to save time by making a double or triple batch of jelly or jam. The extra cooking time required causes the pectin to break down. This will make your jam and jelly runny, change the flavor, and make the product dark and unappealing.

Acid

Just as with pectin, acid content is higher in underripe fruit, so if you're making jam and jelly with ripe fruit, you'll need to add acid to be sure your fruit product gels. Acid also adds flavor. Commercial pectin products contain acid, but you may still need to add more to get to the proper percentage. Follow the directions on the box or bottle exactly to find out if and how much additional acid you'll need.

Acid is measured by the pH scale that ranges from 0 to 14. A pH of 7 is neutral. Numbers less than 7 are acidic, while numbers above 7 are basic. A pH between 3.0 and 3.3 is what you're shooting for, and that's pretty acidic. Below 3.0, the jelly "weeps" or forms drops of water on the surface. Above 3.3, the jelly gets weak and runny.

Lemon juice is what's usually added to fruit to get the correct amount of acidity. If you prefer to use citric acid, you'll use ⅛ teaspoon citric acid for each tablespoon of lemon juice.

General Procedures

Even though there are three different kinds of fruit spreads—jam, jelly, and marmalade—the process for making each is essentially the same. Jam or jelly making adds one more step, as you'll see a little later in the chapter. Here are the basic steps:

1. Check jars to be sure there are no nicks, chips, or cracks. If you find any, throw the jars into the recycle bin.

2. Wash jars in hot, soapy water, rinse, and invert them on a clean, dry towel. If the processing time will be more than 10 minutes, sterilize the jars.

   To sterilize jars, the National Center for Home Food Preservation recommends using your boiling water canner. Place the empty jars on the rack in the canner, fill the jars with hot (not boiling) water, and then fill the canner so the water level is 1 inch above the tops of the jars. Turn the heat on high. When the water comes to a boil, set the timer for 10 minutes (this is for sea level; for each additional 1,000 feet in elevation, add 1 minute to the boiling time). Use your jar lifter to remove each jar and immediately fill it with the food to be processed. You can save the water you used to boil the jars for processing the foods.

3. Prepare the lids and bands.

4. Follow the directions on the pectin box or bottle for the type of jam or jelly you are making.

5. After skimming off foam, fill the jars, leaving ⅛ inch headspace.

6. Wipe the rim of the jar with a damp towel to remove any residue.

7. Cover with the lid and screw the band closed. Do not overtighten.

8. Place the jars in a boiling water bath, making sure the water is 1 inch above the tops of the jars.

9. Process in a boiling water bath. Times, along with adjustments for altitude, are included on the pectin box or bottle.

10. Remove the jars, one at a time, from the canner using a jar lifter.

11. Let the jars cool for at least 8 hours or overnight.

12. Remove the screw bands.

13. Wash the jars to remove any sticky residue. Dry. Check the seal.

14. Store in a cool, dry place away from sunlight.

Safety Check

Paraffin is no longer recommended for sealing jams and jellies. The chance of mold and spoilage occurring is too great with this old method. Scraping off mold and eating the product is also not recommended, as mold spores penetrate into the rest of the product and may make it unsafe as well as unappetizing.

Equipment and Supplies

Setting up your kitchen for a jam or jelly session may remind you of your high school or college chemistry lab. There's acid, for starters, although the acid here is usually plain old lemon juice. There are also funnels and drip mechanisms, but unlike in chemistry class, you can take some shortcuts with the equipment and still get the right result.

In addition to fruit, sugar, pectin, and lemon juice (if specified), you'll need the following:

♦ Kitchen scales. Fruit doesn't come in uniform sizes, so you'll need your kitchen scales to be sure you have accurate measurements.

♦ An 8- to 10-quart cooking pot with a flat bottom and enough depth to contain the jelly as it boils.

♦ A long-handled metal spoon for stir-ring jelly and skimming foam.

♦ A small bowl to hold skimmed foam.

♦ A potato masher, if using soft fruit.

♦ A jelly bag.

♦ A jelly bag holder.

♦ A jelly thermometer, if you're making jelly without added pectin.

In Other Words

I squeeze my own lemons to get the juice for jam or jelly, and then I save the peel to use in marmalade. I think fresh is best.

—Bethany, experienced marma-lade maker

Making Jam

Jam is a fruit spread made from crushed fruits cooked with sugar. Once you've mea-sured everything for your batch of jam, you'll be surprised at how quickly everything happens. For example, suppose you're making strawberry jam. You'll follow the general procedures listed earlier in this chapter, but here's the breakdown of how to combine the fruit, acid, pectin, and sugar:

1. Measure out the exact amount of crushed strawberries called for by the pectin box and put them into the large cooking pot, along with the exact amount of lemon juice specified.

2. Stir in 1 box of pectin. You can add ½ teaspoon butter or margarine at this time, and you'll have practically no foam to skim off.

3. Over high heat, stir the mixture constantly until it comes to a full rolling boil (a boil you can't stir down).

4. Add the sugar in all at once and keep stirring while the mixture once again comes to that full rolling boil.

5. Put on the timer as soon as the mixture comes to that full rolling boil and boil hard for exactly 4 minutes—no more and no less!

Strawberry jam is easy to make. Just remember to measure exactly and use your timer to time correctly.

Making Freezer Jam

Freezer jam has the freshest fruit flavor. If this is your first venture into making jam, freezer jam is a great way to begin. It's quick and it's easy. Assemble everything before you begin. Measure all ingredients and set them aside. Once you begin the process, it goes quickly. Read the directions on the pectin box or bottle carefully. The procedure is different from making cooked jam.

Suppose you want to make peach freezer jam. First wash the fruit in cool water. Remove the stems and peels. Place the fruit in a medium-size cooking pot and, using your potato masher, crush the fruit.

Measure out 3¼ cups of the fruit and place it in a large bowl. Add ¼ cup lemon juice. Gradually stir in 1 box of pectin and set it aside for 30 minutes, stirring every 5 minutes to be sure all the pectin dissolves. Add 1 cup corn syrup and mix well. Add 4½ cups sugar. Stir well until there is no grainy texture. Then pack it into plastic freezer containers or jelly or pint glass canning jars. Leave ½ inch headspace. Seal, label, and date. Let stand for 24 hours to allow to set. Then store in the freezer for up to 1 year.

Supplies for freezer jam.

Making Jelly

Jelly is made from fruit juice cooked with sugar. Perfect jelly is clear and holds its shape when you slip it out of the jar. You can use commercially bottled fruit juice, or you can make your own.

Preparing the Fruit

Heat is what gets the juices started, and jelly is all about fruit juice! You'll be doing some simmering to begin the process. To prepare hard fruits such as apples, peaches, and pears, first wash them thoroughly in cool water. Remove any stems and cut off the blossom ends on apples and pears. Remove the pits from peaches, apricots, or nectarines, but do not core apples or pears. Cut the fruit into quarter sections or smaller. Do not pare fruit. The cores and pares provide pectin.

Measure the exact amount of fruit specified in the instructions on the pectin box or bottle and place it in a large cooking pot. Add 1 cup of water for each quart of prepared fruit, cover with a lid, turn on the heat, and simmer fruit until soft.

To prepare soft fruits such as berries, cherries, or grapes, first wash them gently in cool water. If using frozen berries, allow them to thaw before washing but measure them while they're still frozen to get the right amount.

Place the fruit in a large cooking pot and use a potato masher to lightly crush the fruit. Add ¼ cup of water to the crushed fruit, cover with a lid, turn on the heat, and simmer the fruit until soft.

Extracting Juices

A jelly bag and a jelly bag holder are essential for making jelly, but you can improvise if you don't have this equipment.

If you don't have a jelly bag or cheesecloth, cut off one leg from a clean or new pair of pantyhose or use a clean pillowcase, coffee filters (these don't work quite as well as the others and need to be changed frequently), or a clean white cotton sock. Run the jelly bag or substitute jelly bag under cool water and wring gently to remove excess water. This will prevent the bag from soaking up the juice.

A jelly bag holder is an apparatus with three legs from which the jelly bag is suspended. If you don't have one, you can use your ingenuity. The objective here is height. You want gravity to get all the help it needs to make the juice drip. You can hang the jelly bag from a doorknob (protect the door surface with some plastic wrap) or hang a heavy-duty clothes hanger from a cupboard handle and attach the jelly bag with clothespins. (Again, protect the door surface with some plastic wrap.)

It's actually possible to use an entire pair of new pantyhose and get maximum mileage from all your prepared fruit. Just treat each leg like one jelly bag. You can drape the legs over the aforementioned clothes hangers and collect fruit juice at double speed. It will look strange, but the juice will be perfect.

Preserving Pointers

Don't squeeze the jelly bag! You may be impatient to have it finish dripping, but if you squeeze, your jelly will be cloudy.

Whatever your inventive mind has conjured up, it's time to juice. Using potholders, carefully pour the softened fruit mixture into the jelly bag. Allow it to drip at its own pace.

Once the juice has dripped out, you have some options. You can proceed with making jelly, or you can freeze or can the juice for later. If you decide to freeze it, pour the juice into freezer containers, leave appropriate headspace, label, date, and freeze. If you wish to can the juice, pour it into glass canning jars, leaving appropriate headspace. Adjust the lids and process both pints and quarts in a boiling water bath for 10 minutes to ensure the seal. If you want to make jelly now, it's time for the next step!

Extracting juice.

Will You Need Pectin?

The riper the fruit, the lower the pectin content. Apples are naturally high in pectin, but if the apples you're working with are too ripe, you'll need to add pectin in order to make your jelly set. The Cooperative Extension Service notes that these fruits are usually low in pectin or acid:

- Ripe apples
- Ripe blackberries
- Sour cherries
- Elderberries

- Grapefruit
- Eastern Concord grape juice
- California grapes
- Oranges

The following fruits always need added pectin, acid, or both:

- Apricots
- Figs
- Western Concord grapes
- Guava
- Peaches

- Pears
- Pomegranates
- Prunes
- Raspberries
- Strawberries

Preserving Pointers

If you decide to use fruit juice you've bought at the store, you'll definitely need to add pectin. The commercial processing removes the natural pectins.

Don't feel that somehow you're being less of a purist if you use commercially produced pectin in your jelly. It cuts down on the amount of cooking time and helps preserve the natural fruit flavor. It also increases the amount of jelly you'll get compared to not using added pectin. You also can forego the testing that making jellies without added pectin requires.

Getting By Without Added Pectin

Some fruits contain enough natural pectin and are acidic enough without adding pectin or acid. The Cooperative Extension Service offers this list of those fruits:

- Tart apples
- Crabapples
- Tart blackberries
- Cranberries
- Currants
- Gooseberries

- Eastern Concord grapes
- Lemons
- Loganberries
- Plums (most)
- Prunes (sour)
- Quince

If you decide to make jelly from apples or crabapples without adding pectin, don't peel or core them before simmering. Peels and cores also contain pectin. Take advantage of every source of natural pectin you can!

This jelly will need to boil for a long time; in fact, making jelly without added pectin is sometimes referred to as the "long boil" method. It takes more time to make jelly without added pectin, so be prepared to stir and stir. To test for doneness, turn off the heat under the jelly. Dip a long-handled metal spoon into the jelly and hold the spoon so that the jelly can drip off it. The jelly will be done when it sheets. This means that the jelly separates from the spoon in a sheet, not as individual drops or clusters of drops. You can use a jelly thermometer to let you know when you're getting close, but you'll still need to test.

If it seems close but you're not sure, put a spoonful of jelly on a dish and allow it to cool to room temperature. You can hurry this along by putting it in the freezer for a few minutes to get it to room temperature. If the jelly is set at room temperature, the batch is done.

Making Jelly with Added Pectin

Having the jelly turn out perfectly depends on accurate measuring of all ingredients. Read all the directions on the pectin box or bottle before beginning to make jelly. For example, suppose you're going to make apple jelly using commercially produced pectin. Here's the breakdown for combining the fruit juice, lemon juice (if required), sugar, and pectin:

1. Measure the correct amount of the prepared juice as stated on the pectin box or bottle. This will include lemon juice as well if the apples are ripe.

2. Measure the exact amount of sugar that's required according to the directions into a large bowl and set aside.

3. Pour the juice into an 8- to 10-quart cooking pot. Stir in 1 box of pectin or the required amount of liquid pectin. Turn on the heat.

4. When the mixture comes to a full rolling boil (a boil that can't be stirred down), add sugar all at once, stirring constantly. Keep stirring until the mixture again reaches a full boil, set the timer for 1 minute, and continue to stir. After 1 minute, turn off the heat and remove the pot from the burner.

Preserving Pointers _____

Keep that jam and jelly boiling hard! Slow cooking destroys the pectin. Rapid boiling helps ensure your jam or jelly will set up nicely.

After these steps, the rest is a cinch. Skim off the foam; ladle the jelly into clean, hot jars; wipe rims; adjust lids; and process in the boiling water canner for 5 minutes to ensure the seal.

If you choose not to process in a boiling water bath, you can invert the jars and place on a dry, flat surface for 5 minutes. Then turn the jars right side up and allow to cool.

Ladling jelly into jars.

Remaking Soft Jellies

Sometimes jelly just doesn't set. It happens to everyone at some point. So why does this happen? The fruit could have been too ripe, or perhaps you made a double batch trying to save time, or maybe you didn't add enough acid, or you cut back a little on the sugar. Maybe you overcooked the fruit during the juice extraction phase and this reduced the pectin levels.

If you don't need any more strawberry or peach syrup, you may want to make it over. However, before you plunge in, wait. It's not an emergency. Put the soft jelly aside and give it a week or so. If the jars have sealed, it's not going to go bad on you. Sometimes it just takes a little time.

If you've waited and the jelly still isn't cooperating, you may decide to remake it. If one jar hasn't set, it's likely the whole batch is the same way. Remove the lids and throw them away. Lids cannot be reused. Wash the rings and set them aside.

You'll find directions for remaking soft jellies on the pectin box or bottle. Read the instructions carefully. Then read them again for good measure.

Making Marmalades

Marmalades are traditionally associated with Great Britain, and originally these fruit spreads were used to prevent scurvy. It's how British sailors came to be called "Limeys."

Marmalades combine the best features of jams and jellies. What sets them apart is the small pieces of peel that are suspended in a soft jelly. Orange marmalade is a familiar spread on toast, but you can also try lemon, grapefruit, or lime marmalade as well.

You don't need to add pectin or acid when you're whipping up a batch. All you'll need is citrus, sugar, and water. See the Recipes section at the end of this chapter for a basic marmalade recipe.

Making Reduced-Sugar Fruit Spreads

Sugar helps with the jelling process, so if you use a reduced-sugar recipe, the product will be softer than jams and jellies made with sugar. Recipes for making these fruit spreads are included on the package inserts for pectin. Be sure to follow them carefully.

Low-calorie sugar substitutes vary in their ability to produce a good product, so it's best to check with the manufacturer's website to find specific recipes developed for use with a particular sugar substitute. See the Recipes section at the end of this chapter for instructions.

Troubleshooting

Even if you've faithfully followed every direction, there are times when jams, jellies, and marmalades seem to have minds of their own. They present you with some situations that may be perplexing. Here are some of the most common vexing issues.

What's with All the Foam?

Foam is the syrup with air incorporated into it. As the jam boils, air bubbles move up through the syrup and past the fruit to the top of the cooking pot. It's not harmful, but if you don't skim it off and just pour the entire mixture into jelly jars and seal them, over time the air bubbles collapse and increase the headspace. With all this air inside, your jam can mold and spoil.

You can prevent foam from developing by adding a teaspoon of butter or margarine before the liquid begins to boil.

> **Preserving Pointers**
>
> You can actually heat the foam that arises during jam and jelly making in the microwave or over low heat on the stove and watch it turn back into syrup. You can then save this reconstituted jam in the refrigerator to use within a few days.

Why Is Processing in a Boiling Water Bath Necessary?

Even though the jam or jelly is hot and the jars you're going to put it in are hot, they're probably not hot enough to create a good seal. Processing the jars in a boiling water bath ensures the seal.

You can also try the inversion method, which means that after you fill the jar and put on the lid and screw band, you invert the jar so that the lid is resting on a flat surface. Leave it that way for 5 minutes and then return it to its normal upright position. It will probably seal, but again, it's iffy, and it can be discouraging to check on your jam during the winter and find that the lids have popped and you're growing a mold farm on your jam and jelly. It's not only discouraging, but it's a waste of your time, effort, and money. You should discard any moldy jam or jelly since the mold can penetrate below the visual level.

Why Is the Top Half of the Jar Jam and the Bottom Half Jelly?

This doesn't make the jam unsafe to eat, but it does look a bit strange. You can, of course, open the jar and stir the contents before serving. Prevention is the better tack to take here.

Bigger pieces of fruit are notorious for rising, so be sure to mash or chop your fruit into small enough pieces before you begin. You don't want to turn it into a purée, but you don't want huge hunks either. Also, fruit that is too ripe has a tendency to cause this problem. It's also lower in pectin. Choose ripe fruit but not fruit that's even a shade past its prime.

Follow the directions on the pectin box or bottle to the letter. Set the timer to make sure you're cooking the jam according to the recipe.

When you've finished skimming off the foam, you'll see that the fruit is floating on top of the hot sugar syrup. Let the jam cool for a few minutes and then stir it gently to get the fruit to mix in.

Recipes

You'll find specific recipes for all kinds of jams and jellies on the pectin boxes, but this is an old-time favorite that's worth adding to your file.

Apple Peel Jelly

This recipe has been a standby in many country kitchens for decades. It's thrifty and doesn't waste an essential part of the apple—the peel!

1. When you're cutting up apples for pie slices, don't throw away the peels, especially if you're working with apples that are a bit tart. Put the peels in a large cooking pot as you go along, adding enough cold water just to cover. When you've finished with your peeling, cook the peels over medium heat for about 30 minutes. Then slowly pour the mixture into a jelly bag and allow it to drip out. Do not squeeze the jelly bag.

2. Measure the juice. At this point, you can either use a commercial pectin product and follow the directions on the box or bottle, or you can make the jelly without additional pectin.

3. You'll need 4 cups of juice and 5 cups of sugar. Bring the juice to a boil and boil hard for 5 minutes. Add the sugar all at once and boil hard until the jelly sheets. Remove from the heat, skim the foam, and pour the jelly into hot, sterilized glasses. Adjust the lids and process in a boiling water canner for 5 minutes to ensure the seal. Remove the jars with a jar lifter and allow them to cool on a flat, dry surface.

Makes 4 pints
Prep time: 45 minutes (plus time to allow jelly to drip)
Cook time: About 45 minutes (does not include processing time)

No-Cook Strawberry-Blueberry Jam

Blueberry jam has a nice texture. It's rich and thick and makes a colorful accompaniment at the breakfast table as a spread for scones, biscuits, and toast. This recipe reprinted with permission from Equal. For other recipes, go to www.equal.com.

Makes 40 servings

Prep time: 15 minutes

Cook time: None

1½ cups Equal Spoonful

1 package (1.59 oz.) Ball Fruit Jell Freezer Jam Pectin

2½ cups frozen unsweetened strawberries, thawed, drained, and crushed (or use the same amount of fresh)

1½ cups frozen unsweetened blueberries, thawed, drained, and crushed (or use the same amount of fresh)

1. Combine Equal Spoonful and Ball Fruit Jell in a large bowl until well blended.

2. Add crushed fruit to dry mixture. Stir 3 minutes.

3. Ladle fruit mixture into 5 clean 8-ounce jars, leaving ½ inch of headspace. Cover with lids. Let stand at room temperature until thickened, about 30 minutes. Refrigerate up to 3 weeks. For longer storage, freeze up to 1 year.

Strawberry Jam

This recipe reprinted with permission from Equal. For other recipes, go to www.equal.com.

1½ cups Equal Spoonful

1 package (1.59 oz.) Ball Fruit Jell Freezer Jam Pectin

4 cups frozen unsweetened strawberries, thawed, drained, and crushed (or use the same amount of fresh)

Makes 40 servings
Prep time: 15 minutes
Cook time: No cooking required

1. Combine Equal Spoonful and Ball Fruit Jell in a large bowl until well blended.

2. Add crushed fruit to dry mixture. Stir 3 minutes.

3. Ladle fruit mixture into 5 clean 8-ounce jars, leaving ½ inch of headspace. Cover with lids. Let stand at room temperature until thickened, about 30 minutes. Refrigerate up to 3 weeks. For longer storage, freeze up to 1 year.

Orange Marmalade

Here's a golden opportunity! Capture the sunny color and disposition of fresh oranges and lemons and enjoy the spicy tang of marmalade in the morning.

Makes 4 half-pints
Prep time: 25 minutes
Cook time: 30 minutes (plus time to reach the gel stage)

4 oranges   **Water**

1 lemon   **Sugar**

1. Wash fruit, cut in half, remove seeds and stem end. Slice the oranges and lemon thinly. Add 1½ cups water to each cup of fruit. Let stand 8 hours or overnight.

2. In the morning, cook mixture over until fruit is tender, about 30 minutes. Remove from heat.

3. Measure cooked fruit and liquid. Add 1 cup sugar to each cup of fruit and liquid. Return fruit, liquid, and sugar to cooking pot. Cook over high heat until mixture sheets from a metal spoon. You can also use a jelly thermometer to be sure the mixture has reached the gel stage.

4. Remove from heat and skim any foam from marmalade. Ladle into clean, hot jars, leaving ½ inch of headspace. Wipe rims, seal, and process in a boiling water bath for 5 minutes to ensure the seal.

Chapter 19

Butters, Conserves, and Chutneys

In This Chapter

- ◆ Beyond jam and jelly
- ◆ Starting with purée
- ◆ Weaving flavors and textures
- ◆ Potent products

Here's where you'll find a rich celebration of textures, flavors, and aromas. From the simple to the exotic, these fruit products make excellent accompaniments to any main course. They're also stellar gift items. And what's even better, you can make them for a fraction of what you'd pay for them in a specialty store.

Getting to Know You

Jams, jellies, and marmalades (see Chapter 18) are the Type A personalities of fruit spreads. Everything must be measured accurately and timed correctly. Butters, conserves, and chutneys, however, are the more laid-back members of the fruit spread family. "Take your time" is their motto, and you can do just that. Get a batch started today, finish it tomorrow. No problem. Just keep everything refrigerated, and it will be perfect and ready to go the next day when you are—or the day after, for that matter. Of course, there are reasonable limits, and you'll want to finish up within a few days.

Making Fruit Butters

What's in a name? Actually, fruit butters don't contain butter at all, and you'd never mistake them for butter by their appearance. But they have a smooth, spreadable consistency like butter, and they're great on toast, scones, and muffins—also like butter. They're made, as the name implies, from fruit and also can contain flavorings and sugar. Rich in color, the finished product is much deeper in hue than the raw fruit. Apple butter is a deep, golden amber, for example.

It may seem that it takes forever for certain fruits to begin the ripening process, but once it gets underway, there's no stopping it. You can slow it down by refrigeration, but as the fruit begins to soften, you'd best have a plan in place for using it.

In Other Words

Don't limit yourself to the tried and true. Branch out! My favorite is pumpkin butter.

—Amy, copy editor

Fruit butters are easy to make and a good use for fruit that may be a tad too ripe for eating or for making jam or jelly. Of course, we're definitely not talking about spoiled fruit here. There's only one place for that, and that's the compost pile. We're talking about soft fruit that's peaked and definitely will spoil if you don't do something with it quickly.

Apple butter is the most familiar type, but you can make butters from other fruits, such as apricots, peaches, pears, cherries, blueberries, and plums.

Equipment and Supplies

You don't need much in the way of supplies, but you will need an 8- to 10-quart cooking pot with a bottom that doesn't scorch easily. It's maddening to have to deal with a pot that insists on burning what you're trying to cook.

The other essential item is a food mill, arguably one of the handiest kitchen inventions ever. It's perfect for making smooth applesauce and other fruit purées. Forcing the purée through a sieve helps ensure that you remove any bits of seeds, peels, or stems. A food processor has a purée function, but it tends to incorporate a large volume of air. The old standby, the Foley Food Mill, works like a dream. It's not terribly expensive either, and you can have puréeing perfection for around $50. You'll find food mills at hardware stores, or you can order one online.

Apart from those two items, you'll need fruit, of course, and sugar if your fruit is on the tart side. You'll also need wooden or metal spoons, a peeler, a corer, knives, and a grapefruit spoon for removing the pits from peaches.

Food mill.

Method

Work with 2 to 3 pounds of fruit at a time. It's easier to stir smaller amounts and keep them from burning or sticking to the cooking pot.

First wash the fruit in cool water. Peeling is optional, but some people prefer to peel peaches, apples, and pears before cooking. Cut the fruit into halves and then quarters. Remove pits and core the fruit. If you're working with cherries or blueberries, you can mash them lightly with the potato masher to help them break down more quickly while they're cooking.

Place the cut/mashed fruit in the large cooking pot with just enough water to prevent the fruit from sticking on the bottom of the pot. Turn the heat on low and cook until the fruit is quite soft. When the fruit is mushy, turn off the heat and process the fruit in the food mill. This will give you a nice purée. At this point, you can decide to

Preserving Pointers

Combine fruits to make your own personalized fruit butters. Try apple-pear or cherry-peach. Almost any combination will work well. Mix up a batch with both fruits and make it your signature gift.

proceed with making the fruit butter or transfer the purée to labeled and dated gallon freezer bags and pop them into the freezer for later use.

If you're forging ahead, return the purée to the cooking pot and simmer over low heat until the fruit is thick and a spreadable consistency. This second cooking concentrates the juice and gives fruit butters their intense fruit flavor. You can add sugar to taste at this time or flavoring agents such as vanilla or almond extract, if you wish. There are no cut-and-dried measurements here—it's all a matter of taste.

> **Preserving Pointers**
>
> To test for doneness, take a spoonful of fruit butter from the pot and drop the fruit on a saucer. If no liquid separates out from the butter, it's done.

When you're satisfied with the consistency of the fruit butter, remove it from the heat and spoon it into hot, sterilized pint or half-pint glass canning and freezing jars. Leave ¼ inch of headroom. Process in a boiling water bath for 10 minutes to ensure the seal. Remove the jars from the canner and allow them to cool on a flat, dry surface. Store them in the pantry, away from direct light and heat. They'll keep nicely for a year or longer.

Making Conserves

Conserves are a kind of jam that's usually made from two or more kinds of fruits, with nuts and raisins added for flavor and texture. They're not designed to be spread on bread, but rather to be served as accompaniments to main courses. Fruit pieces are bigger in conserves than in jams, and while some recipes call for pectin, many don't.

If you don't use pectin, cooking times are a bit longer than if you do. If you do use pectin, follow the directions on the pectin box or bottle regarding procedures for adding additional ingredients.

Plums, peaches, apricots, and pears cook up nicely as conserves, and their flavors blend beautifully with each other. Again, don't be afraid to experiment. Add blueberries, cranberries, or grapes. Whatever your favorite fruit is, there's a place for it in your conserves.

The method for making conserves is similar to that of fruit butter, and working with 2 to 3 pounds of fruit at a time is easiest. Peel the fruit, remove the pits, and core the fruit. Then chop or mash it coarsely. You want pieces big enough to fit on a teaspoon. They'll cook down considerably.

Place the fruit in an 8- to 10-quart cooking pot and add raisins and spices. Simmer until thick. Add the nuts during the final 5 minutes of cooking. The amounts of spices and other additions to your conserves are largely a matter of personal taste, so don't be afraid to experiment.

Remove from the heat and ladle into half-pint or pint glass canning and freezing jars. Process in a boiling water bath for 10 minutes to ensure the seal. Remove the jars from the canner and allow them to cool on a flat, dry surface. Store them in the pantry, away from direct light and heat. They'll keep nicely for a year or longer. Just as with butters, conserves make excellent gifts.

In Other Words

If God had intended us to follow recipes, He wouldn't have given us grandmothers.

—Linda Henley-Smith, motivational speaker

Making Chutneys

Chutneys are made with fruits or vegetables, spices, and herbs. They are richer and have a more mellow—some would say exotic—flavor than other fruit spreads. Chutneys have something of the consistency of jam. They use bigger pieces of fruit than conserves, and they have substance to go with their robust flavor.

Like conserves, chutneys are used as accompaniments to main courses. They trace their history back to India, and the days when the British Empire extended nearly around the world. The English took to chutneys, and they soon became known throughout Europe and the New World.

Usually served with curry, Indian chutneys tend to be rather thin and frequently hot. Chutneys have evolved over time, however, and the chutneys we make today are sweeter and thicker.

Fruits that lend themselves to chutney include the following:

- ◆ Peaches
- ◆ Apricots
- ◆ Mangoes
- ◆ Pineapple
- ◆ Papaya

- ◆ Plums
- ◆ Apples
- ◆ Dates
- ◆ Green tomatoes

You can mix and match from this list. Often raisins and nuts are added for texture. Try walnuts, especially black walnuts, if you can find some. They can be difficult to locate but are well worth the effort. There are all kinds of ingredients you can incorporate into chutneys, including garlic, onions, and chilies. Seasonings often include ginger, allspice, cinnamon, cloves, and nutmeg.

The procedure for making chutneys is basically the same as for making conserves. You'll need fruit, sugar, and often you'll find the recipe calls for vinegar. This increases the acidity and gives a bit of a "bite" to the sweetness. Chop the fruit coarsely and place it in an 8- to 10-quart cooking pot. Add spices and other ingredients, bring to a boil, and then simmer until the chutney is thick and the fruit is soft. Add nuts and continue simmering for an additional 5 minutes. Ladle into sterilized half-pint or pint glass canning and freezing jars. Seal. Process in a boiling water bath for 10 minutes to ensure the seal. Remove the jars from the canner and allow them to cool on a flat, dry surface. Store them in the pantry, away from direct light and heat. They'll keep nicely for a year or longer. They make excellent gifts.

> **Preserving Pointers**
>
> The National Center for Home Food Preservation has a delicious mango chutney recipe that is research-based and approved. You can find it at www.uga.edu/nchfp/how/can_06/mango_chutney.html.

Getting Spirited

Brandied fruit (rumtopf) is a traditional German holiday dessert. The name means "rum pot" and refers to the stoneware jar on the kitchen counter that's filled with brandied fruit. Making the rumtopf is a lengthy process, but once you've gotten the mix started, you simply add fruit as it comes into season. The goal is to have a bit of everything thoroughly soused with brandy by Christmastide.

Ingredients

All you need to get started is a large stoneware crock or jar with a tight-fitting lid, fruit, sugar, and your choice of rum or brandy. You want the fruit to be ripe but not overripe. Strawberries are the traditional first fruit to go into the rumtopf. Here are other fruits to add as they come into season:

- Apricots
- Peaches
- Nectarines
- Pears
- Pineapple
- Plums
- Grapes
- Red currants

Method

You'll want about 3 pounds of strawberries to begin. Pull the caps off but don't wash the strawberries. Wet strawberries get mushy superfast. You don't want them saturated with water, but rum! Place them in a large bowl and cover them with 3 pounds of granulated sugar. Let the fruit rest for 1 hour. Then pour the entire mixture into the rumtopf and add brandy or rum to just cover the fruit. Keep the fruit beneath the brandy or rum by weighing it down with a plate. Cover the jar with plastic wrap and put on the lid. (Otherwise, you can secure plastic wrap around the top with an elastic band.) Store the rumtopf in a cool, dark place.

Additional Layers

A good rumtopf is not fast food. It cannot be rushed. Traditionally each new layer was set down as each fruit came into season. That meant a few weeks between layers, for the most part. Today we can buy almost any fruit at any time of the year if we're willing to pay a premium price. However, this is not the way to construct the rumtopf. Slow and easy does the trick. Think strawberries today and apricots in a few weeks. Pace yourself and you'll reap the rewards at holiday time.

You are constructing a vertical, spirited fruit salad. That means to prepare the fruit for eating. Pit and core and remove stems as necessary.

The first layer had equal amounts of fruit and sugar, but each additional layer will use half that amount of sugar. For example, all the remaining layers will have 3 pounds of fruit and 1½ pounds of sugar. To prepare the second layer, measure 3 pounds of fruit into a large bowl and add 1½ pounds of sugar. Allow it to rest for 1 hour. Then pour the mix into the rumtopf. Do not mix this layer with the first one. Add brandy or rum to cover the fruit. Cover the jar again and store it in a cool, dry place.

Throughout the spring and summer, add to the rumtopf until the jar is full. Then let the rumtopf rest for 4 to 6 weeks. Depending on when you start it, it will be ready just in time for the holiday season.

Using the Rumtopf

The brandied fruit can be served with whipped cream or as a topping for ice cream or cake. You can also try some on cheesecake. Try using the brandied fruit as an accompaniment to roast duckling or goose. It also goes well with roast beef.

You can also drink the brandy or rum—and for many folks, this is what they've been waiting for. The liquid is flavored with all kinds of good fruit juices. Strain it and serve it as an after-dinner cordial.

Recipes

With so many combinations of fruits possible, the recipes you can create are nearly endless. Here are some traditional favorites for butter, conserve, and chutney.

Apple Butter

Nothing says autumn more clearly than apples simmering on the stove and filling the kitchen with their scrumptious aroma.

Makes 5 pints
Prep time: 20 minutes
Cook time: 2 to 3 hours (does not include processing time)

5 to 6 lb. apples   Sugar

1 qt. apple cider   **Cinnamon**

Wash and quarter apples, retaining skins and cores. Place in an 8- to 10-quart cooking pot and add just enough water to cover. Cook over low heat until apples are quite soft—about 30 minutes. Remove from heat and process in a food mill. Return apple purée to the cooking pot, add apple cider, and cook over low heat, stirring often to prevent scorching. When fruit butter is of desired consistency, add sugar and cinnamon to taste. Ladle into sterilized pint or half-pint jars, leaving ¼ inch of headspace, seal, and process in a boiling water bath for 10 minutes to ensure the seal.

Pumpkin Butter

The plant world is always teasing us with blurred definitions of what's a fruit and what's a vegetable. Pumpkins are fruit, sort of, even though they belong to the squash family and are treated like vegetables in canning. With that in mind, here's an interesting variation on fruit butter made with pumpkin. You can cheat on this recipe by buying a can of pumpkin at the store, but it's easy enough to make your own.

1 small- to medium-size pumpkin (or 1 28 oz. can pumpkin)

¾ cup apple juice

1½ cups sugar

1½ tsp. pumpkin pie spice

Makes 5 pints
Prep time: 15 minutes with commercially canned pumpkin; 45 minutes with homemade pumpkin purée
Cook time: 1 to 2 hours (does not include processing time)

If using whole pumpkin, remove seeds and rind and cut into pieces. Place in an 8- to 10-quart cooking pot and cover with water. Cook until tender—about 20 minutes. Remove from heat and process in a food mill. Return purée to the cooking pot and add apple juice, sugar, and pumpkin pie spice. Simmer over low heat until thick—1 to 2 hours, stirring frequently to prevent scorching. Ladle into sterilized pint or half-pint jars, leaving ¼ inch of headspace. Seal and process in a boiling water bath for 10 minutes to ensure the seal.

Safety Check

The Cooperative Extension Service does not recommend canning pumpkin purée because its density doesn't allow the product to reach sufficiently high interior temperatures to be safe. However, pumpkin butter processed with sugar and apple juice in half-pint or pint containers is a safe product.

Peach Conserve

This is a good use for peaches that may be a bit bruised and that you don't want to use for canning. Cut away the bruises, toss them away, and use the trimmed fruit for making conserves.

Makes 4 to 5 pints

Prep time: 45 minutes

Cook time: 1 to 2 hours (does not include processing time)

---

8 cups peaches

1 cup dried plums or prunes, coarsely chopped

½ cup raisins

4 cups orange juice (with pulp)

2 cups brown sugar

½ tsp. ginger

¼ tsp. cloves

½ cup walnuts, coarsely chopped

½ cup pecans, coarsely chopped

Remove skins from peaches and use potato masher to mash peaches coarsely. Place peaches in 8- to 10-quart cooking pot, add dried plums or prunes, raisins, orange juice, brown sugar, ginger, and cloves. Bring to a boil and then simmer 1 to 2 hours until thick. Add nuts and continue to simmer for an additional 5 minutes. Pack into hot, sterilized half-pint or pint glass canning and freezing jars, leaving ¼ inch of headspace. Process in a boiling water bath for 10 minutes to ensure the seal. Remove from the canner and allow to cool on a flat, dry surface.

Pear Chutney

Windfalls are a great source of pears for making chutneys. Orchards and farmers' markets often have good buys on fruit that has blown down in a windstorm before it could be picked. Even if they've got some bruises, you can cut them away and use the good parts. Pears are also readily available at farmers' markets and local grocery stores during the late fall.

8 cups pears

2 cups dates, coarsely chopped

1 onion, coarsely chopped

4 celery stalks, coarsely chopped

1 cup crystallized ginger, chopped fine

2 cups brown sugar

1 qt. apple cider vinegar

2 tsp. ground mustard

½ tsp. cinnamon

¼ tsp. ground cloves

Makes 4 to 5 pints, depending on size of pears
Prep time: 45 minutes
Cook time: 1 to 2 hours (does not include processing time)

Wash and peel pears. Remove cores. Chop into teaspoon-size pieces and place in an 8- to 10-quart cooking pot. Add dates, onion, celery, ginger, brown sugar, vinegar, mustard, cinnamon, and cloves and cook over high heat until mixture begins to boil. Then reduce heat and simmer until thickened, about 1 to 2 hours. Add salt to taste. Ladle into half-pint or pint glass canning and freezing jars, leaving ¼ inch of headspace. Seal, and process in a boiling water bath for 10 minutes to ensure the seal. Remove the jars from the canner and allow them to cool on a flat, dry surface.

Sweet-Hot Chutney

This is tangy, just a bit hot, and oh so delicious! The mangoes give it a subtle, exotic flavor.

Makes 4 to 5 pints

Prep time: 45 minutes

Cook time: 45 minutes (does not include processing time)

---

1 orange

3 medium apples

2 peaches, nectarines, or mangoes

1 lemon

1 onion

2¼ cups sugar

1 cup white vinegar

1 cup water

Tie in a bag 2 chiles (small, hot peppers), cut lengthwise, along with 1 tsp. each of:

Whole black peppers

Whole allspice

Mustard seed

Whole cloves

Celery seed

⅓ cup sliced blanched almonds (about 50)

Peel, core, and remove seeds from fruit and onion. Chop fruit and onion into small pieces and place in 8- to 10-quart cooking pot. In a medium mixing bowl, combine sugar, vinegar, and water. Add to the fruit and onion and stir thoroughly. Add bag of spices. Cook over medium heat for 20 minutes. Add almonds and continue cooking for 10 minutes or until desired consistency. Remove spice bag and discard. Pack into hot, sterilized half-pint or pint glass canning and freezing jars, leaving ¼ inch of headspace. Seal and process in boiling water bath for 10 minutes to ensure seal. Remove jars from the canner and allow them to cool on a flat, dry surface.

Part 6 Drying, Salting, Smoking, and Root Cellaring

These are the oldest methods of food preserving, although some of them have become new again thanks to modern technology. Smoking adds a wonderful layer of aroma and flavor to meat and fish, but it's just the first step in the preserving process. With smoking and salting, it's vital that you adhere to strict safety guidelines and research-based practices in order to get a good, safe product.

Chapter 20

Drying/Dehydrating

In This Chapter

◆ Suitable foods for drying

◆ Different methods for drying

◆ Basic procedures

◆ All about jerky

Drying is probably the oldest and simplest method of preserving foods. It operates on a simple premise: if you remove as much moisture as possible from food, you stop the growth of yeasts, molds, and bacteria that cause food to spoil. The earliest means of drying was provided courtesy of the sun. Today there are many options, ranging from oven drying to portable dehydrators.

What can you dry? Just about anything. If you love fruit leathers or jerky, you can make your own for a fraction of what you'd pay even at the super-warehouse grocery outlets. And if you've got a kitchen herb garden, experiment with drying your own herbs to add zest and freshness to your cooking.

General Procedures

Fruits, veggies, and meats are handled differently, but a few basic principles apply to whatever you're planning on drying. First, start with the best. That means fruits and vegetables should be ripe but not overripe and should be free from bruising and other blemishes. Fish should be handled gently and as quickly as possible after being reeled in. Meat and poultry products should be lean and fresh.

Fruit

Fruits that dry well include the following:

- Blueberries, cranberries, and huckleberries
- Apples
- Cherries
- Figs

- Grapes
- Peaches
- Plums
- Pears
- Tomatoes

Wash and sort the fruit. Select only ripe, firm fruit without blemishes or bruising. Larger fruit should be sliced or halved so it dries evenly. The thinner the slice, the quicker the drying time.

> **Safety Check**
>
> Once you begin the drying process, keep at it until you're finished. Food that's only partially dried is a breeding ground for bacteria and molds and can spoil very quickly. If you don't have time to finish, don't start until you do.

Peel, core, and slice apples. Cut peaches and apricots in half and remove pits. Pit cherries. Cut pears in half and scoop out stringy center. Slice tomatoes.

If you're working with light-colored fruit, you'll want to treat it to prevent it from darkening. You can use a commercial antidiscoloration product (follow directions on the label), ascorbic acid, or vitamin C. If you're using ascorbic acid, use $1/2$ teaspoon ascorbic acid crystals or 3 crushed 500 mg vitamin C tablets in 1 quart of water.

Plums, cherries, grapes, and blueberries are usually dried whole, but their skins are tough and keep moisture trapped inside. They need to be "cracked" or "checked." Cracking means dipping them in boiling water for about 30 seconds and then plunging them into ice water. Remove them from the ice water and allow them to dry. This method works well with smaller fruits. Checking means scoring them with a paring knife in several places to give inner moisture an outlet. This method is more easily used on larger fruits.

Vegetables

Vegetables that dry well include the following:

◆ Beets

◆ Cabbage

◆ Carrots

◆ Celery

◆ Corn

◆ Peas

◆ Green peppers

◆ Mushrooms

◆ Onions

◆ Potatoes

◆ Turnips

Wash vegetables thoroughly, using a brush if needed to remove dirt. Core cabbage; peel beets, potatoes, and turnips. Carrots may be scraped, if desired. Shell peas. Remove seeds and white membrane from peppers. Remove corn kernels from cob.

Chop or slice vegetables into uniform sizes. If a vegetable needs to be blanched before being frozen, it should be blanched before being dried. Drying does not stop the enzymes from causing flavor and color changes in veggies. See Chapter 5 for recommended blanching times for vegetables. Peppers, onions, and mushrooms don't need blanching.

Meats and Poultry

Select fresh or frozen lean meats and poultry. Partially frozen meats and poultry are easier to slice and give more uniform results.

For beef, the leaner grades, such as standard and select, have less fat and are more suitable for drying. Rump, flank, round, and sirloin cuts are good choices.

Game meats make excellent jerky. Most people are familiar with venison and elk jerky, but the possibilities are almost limitless. Depending on where you live, you may find alligator, emu, buffalo, antelope, or bear.

Meats and poultry should be cut into long slices and shouldn't be thicker than ¼ inch. Cutting with the grain makes a chewier jerky, while cutting against the grain makes a more tender product. Remove all fat.

Fish

Most fish are first dry salted or brine salted and then either smoked or canned (see Chapters 22 and 12 respectively). Air drying (discussed in the next section) is an old method for preserving fish.

Herbs

Clip herbs for drying before they flower and early in the morning right after the dew is off. The exception is dill, which should be harvested after the seeds have developed.

Different Methods of Drying

There are so many different ways to dry foods, you're almost certain to find the right one for what you want to do. Foods can be dried outdoors and indoors. Outdoors you can take advantage of air movement and the heat of the sun; indoors, you can use a portable dehydrator, microwave, oven, and even the air inside your home.

Air Drying

In warm climates with low humidity, outdoor air drying works quite well for certain foods, including herbs, mushrooms, green beans, onions, and garlic. These foods are hung away from the sun in a place with good air circulation. Moisture is the enemy, and it's essential to bring drying foods indoors overnight if there's any chance of dew or increased humidity, as this can cause the foods to turn moldy and spoil.

To prepare green beans and mushrooms for outside air drying, string them together. It's the same procedure you use if you've ever strung popcorn for decorating the Christmas tree. Use a sturdy needle and strong thread. When you've got a string completed, hang it from a hook out of the sun and in a place with good air circulation.

Onions and garlic can be braided before hanging. Just remember to leave the long stems attached so you'll have something to braid.

Air drying works indoors as well, and you don't have to worry about a nocturnal rainstorm or sudden jump in the humidity. Herbs, garlic, and onions are good candidates for this type of home food preservation.

Herbs are an essential part of the home food preserver's pantry. Air drying works well for herbs, which shouldn't be dried in the sun. You'll need scissors, small paper bags (lunch size), large paper clips or Christmas ornament hangers, and yarn or twine.

Herbs need to be completely dry before you begin the drying process (sort of a paradox!) because the slightest bit of mold will ruin them. Cut a stem about 6 inches long and remove the lower leaves. If the herbs are dusty, rinse them off but be sure they are completely dry before you work with them. You can set a hairdryer on low and wave it around the herbs to make sure.

Use the twine or yarn to bundle several stems together and then insert the bundle into a paper bag. Tie the bag around the stems and be sure the herbs are not touching the sides of the bag. If they do, they may adhere to the bag during the drying process and refuse to separate.

Bend a large paper clip into a hook or use a Christmas ornament hanger to snag the twine around the paper bag. Hang the bag away from light in an airy location. You can run a string across a doorway in a seldom-used room and hang the bags from the string. The bags will protect the herbs from sunlight and dust and will also catch any stray leaves that decide to jump ship. It will take about 2 weeks for the herbs to air dry.

In Other Words

I like to combine herbs when I store them. Parsley, sage, rosemary, and thyme are my favorites, and I crumble the leaves together and store them in decorative glass jars. They make great gifts.

—Janet, master gardener

When they're dry, you can separate the leaves from the stems and store them away from direct heat or sunlight in a glass jar with a secure lid. They'll keep for about a year.

You can also dry herbs in the oven, which is covered later in this chapter.

Sun Drying

Sun drying uses the sun's heat and air movement and is the most inexpensive method for drying foods. Because of their sugar and acid content, fruits are recommended for sun drying. Vegetables and meat products are low-acid and low-sugar foods and are not recommended for this process. They can easily become reservoirs for harmful bacteria and spoilage.

Apricots and peaches set out to dry on wooden, slatted trays used to be a common sight in California orchards at picking time. Today the orchards are fewer and outdoor drying is rarer, but if you venture out into the country, you may be lucky enough to spot some.

Drying outdoors requires several consecutive days of high temperatures—from the mid-90s to the 100-degree mark—accompanied by low humidity (below 60 percent) and brisk winds. If your climate lends itself to outdoor drying and the air is clean where you live, you might want to give it a try.

You'll need drying trays, which are wood frames with wood slats far enough apart to allow the air to circulate but close enough together to keep the food from falling through the cracks. Stay away from redwood or other evergreen woods. These can cause the fruit to have an off flavor and can also stain the fruit.

You'll need bird netting or cheesecloth to keep dust and insects from the food. If you'll be drying light-colored fruits such as peaches, pears, or apples, the best candidates for outdoor drying, you'll need ascorbic acid (vitamin C) or a commercial antidiscoloration preparation and pans for holding the antidiscoloration agent.

Safety Check

Light-colored fruits dried outdoors used to be dusted with sulfur to keep them from darkening during the drying process. This process is no longer recommended as sulfur can have serious health consequences in some people. You can pretreat light-colored fruits with a commercial antidiscoloring preparation, ascorbic acid, or vitamin C, but these methods tend not to be totally satisfactory.

Solar Drying

This is one step up from sun drying. A solar dryer is a structure that uses reflectors to intensify the sun's heat and a ventilation system that increases air flow to speed up the drying process. This is useful if your area tends to be more humid or if temperatures aren't optimal for sun drying, although it's still iffy as a solution. Foods that are suitable for sun drying, such as fruits, are good choices for solar drying. Even though solar drying speeds up the process, it's not reliable enough to ensure that vegetables won't become contaminated by bacterial growth and spoil.

If you're handy with materials, you can make your own solar dryer using found materials. For example, gardeners who like to get a head start on the season are likely to use a *cold frame*. Lining this with foil and propping the glass open to allow air circulation will serve as a makeshift solar dryer. See Appendix G for further information.

def•i•ni•tion

A **cold frame** is simply a wooden box minus the top and bottom. It's set outdoors on the ground, and plants are set inside it for shelter. The top is usually an old window that's attached with a hinge and propped up with a piece of wood during the day and closed down at night. It provides protection from wind and cold.

Oven Drying

This takes the drying process indoors where climate doesn't matter. It also expands your options since you can dry veggies, fish, and herbs and make fruit leather and jerky by this method. The major drawback to drying foods in the oven is limited space. You can generally dry about 5 pounds of food at a time, and the only additional items you'll need are a wooden spoon or an oven mitt to prop the door open a smidge while the foods are drying and a thermometer to check the internal temperature. You want to keep that between 140°F and 160°F. Air circulation is essential, hence the slightly open door. Heat is required, hence the thermometer. You'll need to keep an eye on the temperature and turn it up or down accordingly to maintain an even flow.

The temperature is warmest closest to the heating element. If you have a gas stove with a pilot light, that may be enough to give you the temperature you need. The way to check is to put a thermometer on the top rack and close the door. Check in an hour and see what the reading is. If it's not high enough, you'll need to turn the oven on warm. Check the temperature after half an hour.

Oven drying isn't difficult, but it requires some finessing to settle at the proper temperature. You may need to do some fiddling with the temperature control until you hit on just the right setting. Do this part of the preparation work before you commit food to the oven.

Trays

Air circulation is essential to getting a good product, so you'll need trays made with wood slats or stainless steel screening. Most ovens have two or three racks, and if you use all three, you'll have pretty close to a full load without rigging an additional rack. Cookie sheets and other solid trays aren't suitable because they block the air flow.

Method

As you'll see shortly, oven drying is best begun early in the day. Place the cut food in a single layer on each tray and place each tray on an oven rack. Be sure there's room for the air to circulate around each piece of food. Prop the door open so that the air can circulate, but keep an eye on the thermometer so that the temperature remains between 140°F and 160°F.

> **Safety Check**
>
> Be careful about the materials you use when making your trays. Keep to stainless steel or wood to prevent harmful chemicals from coming in contact with your food. Aluminum, copper, vinyl, fiberglass, and galvanized metal should be avoided.

You can speed up the process a bit if you have a small electric fan to set up so that the stream of air blows into the oven. Once you've got everything nicely settled, set the timer for 30 minutes.

When the timer buzzes, it's time to rotate the racks. Move each rack down one space and put the bottom rack on the top. Reset the timer. Each time you check you repeat this process so that every rack will have equal time. This will correct for any temperature differences inside the oven.

You can also take this opportunity to turn the food over so it dries more evenly. You can expect the process to take several hours, and veggies can take up to 12 hours. This is why it's best to get an early start. You don't want to be rotating racks and flipping food late at night.

Drying Herbs in the Oven

Just about any herb you can grow will dry well in the oven. Harvest the herbs when mature but before they've begun to flower, as the flowering takes strength from the leaves. The most potent leaves are found at the ends of the stems, and they decrease in strength as you get closer to the stem.

Throw away any discolored or dead leaves. Remove the leaves from the stems and place the leaves on a drying rack, allowing space for the air to circulate. Follow the general procedures for oven drying as outlined in the preceding section. Herbs will dry in 2 to 4 hours in the oven.

You can dry herbs in the microwave, but this has a strong tendency to cook the leaves instead of drying them. If you want to try it, place a few stems on a paper towel and cover them with another paper towel. Cook on high for 2 to 3 minutes and then check them. If you're working with mint, parsley, thyme, or any other tender leaves, check them more frequently and turn them over every 30 seconds or so. They're done when they crumble. If you need to nuke them a bit more, try 15-second intervals so you don't end up scorching them.

Fruit Leather

Get out those cookie sheets again! (Be sure they're the kind with sides.) Smooth a piece of plastic wrap across the inside of the cookie sheet, making sure it comes up the sides. Don't use waxed paper or aluminum foil. They'll stick to the leather, and you'll end up with pieces of foil or paper in your teeth.

Spread fruit purée on top to a depth of ¼ inch. For each 2 cups of light-colored fruit (such as peaches, apples, or pears), add 2 teaspoons of lemon juice or ⅛ teaspoon of ascorbic acid (vitamin C) to keep the purée from darkening.

Place the cookie sheets on the oven racks and follow the general procedures for oven drying discussed earlier. The edges of the leather will dry first, so check for doneness by touching a finger to the middle of the cookie sheet. The fruit leather will be done when it isn't sticky in the middle, but don't overdry it. You don't want it to crack when you try to roll it up.

When it's ready, remove the tray from the oven, peel the fruit away from the plastic, and roll it up. After it has cooled off, you can reroll it in plastic for storage. Fruit leather will keep up to a month unrefrigerated or up to a year in the freezer.

Dehydrators

These units are freestanding, are electric, have automatic temperature selection, are programmable, and come in a variety of sizes and price ranges. They're available at hardware stores, retail outlets that sell small appliances, natural food stores, catalogues, and online.

Preserving Pointers

You don't need to spend a fortune on fancy dehydrators if you don't want to. If you'd like to make your own, the University of California Extension Service has dehydrator plans on its website: http://ucce.ucdavis.edu/files/filelibrary/1808/65.PDF.

The bigger the dehydrator, the more trays it can hold. Smaller units will have 4 shelves, while the larger models can accommodate up to 12. If your unit has stackable trays, check to see if you have the option of ordering additional trays from the manufacturer.

The unit pictured here has a vertical air flow. That means the heating element and fan are in the base of the unit. The one drawback to this arrangement is that foods can drip or fall into the fan vents. This can be potentially a problem if you're making fruit leather and accidentally dump purée into the heating element and fan. If this does happen, turn off the unit and use a damp cloth to soak up the spill. Be careful not to get water into the heating element.

Dehydrator with stackable trays.

Safety Check

It may seem truly odd, but people have tried to dry food in the clothes dryer. Don't! The idea of tumble-drying jerky makes the head spin. Also, if you have forced-air heat, resist the impulse to spread your apple slices on an air vent. It may work for drying socks, but the dust and other contaminants in the air aren't good for food.

Pouring peach purée into the dehydrator tray.

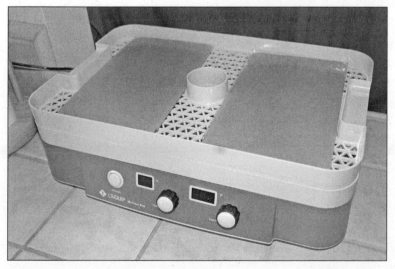

Fruit leather.

The other option is a unit with the heating unit and fan built into the side. This creates a horizontal air flow. With this design, you don't have to worry about the spills, and all the foods get the same amount of heat and air flow. It might be the better choice, especially if you want to dry different types of foods at the same time or are seriously into making fruit leathers. A dehydrator is more economical to operate than an electric oven, but it's slightly less economical than gas.

Regardless of what you're drying, you'll need to keep tabs on the temperature. It needs to be high enough to cause moisture to evaporate but not so high as to cook the food.

If the temperature is too high at the beginning of the drying process, the outer layer of what you're drying will develop a hard shell, while moisture is trapped inside the inner layers with no way out. This is called "case hardening," and it's not good. It's all about striking a balance and understanding how the process works.

Preheat the dehydrator to 125°F. Then add the food to the trays and stack them in the dehydrator. After an hour or so, when you can see that the exterior of the food has begun to dry, increase the temperature to 140°F and hold it there until the food is done. The drying process can take from 4 to 12 hours.

Making Jerky

This is the backpacker's staple food, along with granola and dried fruit. You can make jerky from a wide variety of meats, including game meats, poultry, and fish. Lean meats are best, and the leaner the meat, the better the finished product. This means that, for beef, you'll be looking at standard and select grades as opposed to choice or prime grade, which have more marbling.

One of the difficulties of rediscovering the old ways of preserving foods is that we often approach them without the knowledge gained over the long run by those who perfected the process. We don't have a healthy respect for the need to do the job right and want to take some shortcuts. Here are two cases in point:

1. Game meats pose their own special considerations. The length of time the animal is held at ambient temperatures before getting to the cooler can allow harmful bacteria to grow and multiply. Additionally, there is the possibility of fecal contamination of the meat when the animal is being field dressed.

   Bottom line: Get the game to the cooler as quickly as possible and observe strict cleanliness during field dressing.

2. We want to reduce the amount of salt in our diets and don't understand that that principle can't always be applied across the board. Making low-salt or no-salt jerky is not a recommended practice. Salt binds moisture in the meat, and this kills any bacteria present more quickly if water isn't available for them to grow and multiply.

Salt is just one consideration, however. There have been cases of illness associated with homemade jerky. The USDA recommends that, to destroy harmful microorganisms, meat should be heated to 160°F before the dehydrating process begins.

Bottom line: Follow approved safety practices and approved methods for making jerky.

The following method is approved by Oregon State University and will give you an excellent product. To begin, you'll find it easier to work with meat that's been slightly frozen. If you slice the meat with the grain (along the muscle), you'll get longer strips that are chewy. If you slice against the grain (at right angles to the long muscles), the strips will be shorter and more brittle. It's strictly a matter of personal preference.

Follow these steps to make jerky:

1. Remove all visible fat and tendons. Fat that's left on the meat can turn rancid and spoil the jerky.

2. Cut long, thin strips—⅛ to ¼ inch thick—about 1 to 1½ inches wide. Longer strips are easier to work with.

3. Prepare the marinade of your choice in a large saucepan and bring it to a full rolling boil. You'll need 2 to 3 cups.

4. Add a few meat strips, making sure they are covered with the marinade. Let the marinade return to a full boil.

5. Turn off the heat and use tongs to remove the meat strips from the marinade. Place them immediately on drying racks in single, nonoverlapping rows.

6. Continue the process until all meat strips have been precooked in the marinade.

Safety Check _____

Dipping the meat pieces into boiling marinade keeps any bacteria present on the meat from contaminating the marinade. This precooking process helps to ensure a safe product.

7. Process them in the dehydrator at 140°F to 150°F until done.

8. Test for doneness. Remove one piece from the dehydrator and allow it to cool. It should crack but not break when you bend it, and there should be no moist or underdone portions.

9. Refrigerate the jerky overnight. In the morning, test for doneness again. If required, return strips to the dehydrator to complete the drying process.

Testing for Dryness

You can follow a recipe or the manufacturer's instructions on your dehydrator to the letter, but many factors play a role in determining when your foods are dry:

◆ The kind of food being dried

◆ The thickness of the food

◆ Humidity

◆ The amount of air circulation

◆ The amount of food on the tray, in the oven, or in the dehydrator

Whatever you're drying, however, will follow a basic pattern: the edges will dry before the middle. This also means that foods on the outside edge of each tray may dry more quickly than foods crowded into the middle. To even this out, it's important to move the food around to even out the process.

Each batch will be different. Just because the last 4 batches of dried pears took 2 hours to reach perfection doesn't mean that this batch won't need 3 hours or the following batch will be done in an hour and a half. You need to check. That means taking a few pieces out of the dehydrator and allowing them to cool. If the food is warm, it will feel soft. Only after it has cooled down will you be able to determine if it's dry.

Fruit will be pliable when it's dried. You can put a pear half or other large piece in your hand and squeeze. The fruit should bend when your hand bends and open back up when you open your hand. It shouldn't feel or look wet at all.

Testing veggies for dryness is fun and also therapeutic. You hit a test piece with a hammer. The vegetable should shatter. A word of caution here: don't use your kitchen counter for a test surface. Take the veggie outside or use a wooden block. Mushrooms, peppers, and squash don't test this way. They'll be softer.

The Final Step: Conditioning

Think of conditioning as the great evening-out process. Even if a couple of pieces in a batch are too dry and a couple of others aren't dry enough, you can fix it!

When everything has cooled, put the pieces in large freezer bags or a glass jar with a snugly fitting lid. Put the container in a warm, dry place and check it every day. Stir or shake it up to redistribute the pieces of food. It will take about a week or so for the conditioning process to be complete. During this time, the moisture from the underdone pieces is absorbed by the overdone pieces.

Safety Check

If you notice sweating on the glass or moisture forming on the inside of the plastic freezer bag during the conditioning process, you'll need to send the whole batch back to the dryer to finish drying; otherwise, you'll start growing mold.

The Importance of Pasteurizing

If you dried your food outdoors, there's a good chance a stray insect decided to use it for a nursery. Destroying any insect eggs is important to keep your food safe. It needs to be pasteurized. Also, if you're worried about the possibility of mold, you can pop your dried foods into the oven or the freezer and pasteurize them.

For the oven: Preheat to 175°F. Arrange the dried food in a single layer on a tray. Close the oven door and leave the food in the oven for 15 minutes. Remove and allow it to cool before packaging.

For the freezer: Place food in freezer containers and leave in the freezer for 1 to 2 weeks.

Storage Options

Moisture/vapor-proof containers are good choices for storing dried foods. You want to store food away from light in a cool, dry location. You can keep dried foods in the freezer for extra insurance.

Choose smaller containers over big ones. Each time you open the container moisture can creep in, and with moisture comes the possibility of mold taking hold. If you spot any mold on the food, toss the entire batch. Eating anything with mold on it is not smart and can make you very, very sick.

Properly stored, dried foods keep up to a year, with jerky maxing out at about 6 months. As with other preserved foods, remember that the goal is not to stockpile forever but to put foods aside for use when you want them. Use your dried foods—don't let them pine away on the pantry shelf.

Recipes

Corn dries well and is handy for all kinds of recipes, from soups to desserts.

Corn Chowder

This is a cheerful chowder—golden and hearty. The salt pork gives it a nice smoky flavor and the onion adds some crunch.

Serves 6
Prep time: 30 minutes
Cook time: 1 hour

½ cup dried corn

1½ cups water

½ cup salt pork, diced

1 medium onion, chopped

2 cups water

1 medium potato, diced

2 cups milk

2½ TB. flour

Salt and pepper to taste

¼ tsp. paprika

1. Place corn in medium-size mixing bowl. Add 1½ cups water. Allow 30 minutes for corn to rehydrate.

2. Brown salt pork in skillet. Add onion and sauté until translucent. Transfer salt pork and onion to soup pot. Add corn and any remaining liquid. Add potato and 2 cups water. Turn heat on high and bring ingredients to a boil. Reduce heat and simmer about 45 minutes, or until potatoes are tender.

3. Combine milk, flour, and salt and pepper to taste and mix well. Add milk mixture to the pot and bring to a simmer, stirring occasionally. Sprinkle with paprika before serving. Serve with crackers or homemade bread.

Corn Pudding

Corn pudding is a traditional New England dish, and it's also claimed by Southern cooks. Often served at Thanksgiving dinner, it's a good dish for any time of the year.

¾ **cup dried corn**

3 cups water

3 eggs, beaten

2 TB. butter, melted

2 cups milk or light cream

2 TB. sugar

1 tsp. salt

Serves 6	
Prep time: 30 minutes	
Cook time: 1 hour	

Place dried corn in a medium-size cooking pot and add 3 cups water. Allow 30 minutes for corn to rehydrate. Then turn heat on medium and simmer corn until tender, about 1 hour. Drain. Preheat the oven to 350°F. Spray a 1-quart casserole dish with nonstick cooking oil. In a large mixing bowl, combine corn, eggs, melted butter, milk or light cream, sugar, and salt. Pour mixture into the greased casserole dish and bake for 45 to 60 minutes or until a knife inserted in the center comes out clean.

Chapter 21

Salting

In This Chapter

- ◆ The history behind salting
- ◆ Salting vegetables
- ◆ Salting meats
- ◆ Salting fish

Salting as a process for preserving meat and vegetables has been around for a very long time. In fact, it's probably as old as using the sun to dry foods. Today, however, as far as vegetables are concerned it's more of a curiosity, and for meat it's usually just one step in the preservation process.

Salt dries things out. That's not exactly a news flash, but it's important when it comes to preserving foods. Certain types of bacteria and other spoilage microorganisms thrive in moist environments. By depriving them of water, you cause them to dry up and either go dormant or die.

Historical Perspective on Salting

The exact moment when salting food became a common practice is lost in the mists of history, but we do know that the Chinese and Egyptians were among the earliest users of this product of the earth and the sea.

A salt lake in northern China, Lake Yuncheng, was a source of salt for the Chinese at least as early as about 6000 B.C.E. The ancient Egyptians were also salt consumers. They probably deduced that if salt was good for preserving mummies, it might work equally well on meat they were planning to eat at some later date.

At any rate, the practice caught on, and salt mining became a major trade. Salt became so important that the money the Romans paid their military so they could purchase salt was known as *salarium*, thus the word "salary."

Salt also played an important role in the Age of Exploration. Once it was discovered that salt could be used to preserve fish and that the salted fish kept almost indefinitely, it became a staple for sailors' diets and allowed long ocean voyages to get underway.

Salt was expensive because it wasn't easily obtained. It had to be evaporated from seawater or mined from salt beds, so if a meat were to be "worth its salt," it would have to be worth the trouble of salting it in the first place. It would need to be meaty and fat.

def•i•ni•tion

Freshening is the process of rinsing and soaking meat or vegetables in cold water to remove as much salt as possible before cooking.

Today, salting is more of a decision point in food preservation than a goal. It's the fork in the road at the intersection of pickling and smoking. It's a useful emergency measure if you've no other way to put up food, but it leaches nutrients out of foods that then require *freshening* to remove as much salt as possible before the food is usable.

General Principles and Procedures for Veggies

There are two main ways to go about salting vegetables: brine salting or dry salting. Actually, to be more precise, there are two subgroups as well that involve using either a lot of salt or using less salt. Dry salting works with vegetables that contain quite a bit of moisture or that have been cut into small pieces, and brining is used for vegetables that don't have sufficient moisture in them to make enough liquid during curing. Brining is the process of preserving foods by immersing them in a saltwater solution.

When brining involves vinegar in addition to salt, it causes fermentation. It's the way corned beef and pastrami are made. The corning process is discussed in Chapter 15. If you don't want fermented veggies, then you'll forego the vinegar and pack in the salt—lots of salt.

Dry salting is the process of combining salt with the juices from the food being salted to form a concentrated brine. The stronger the salt solution, the greater its ability to reduce or destroy spoilage microorganisms. The weaker the salt solution, the greater the tendency for the vegetables to ferment. This is desirable if you're making sauerkraut; it's not desirable if you're trying to preserve your green beans.

Equipment and Supplies

In addition to regular kitchen utensils, you'll need your kitchen scales, a crock, and something to weigh down the top layer of veggies. You can use a glass or wood container if you don't have a crock, but don't use anything metal because it will react with the acid created during brining. A plate works well. So does a plastic bag filled with water and securely tied.

Dry Salting Vegetables

Wash the veggies and discard any that aren't in great shape. Just as with other forms of preserving food, you're not going to improve what you start with, so always start with the best. Weigh the vegetables. You'll be working with a ratio of 4:1. That means for every 4 pounds of veggies, you'll use 1 pound of salt.

Next, prepare the veggies as follows:

◆ Cabbage—shred

◆ Celery and okra—cut into pieces

◆ Corn—cut from cob

◆ Peas and lima beans—shell and blanch

◆ Green beans—snip off tips and tails, cut into pieces, blanch

◆ Turnips and rutabagas—peel and shred

Preserving Pointers

Use medium-coarse pickling salt or kosher salt for curing. These have larger-size crystals than other salts, and their greater surface area absorbs moisture quickly. Do not use iodized or regular table salt. Iodized salt can turn foods dark, and regular salt will cake. You need to have the salt dissolve quickly and evenly to achieve a good brine.

Place a layer of veggies on the bottom of the crock. Cover this with a layer of salt. Repeat the layers until you've used up all the veggies and all the salt, ending with a layer of salt. Cover with a clean cloth or dish towel and weight it down with a plate. Set the crock in a cool location and let it rest overnight. The next morning check to be sure that brine has formed and is covering the top layer of vegetables. This brine comes from the moisture in the veggies being drawn out by the salt. The vegetables need to be covered with the brine to prevent mold from forming.

If you need to add more brine to make sure the veggies are covered, dissolve 1 pound of salt in 2 quarts of water and pour it into the crock. You may notice some bubbling. Any bubbling will stop within a few days. This bubbling isn't an indicator of fermentation. It's gas and air escaping from the veggies. Do skim off any scum that forms early on in the salting process.

Store the crock in a cool location away from direct sunlight until you're ready to use the veggies. Their storage life varies according to many factors. Many will keep a year or more, while others need to be used up within a few months. As with all methods of home food preservation, it's good sense to have a plan for your produce in mind as you put it up. Nothing is meant to keep forever.

Safety Check

Never taste veggies that have been preserved by salting without first boiling them for 10 minutes to be sure they are safe to eat.

When it's time to dip into the crock, you'll notice that the veggies have shrunk. That's because the salt drew out the moisture they contained. When you soak them in cool water they'll plump out again, so take about $\frac{1}{3}$ the amount you'll need: if you ultimately want 1 cup of veggies, take $\frac{1}{3}$ cup out of the crock. To use them, rinse them in cool water. If they're saltier than you like, you can soak them in cool water briefly and then drain and use.

Brining Vegetables

"As a method of emergency preservation, requiring a minimum amount of labor and critical materials, and offering the possibility of storing large quantities of vegetable material in bulk until further processing can be brought about, brine preservation justly deserves adequate consideration in our war program." Thus were the conclusions of J. L. Etchells, I. D. Jones, and M. A. Hoffman as reported in the 1943 Proceedings of Institute of Food Technologists and reprinted online at http://fsweb2. schaub.ncsu.edu/usdaars/Acrobatpubs/P1-29/P22.pdf.

World War II brought all kinds of challenges to the food industry and the home food preserver. Preserving vegetables by brining was one solution to the problem, and the information contained in this report hasn't altered much in the intervening years. If you're interested in trying your hand at this technique, you'll begin by making your brining solution.

Prepare the brining solution by combining ½ pound of salt and 1 cup 5 percent strength vinegar to each gallon of water. Then prepare the vegetables as follows:

- Beets, carrots, okra, and onions—leave whole

- Cauliflower—cut into pieces or leave whole

- Greens—wash

- Lima beans and peas—leave in the pods

- Rutabagas and turnips—peel and slice or cube

- Green beans—leave whole and blanch

Place the vegetables in the container and cover with the brine solution. Place a weight on top of the vegetables and cover this with the brine solution as well. As liquid is drawn out of the vegetables by the brine, the brine strength will become diluted. Add 2 pounds of salt to the plate serving as the weight for each 10 pounds of vegetables in the crock. By keeping the plate under the crock, the salt will slowly dissolve over time.

Remove any scum as it forms. Fermentation will take several weeks to be complete. When the bubbles stop rising to the surface, fermentation is complete. Many variables affect the length of time these vegetables will keep, and even if you've followed recommended procedures, you may find that some of the produce will spoil.

To use salted vegetables, remove them from the crock and freshen them by rinsing in several changes of cool water. Then cook as usual.

General Principles and Procedures for Salting Meats

To get the best product, meat must be handled quickly and carefully after slaughter and strict cleanliness must be observed to avoid contamination. Chilling the carcass as soon after slaughter as possible is also an essential step, since warm meat will begin to spoil before the salting process can take effect.

Certain cuts of meat lend themselves more readily to salting than others. For example, in beef, the brisket, round, chuck, and plate cuts are the most common. In pork, the ham, shoulders, and belly are good candidates.

Historically, salted meats have traveled with Native Americans and polar explorers. As a source of protein, these meats were all that was available. Native Americans improved on the basic recipe and made pemmican from dried meats by pounding in grease and berries. Kept dry, the pemmican didn't spoil.

Today the process has been adapted somewhat, and you will find recipes that call for brined meats. This kind of brining isn't done for preserving but rather more as a marinade, allowing moisture and flavorings to penetrate deep into the tissues of the meat or poultry to make it moister during cooking.

If you're interested in traditional salting of meat, this is more easily done outside if the weather is cool. The process can be messy and take up considerable room. Salting is usually the step before smoking.

The purpose is to draw out as much moisture as possible from the meat to prevent spoilage. To accomplish this you'll dry salt the meat, packing in as much salt as necessary to create your own version of the Gobi Desert.

Equipment and Supplies

You won't need much in the way of supplies: meat, salt, sugar in some cases, and a salting box. If you've got a small shed or workroom, that's to the good.

Salting Meats

The Oklahoma Cooperative Extension Service Bulletin ANSI-3994, "Meat Curing," gives straightforward directions for curing meat by the salting process. The first order of business is to prepare the dry-cure rub, which consists of 8 pounds of salt and 3 pounds of sugar. These recommendations include 2 ounces of sodium nitrate and $\frac{1}{2}$ ounce of sodium nitrite as well. These latter two ingredients are not essential to the cure.

For pork, use 1 ounce of the cure mixture per each pound of meat. Divide this amount by the number of times the meat needs to be rubbed with it. Rub this into the meat at 3- to 5-day intervals. Hams should get the rub three times, picnic and butt roasts need two rubs, and the belly gets just one. The cure takes 1 week for each inch of thickness of the meat.

Preserving Pointers

You can purchase salt especially formulated for seasoning meats during the salting process. This salt is available at most major grocery stores and at hardware stores during canning season.

The process is simple: lay down a layer of salt in a wooden box, barrel, or crate. Then rub salt into the pieces of meat and place them on top of the salt layer in the salting box. Add a layer of salt on top of the meat. Then rub salt and whatever spices you want into the meat that's going into the next layer, add it to the salting box, and add a layer of salt to that.

Continue the layering process until all the meat has been salted and boxed, ending with a layer of salt. Be careful that the pieces of meat do not touch each other. Keep the meat between 32°F to 40°F during the curing process.

You can also dissolve the dry-cure mix in water to make a brine or pickling solution. Place the meat in a watertight container or vat and cover it with the brine. Change the brine every 7 days to prevent spoilage. This process takes longer than dry curing— a minimum of 28 days. You can expect it take about 4 days for each pound of meat.

When you're ready to use the meat, check each piece over carefully to be sure it has not spoiled. If the meat is bone-in, pierce the meat along the bone and check for a fresh smell. If you detect any off odor, dispose of the meat. If the meat is good, rinse it thoroughly and check it again. Look for soft spots, an off odor, or other signs of spoilage. If you detect any, throw the meat away.

After the cure is completed, the meat should be either eaten, frozen, or smoked.

General Principles and Procedures for Salting Fish

It's important to begin with fresh fish. Catch it, ice it, and salt it quickly. Fish can spoil either because they break down organically or because bacteria get involved. Salting can stop both of these processes, and the more quickly the fish can absorb the salt, the better the quality will be. You can choose two types of cures.

Heavy Cure

This is the preferred method for working with fatty fish such as mackerel, trout, and bluefish. Scale, gut, and remove the heads if you're working with small- to medium-size fish. Split each fish down the backbone and flatten it out.

Now it's time for a thorough cleaning. Wash the fish in cool, running water and follow this with a 60-minute soak in a brine of 1 quart salt per gallon of water. This takes care of any slime that's stubbornly hanging around the skin, and it also ensures that any residual blood has been washed away. Remove the fish from the brine and pat it dry with paper towels. It's time to salt.

Generally you'll work with a ratio of 1 pound of salt to 4 pounds of fish. That means you'll need to weigh the fish you have and then do the math. A kitchen scale works well here. Once you've determined how many pounds of fish you have, dredge each piece of fish in salt. Then place a layer of salt in the bottom of a crock and add a layer of fish, skin side down, on top of the salt. Add another layer of salt, layer of fish, and so on until all fish have been placed in the crock. Finish with a layer of salt.

While you're layering, try to keep the fish from touching each other. It's also helpful if you stagger the position of the fish from layer to layer so that the levels even out.

Place a plate on top of the crock to weigh down the fish. The weight will also help push the moisture out of the fish. Small fish should be sufficiently brined in 2 days, while it can take up to 2 weeks for large fish to be *struck through*. When the brining process is finished, remove the fish and wash them in a brine solution made of 1 quart of salt to a gallon of water.

> ## def•i•ni•tion
>
> **Struck through** is the term used to indicate that a fish has been completely salted and will not accept anymore salt.

Use a stiff brush to thoroughly clean the fish. Then repack them in the crock as before, alternating layers of salt and fish, beginning and ending with a layer of salt. Then fill the crock with a fresh brine solution of 1 quart of salt per gallon of water.

> ### Safety Check
>
> Even after salting, the fatty tissues in fish can still turn rancid because of oxidation. Fish need to be held at cold temperatures to prevent this oxidation process.

Store the crock in a cool location away from light. Fish should keep up to 9 months. Check periodically to be sure the brine is covering the fish. If you detect any signs of fermentation, remove the fish, wash them, refill the crock with a fresh brine solution, and then repack.

Light Cure

If you're working with freshly caught lean fish such as bass, haddock, mahi-mahi, cod, perch, or sole, you can use a light cure. You'll follow the same procedures as for a heavy cure, except the salt is used in a ratio of 1:10 (1 pound of salt to 10 pounds of fish). Fish cured by this method will keep several months.

Curing Herring

Herring spoil so quickly that they almost seem to want to go bad the moment they're hauled in. Take them from the hook to the brine. Of course, pause a moment to clean, gut, and scale them first. You can scale herring in the brine solution, which also gets rid of any residual blood. Drain, pat dry with paper towels, and then begin the layering process. Put them in backs down for each layer except the top one, which should be backs up. Cover with the brine and change the brine solution every 2 months.

Using Salted Fish

Freshen the fish by soaking them in cool, fresh water until they're the right texture for their intended use. This can take from half an hour to most of the day, depending on the size of the fish and the amount of salt you want to remove. After freshening, they're ready to be used in many recipes calling for fish.

Recipes

You shouldn't have to add any salt to these recipes. Indeed, removing salt by freshening is the first step in preparation.

Cabbage and Salt Pork

Cabbage is usually reserved for sauerkraut, cole slaw, or as a bland vegetable side dish. This is a hearty meal that's simple to fix and just right for a cold night.

½ lb. salt pork, cut into small pieces

1 TB. oil

1 medium onion, chopped

1 medium head cabbage, cored and loosely shredded

Serves 4
Prep time: 10 minutes
Cook time: 25 to 30 minutes

Freshen salt pork by rinsing it in cool water. Place oil in a cast-iron skillet and sauté onion until transparent. Add salt pork and cabbage. Cook over medium heat until cabbage is wilted. Serve hot with warm rolls.

Sillgratin
(Herring and Potato Casserole)

The name is Scandinavian, and that's fitting because this is a traditional herring dish, and herring is to Scandinavia what apple pie is to the United States.

Serves 4
Prep time: 45 minutes
Cook time: 1 hour

2 large salt herring

4 medium potatoes, peeled and sliced into ¼-inch slices

4 TB. butter

1 large yellow onion, sliced into ¼-inch slices

Salt and pepper to taste

⅓ cup light cream

2 TB. breadcrumbs

1. Preheat oven to 350°F. Freshen the salt herring by soaking overnight in cool water. In the morning, rinse and drain. Make a slice along the backbone and spread the herring apart. Remove the skin and all bones. Slice the herring diagonally into ½-inch pieces.

2. Place sliced potatoes in small saucepan filled with cool water to prevent them from darkening. In another small saucepan, melt 2 tablespoons of butter and add the sliced onion. Sauté until onion is soft.

3. Spray a 1-quart baking dish with nonstick cooking spray. Drain potatoes and remove excess moisture with paper towels. Place a layer of potatoes in the bottom of the casserole, then add a layer of herring and a layer of onions. Sprinkle each layer with salt and pepper to taste. Repeat layers, ending with potato layer. Pour in cream. Add breadcrumbs and dot with remaining 2 tablespoons of butter. Bake for 1 hour or until potatoes are done.

Mackerel Run Down

Not every recipe using salted fish comes from Scandinavia. Here is a sensational taste treat from Jamaica, courtesy of JamaicaTravelandCulture.com.

2 lb. salted mackerel	2 tomatoes, chopped
1 can coconut milk	3 cloves garlic, chopped
1 cup water	4 to 5 sprigs thyme
1 onion, chopped	1 to 2 tsp. each vinegar, black
3 scallions, chopped	pepper, and salt to taste

Serves 4
Prep time: 45 minutes
Cook time: 40 minutes

1. Freshen mackerel by soaking overnight in cool water. In the morning, drain the mackerel and boil for 15 minutes. Remove from heat and allow to cool. Remove heads (optional) and bones and cut fish into small pieces.

2. Combine coconut milk and water in a medium-size saucepan. Bring to a boil, then reduce heat. Add mackerel and simmer 15 minutes. Add chopped onion, scallions, tomato, garlic, and thyme and cook an additional 10 minutes. Add vinegar, black pepper, and salt to taste. If necessary to thicken sauce, mix 1 tablespoon flour in ¼ cup water and stir into mixture. Serve with boiled green bananas and dumplings.

Chapter 22

Smoking

In This Chapter

◆ Smoking hot (or cold!)

◆ Smoking meat in a smokehouse

◆ Using portable smokers

◆ Think fatty: smoking fish

◆ Your goose is cooked: smoking poultry

Not so long ago, the smokehouse was a familiar sight on farms and ranches. The size of a small shed, it was generally constructed of wood. The earthen floor held a fire pit, and in the roof was a vent that provided air circulation. A fire was kept smoldering in the pit, occasionally fed with hickory to keep the smoke coming.

This was the final step in preserving food for families who raised their own poultry, beef, and pork. If fishing had gone exceptionally well, the surplus would also find its way to the smokehouse. The smoking was finished by the holidays, providing smoked ham for Christmas dinner.

The Science Behind Smoking

Smoking not only imparts a wonderful aroma to food, it's also a preservative. Heat produced by the smoking process helps to dry the food, and this keeps harmful water-dependent microorganisms from growing and multiplying. Additionally, chemicals produced by the smoke kill insects or insect eggs.

> **Safety Check** _____
>
> Smoked foods, such as fish and fowl, need to be cooked before being consumed. The smoking process helps preserve the food, but it does not destroy potentially dangerous bacteria. Be safe and always follow approved, research-based instructions for home smoking.

Smoking generally follows salting, which I covered in Chapter 21. Once foods have been salted, they are ready for the finishing touch of the smokehouse. Meat, poultry, fish, and occasionally cheeses are good candidates for smoking.

If you plan to do quite a bit of smoking, you might consider building your own smokehouse. North Dakota State University Extension Service has several plans for smokehouses, and you can research and order them at www.ag.ndsu.nodak.edu/abeng/miscplans.htm.

Before you begin, check to see what your local ordinances require so that you will be in compliance. These requirements may include permits and inspections. Generally, the smokehouse must be made of noncombustible materials and must be located at a safe distance from other structures. The fire marshal is the one who makes those determinations.

The smokehouse will need a roof vent and a fire pit in the center of the floor. Generally, the pit is about 2 feet deep and 2 feet wide. You're not going to have a raging fire in the pit—the process is to make a cold smoke. That means a bed of coals that smoke and smolder while the meat is being smoked.

Line is strung across the inside of the smokehouse, and the meat gets hung from that. Each piece of meat should hang freely and not touch another piece. Keeping the meat separate helps prevent spoiling. Meat usually hangs 4 to 5 feet above the pit. When the smoking has been completed, the smokehouse can serve as a storage facility.

Let the Chips Fall Where They May

The most commonly used woods for smoking are apple, hickory, and maple, and if you don't cut and split your own wood, you can purchase them at the hardware store as chips or flakes. Before using chips or flakes, soak them in water to prevent them from burning up the minute you set them on the fire. You add these chips to the charcoal in small amounts—about ½ cup—to get that good aroma going.

Charcoal is also useful for smoking, but be selective in the kind of charcoal you use. Cheaper charcoal can be made from compressed sawdust and other wood waste products that are glued together and then burned to achieve the charcoal appearance. Following the firing process, they're saturated with lighter fluid—these are the "quick start" briquettes. Avoid them.

You may need to search a bit more diligently to find real charcoal and it may cost a bit more, but the search is worth it. Real charcoal is simply wood that's been cooked in a metal kiln or metal barrel by indirect heat so that the gases are driven out.

Cold Smoke

This is the process most often used with foods that have been salted. Cold smoking is the traditional method used in the smokehouse, and if you choose to build your own, it's what you'll most likely be doing. Cold smoking in the smokehouse needs to be done during cool, but not freezing, weather. Late autumn and early spring usually provide the best chances for temperatures to hover in the 30s and 40s.

Cold smoking doesn't cook the cured meat; rather, it helps to increase its dryness and keeps it from turning rancid while at the same time giving it that characteristic smoky flavor.

Temperatures in a cold smoke for meats range from 70°F to 120°F—most are usually around 100°F. It's best not to interrupt the smoking process, but if you must, refrigerate the meat until you can resume. After smoking is completed (and the process generally takes several days), the meat is wrapped for storing in a cool, dry place or is placed in the freezer (the better choice). If your winter climate is severe, you want to avoid having your smoked meat freeze, thaw, refreeze, etc. This causes the quality to deteriorate, so it's best to either use the meat or freeze it.

Smoking Beef in the Smokehouse

Select the cut of meat you want to smoke and then cut out the joints and other large bones to keep the meat from turning sour while it's smoking. Trim as much fat as you can from the outside of the meat to help prevent it from turning the meat rancid.

Cut the meat into sections. Always cut across the grain. This will give you more tender meat and will hasten the smoking process. Then pierce the meat with a hook and insert a piece of heavy twine. Be sure you have allowed enough space so that the twine doesn't rip through the meat and dump the meat into the pit. String the meat up on the line.

Smoking Pork in the Smokehouse

Pork is handled a bit differently from beef in that you don't remove the fat or the bone, except for ball and socket joints. Pierce the meat with a hook and insert a piece of heavy twine. Hang the meat from the line. During the smoking process, fat will render from the carcass, and this should not be disturbed.

Portable Smokers

If your plans aren't quite so elaborate that they require a smokehouse, electric and gas portable smokers are available at sporting goods and outdoor supply stores. These are stainless steel with digital controls, weigh around a hundred pounds, and are generally the size of a dishwasher. Prices vary according to size and features.

Hot Smoke

This is the process most often used with foods that are fresh or have been previously frozen. Hot smoking, as the name implies, uses higher temperatures than cold smoking. In addition to giving the meat a smoky flavor, this process cures the meat so that, at the end of the smoking period, it's either ready to eat or requires minimal cooking to make it table ready. If you're interested in hot smoking, you'll probably purchase a portable smoker.

> **Preserving Pointers**
>
> Have two thermometers at the ready when you're smoking meats. One thermometer keeps tabs on the air temperature inside the smoker, and the other tells you the internal temperature of the meat.

The unit you purchase should come with detailed instructions for its use, along with recipes specifically developed for that unit for smoking meat, poultry, and fish.

Thawing and Marinating

If you'll be working with meat that's frozen, it's important to thaw it first. The safest way to do this is in the refrigerator. Smaller cuts will thaw overnight, but larger cuts may take a day or two to thaw. Planning ahead becomes an important part of smoking.

Why thaw first? Because smoking uses low heat, frozen meat will linger too long in the danger zone of 40°F to 140°F, and that encourages harmful bacteria to grow.

If your recipe calls for marinating the meat for a period of time, be sure to do that marinating in the refrigerator. Again, you want to keep meat in the temperature safety zone. And always boil any leftover marinade that's been used for meat and poultry before you serve it at the table.

If you're using a commercial smoker, be sure to follow all directions carefully. It can save time, effort, and money if you take the time to read the directions before you begin.

Common Sense and Safety

Common sense sometimes isn't all that common. Whether you're using a commercially manufactured portable smoker or have improvised one on your own, don't be tempted to cut corners or take shortcuts when you're smoking meats. Where there's smoke, there's fire. Heed these general cautions:

- Don't use galvanized steel cans or garbage cans as improvised smokers. Chemicals released by them during smoking can contaminate your foods.

- Use approved fire starters. Don't use gasoline or paint thinner to get the fire going. And never squirt a shot of lighter fluid onto a smoldering charcoal bed to get it flaming. You may end up with more flame than you anticipated.

- Set up the smoker in a well-ventilated area that's away from any flammable structures such as shrubbery or your home.

- Don't work in the dark. Be sure you have plenty of light.

- Use insulated mitts to transfer hot items.

- Roll up your sleeves or, even better, don't wear long sleeves or baggy clothes when working with fire.

Safety Check

Evergreen woods, such as pine, spruce, and fir, are high in resins and aren't suitable as smoking materials. During the smoking process, creosote and other resinous products could deposit themselves on the food. Not good or good for you! Use hickory, oak, apple, alder, birch, beech, or maple instead.

The Finished Product

How long you'll smoke the meat depends on the size and shape of the cut as well as the temperature of the coals and the size of the smoker. The goal is to arrive at the safe minimum internal temperature:

- ◆ 145°F for chops, roasts, and whole cuts of beef, veal, and lamb
- ◆ 160°F for all pork, ground beef, ground veal, and ground lamb
- ◆ 165°F for all poultry

Smoking Fish

Unlike meats, which you want to be lean, you want fish to be the high-fat varieties. This means that salmon and trout smoke quite well. Fat absorbs smoke more readily than lean tissues, and this means that lean fish can be dry and tough when you're done with them. For fish: think fat!

Preparation

Fresh. That's the first rule of working with fish. If you've caught the fish, keep them iced until you're able to clean them—and don't wait too long to clean them. Fish to be smoked should be in excellent condition without rips, bruising, and other damage to the flesh. As with any other means of preserving foods, the process of preserving will not improve on the quality of what you've started with. As soon as you can, prepare the fish for brining (see Chapter 21).

When brining is completed, remove the fish from the brine, rinse them in cool water, and let them dry—skin side down—on greased racks. The grease keeps the skins from sticking to the rack. Fish should be dry within a couple of hours. You'll know they're ready for the smoker when the flesh has a shine, known as a pellicle.

Method

Hot smoking uses a short time in the brine followed by a short time in the smoker. Cold smoking uses longer brining time and longer smoking time. In any case, you're looking for a uniform brown color on the fish.

For hot smoking, you'll set the temperature at 90°F for the initial 2 hours and then raise it to 150°F until the fish is finished (anywhere from 4 to 8 hours). Hot smoking will kill parasites that fish are notorious for harboring. The fish will need to be refrigerated after the smoking process and should be used within a few days.

If you won't be using the fish immediately, it's best to freeze it. Coat the fish lightly with vegetable oil to prevent it from drying out and oxidizing during storage. Then wrap it in moisture/vapor-resistant freezer wrap and overwrap with foil or place in freezer bag. Seal, label, date, and freeze.

For cold smoking, you'll set the temperature between 80°F and 90°F for the first day and then check each day until the fish is smoked to your liking. This can take up to a week. These fish will be saltier and dryer than hot smoked fish. Cold smoking doesn't kill parasites, so you'll need to thoroughly cook the fish before consuming them. They'll keep in the fridge for up to several months.

You can also freeze fish that has been cold smoked. Follow the same procedures described previously.

> **Preserving Pointers**
>
> Smoked fish cans beautifully, and you'll have a supply that won't need to be thawed before you use it. See Chapter 12 for directions.

In either hot smoking or cold smoking, be sure there's enough room in the smoker for the air to circulate around the fish. Also make sure they're not touching each other.

If you love lox, you'll enjoy smoking your own. Rinse the salmon in cool water. Then make a brine of 2½ tablespoons of sea salt or kosher salt to 1 cup water. You can hasten the dissolving process by using warm (not hot) water. Depending on the amount of salmon you'll be smoking, you'll increase the amount of brine so that the fish is completely covered by the brine. Soak the fish in the brine for 25 to 30 minutes.

Remove the fish from the brine and rinse in several changes of cool water. This is called freshening and is an important step in the process. Using paper towels, blot the excess water from the fish and then fillet it.

Arrange the salmon on wire racks to allow the fish to dry completely. When the skin has a pellicle (glaze), transfer the fish to the smoker racks. If you place the fish on a piece of aluminum foil that has been sprayed with vegetable oil, the fish won't stubbornly cling to the foil after smoking has been completed.

Smoke the salmon at 70°F to 80°F for 6 to 8 hours. If you prefer a smokier taste, return it to the smoker for a bit longer. Getting the right degree of smoke takes some practice. When you're satisfied, remove the salmon from the smoker and store it in the refrigerator for use within a few days. Freeze what you don't use immediately.

Smoking Poultry

Think beyond chicken when you're envisioning smoked poultry. Goose and duck are excellent when smoked, and they're no more trouble than a chicken. Again, fresh is best. If you're butchering your own chicken, had a successful bird season, or are using commercially raised poultry, keep the birds refrigerated until you're ready to brine—and get to the brining within a couple of days to get the best results.

You can purchase special poultry bags for hanging poultry from farm or hunting supply stores, or you can wrap the birds in cheesecloth. This keeps them from drying out during smoking. Hang them tail up and with enough room between them for the air to circulate. You'll be using a hot smoke method, and the poultry will be ready to eat when you're finished.

In Other Words

Don't be chicken! Try your hand at making smoked duck or smoked goose. You're in for a taste treat.

—Grant, hunter and member of Ducks Unlimited

Set the temperature to 170°F for 6 to 10 hours to allow the skin to turn a light brown. Then raise the temperature to 185°F to 200°F and hold it at this level until the interior of the bird is 165°F, as determined by a meat thermometer inserted into the thickest portion of the breast.

After smoking, the poultry is ready to eat. It will keep in the refrigerator for several days, but if you aren't going to be eating it by then, it's best to freeze it.

Recipes

Smoked foods add a wonderful dimension to ordinary dishes. Flavor and aroma are enhanced, and they're a treat to be savored.

Smoked Chicken Salad

To give this old favorite a new twist, substitute smoked duck or goose for the chicken or substitute goat cheese for the feta.

Romaine lettuce leaves, torn into pieces

2 cups smoked chicken, cut into 1-inch cubes

1 cup shredded carrots

1 small red onion, sliced

¾ cup crumbled feta cheese

Vinaigrette dressing

Serves 4
Prep time: 20 minutes
Cook time: None

Put Romaine lettuce into a large salad bowl. Add smoked chicken, carrots, onion, and cheese. Drizzle vinaigrette dressing across the top.

Smoked Salmon Bisque

This is a good use for any leftover smoked salmon fillets. It's also an excellent first use for your smoked salmon. It's rich, hearty, and satisfying.

1 lb. smoked salmon, cut into bite-size pieces

1 cup canned tomatoes

½ cup chopped onion

2 TB. chopped parsley

2 cups water

4 TB. butter

4 TB. flour

1½ cups milk

1½ cups half and half

1½ tsp. salt

½ tsp. paprika

Serves 5
Prep time: 45 minutes
Cook time: 40 minutes

1. Drain tomatoes, reserving liquid. Pour liquid into a measuring cup and add enough water to make 2 cups liquid. Simmer salmon, tomatoes, onion, parsley, and the 2 cups liquid in a large saucepan for 20 minutes.

2. In another large saucepan, make a roux, melting butter and adding in flour. Add milk and half and half, stirring continuously. Add salt and paprika and continue to cook, stirring until smooth and creamy. When the mixture boils, add the salmon mixture and stir until well blended. Serve with crusty bread.

Chapter 23

Root Cellaring

In This Chapter

◆ Going underground—dig it!

◆ Keeping your cool: storage options

◆ Patrolling your produce

◆ Extending the life of your veggies

From the moment a seed is planted in the ground, fruits and vegetables are programmed to sprout, grow, ripen, and eventually—if they aren't consumed or preserved in some way—rot, thus returning nutrients to the earth so that the cycle may begin again. The home food preserver's goal is to delay the onset of that final step as long as possible.

Root cellaring is an old-time method of preserving food. It doesn't require electricity or take up room in your pantry. It's just what the name implies, storing root crops in the cellar, although there's a bit more involved than hurling your turnips under the house. Apples are prime candidates for root cellaring, along with root crops such as carrots, potatoes, beets, and turnips. They store quite nicely under conditions of controlled temperature and humidity. Other crops fit this category as well, especially winter squash—including those giant-size Hubbards!

The Science Behind Root Cellaring

Root cellaring operates on a simple premise that walks a fine line: keep foods cold enough so they don't deteriorate, but not so cold that they freeze. This discovery was probably an accidental one. Just as someone thousands of years ago discovered that the sun could be used to dry foods and thus preserve them, someone else undoubtedly noticed that cold temperatures helped keep food edible for long periods of time. Home food preservers, even the earliest ones, are keen observers of nature.

Knowing that a certain process works usually comes before understanding how that process works. Early on, it's enough to know that it just does—most of the time. Until we understand the *why*, it can be a hit-or-miss affair. Eventually, scientists discover the whys and the wherefores, and this allows some refinements and adjustments to be made to help us become more successful at preserving food.

Preserving Pointers

Some vegetables get too cold at refrigerator-type temperatures. They like it warmer. Some winter squash prefer a balmy 50°F to 55°F.

As with other methods of preserving food, root cellaring works to slow down the enzymes that are responsible for ripening and eventually overripening and rotting foods. It also keeps in check other microorganisms responsible for food spoilage. In the case of root cellaring, that means holding fruits and vegetables at temperatures generally between freezing and 40°F.

This is essentially how your refrigerator operates. Harnessing the principles of refrigeration and putting them to use in an environment that's not dependent upon electricity is the theory behind root cellaring.

Generally speaking, in the Northern Hemisphere, winter temperatures are colder than summer temperatures. They're also widely variable, depending on what part of the country you call home. Elevation plays a role, as does latitude. At the heart of the issue, however, is the capricious temperament of Mother Nature. Even if your temperatures in winter average in the high 40s, that average is just that, an average. You can have days in the teens and days in the 50s. Consistency is not one of nature's prime descriptive terms. That means you can't just consign your vegetables to the outdoors if you live in a cold climate and be confident they'll keep safely until you're ready to use them. They have specific requirements.

Ripening fruits and vegetables respire (breathe) and transpire (give off moisture and a certain amount of heat), so controlling the temperature and humidity of their storage environment is important. Nutrients can be lost during transpiration, so it's important to have a means of controlling the air flow to optimize your storage conditions.

General Principles and Procedures

If you've grown a garden that has blessed you with a good harvest, or if you've taken advantage of fresh produce from a local farmers' market, root cellaring can be an economical way to hold that produce until you're ready to use it. Location is the first consideration, determining the dimensions and type of root cellar is next, and deciding what you'll store is third.

All types of food preservation techniques require some effort. That's a given. With root cellaring, the time and effort revolves around preparing an area that will give you the right amount of air circulation so you can control the humidity. You also want the cellar to be dark and free from insects and rodents. Mice are notorious for their ability to slip through a hole the size of a quarter. You don't need to create a fortress, but a snug bunker is definitely the way to go.

Preserving Pointers

You don't need to have a cellar to preserve food by root cellaring. A shed, a pit dug into the ground on a sheltered side of the house, an unheated breezeway between the house and garage, or a section of the garage that's free from fumes works for many people.

Where do you live? More specifically, what's the winter weather like where you live? If winters are relatively mild, you have more options than folks who live in areas that receive the brunt of winter storms and subzero temperatures. It's not fun struggling to uncover your produce when the temperature is –35°F and the wind is whipping the snow into stinging nettles that burn your cheeks.

The U.S. Department of Agriculture has an excellent resource for home food preservers interested in root cellaring fruits and vegetables. It's USDA FB1939. You can request this bulletin from your County Cooperative Extension Office or directly from the USDA. Their website is www.nal.usda.gov/ref/USDApubs/aib.htm.

Storage Options

You have two basic options when deciding where to locate your root cellar: outdoors or indoors. Outdoor storage generally entails some type of pit dug into the side of an earthen bank or barrels sunk into the earth. If you enjoy the digging and your climate allows you to retrieve your produce during the winter, this could be feasible. However, outdoor storage is more than just digging a minor hole or two. You'll need to provide for drainage, remove any rocks around the barrels (they could be frost conductors), lay in a bed of straw, and create some type of door that will allow you to get at the produce while at the same time being rodent proof. If you enjoy a challenge, you've got one here.

Indoor storage is the other option, and there are several ways to go about creating a root cellar that will serve your needs. The essential components for an indoor root cellar are the following:

 ♦ **Accessibility.** You won't use the foods if it's a pain to get to them.

 ♦ **Room.** Plan a cellar big enough to keep your vegetables and fruits separated.

 ♦ **Air.** You'll also need a way to circulate the air, such as a window.

 ♦ **Coolness.** A storage area with an exterior north-facing wall can help here.

 ♦ **Thermometer.** This is helpful to keep track of the coolness.

 ♦ **Heat source.** A heat source, such as a 100-watt lightbulb, will prevent the cellar from getting too cold.

 ♦ **Humidity.** You'll need an area with between 80 to 95 percent humidity in general (the actual water composition of most veggies) and a way to control that humidity. This can mean either increasing it or decreasing it. A dirt floor is a plus. Onions and squash, however, don't like humidity (they will mold) and need a dry environment.

 ♦ **Darkness.** When it comes to root cellaring, light is the enemy.

Just as with your freezer, a full root cellar operates better than one that isn't full. You'll also need to keep tabs on it. You can't just fill it and neglect it. There is maintenance required.

The Cooperative Extension Service, Fairbanks, Alaska, bulletin HGA-00331 has an excellent diagram to help you construct a root cellar in your basement. You can access this information at their website: www.uaf.edu/ces/publications/freepubs/HGA-00331. pdf.

If you're handy with home improvement projects and have a basement, you're already halfway there. Select a corner away from heating ducts and water pipes, preferably one with a window. You'll need a source for air circulation, and this is where a window comes in handy. Without a window, you'll be forced to create a system of vents and this can get tiresome. You'll build two more walls to complete the storeroom. This is the time to decide how big to make the room since fruits and vegetables should be separated.

Finishing the storeroom involves insulating the inner walls, installing a door (insulated on the inside), and building an air duct box for the window. This box helps with air circulation—getting the cooler air down at ground level and allowing the warmer air a way to vent out.

Organic Gardening (www.organicgardening.com/feature/0,7518,s1-5-19-173,00.html) is another good source for excellent directions for constructing a basement root cellar. You can find a wealth of information from their publication.

Even if you don't have a basement, a breezeway between the garage and the house can work well for storage. The main factor here is keeping the temperature cool and providing a means for air circulation. New shelving available at home supply stores is made of vinyl-coated metal slats and works well; so does wooden shelving with slats. The objective here is to keep your fruits and vegetables from sitting on solid wood or metal and rotting.

Lower shelves will be cooler and higher shelves will be warmer. Situate your foods accordingly. Different foods have different temperature requirements.

If you've just bought a new refrigerator and still have the old one, move it to the garage, plug it in, and set the temperature gauge for 40°F. It's the perfect temperature for holding potatoes. You can keep potatoes in the refrigerator throughout the winter, and they won't spoil. Toward spring you'll notice some sprouting, but old folk wisdom says that if you remove the sprouts three times, they won't trouble you anymore. Whether or not this happens to be true, keep your spuds free of sprouts. These draw nourishment from the potatoes and can eventually cause them to shrivel up.

Preserving Pointers

For best results in root cellaring, select fruits and vegetables that mature late in the season and that have been allowed to fully ripen on the tree, on the plant, or in the ground. Earlier maturing produce doesn't hold up as well.

Root Cellaring Fruits

Apples and pears are the most commonly root-cellared fruits. You'll need to keep an eye on them and remove any fruit that's showing signs of spoiling. As with all the other types of preserving, have a plan to use your food. Nothing lasts forever!

Boxes work well for keeping apples and pears from rolling around the shelves in the root cellar. You'll need some nesting material, such as dried leaves, straw, or newspaper.

Apples

Apples are far and away the most commonly root-cellared fruit, and those that ripen latest in the season are the best choices. These include the following:

- Jonathan
- Delicious
- Cortland
- Winesap
- McIntosh

In Other Words

The adage "One rotten apple spoils the whole barrel" is very true. The same goes for potatoes.

Check apples carefully before storing and be sure they are cool going into storage. Trapping any warmth will accelerate enzyme activity and shorten their storage life. Select only unblemished, firm apples and bed them down on a layer of straw or dried leaves. You can layer them as apples, straw, apples, straw, etc.

Pears

Late-season pears such as Anjou are the best choice for root cellaring. Comice and Bosc have shorter shelf lives. You want these pears to be ready to pick but still hard and green. If they've begun the ripening process before you pop them into storage, you'll be disappointed. They'll rot from the inside out. Store them just like apples.

Citrus

Around holiday time, you'll generally find good deals on oranges and grapefruits. These can also go into the root cellar in their boxes. Keep an eye on them and, if any get moldy, toss them. Clean off any stray mold that's come in contact with the good fruit.

Tomatoes

Tomatoes are good candidates for the root cellar. They need high moisture. Harvest them before a killing frost, since once they've frosted, they will rot. They can be dark,

dark green and will still ripen nicely. You'll be eating delicious, red, ripe tomatoes in December and they'll be far superior to anything available at the grocery store.

Leave the stem on—at least enough to make a handle to carry. Spread newspaper on a shelf and arrange the tomatoes so there's a bit of space between. They'll ripen gradually, so be sure to check on them frequently and remove the ones that are ready for eating. If you have an overabundance of ripe ones at any time, cover them with newspaper to help keep in the moisture.

Root Cellaring Vegetables

Keep it simple: potatoes, beets, turnips, carrots, cabbage, cauliflower, onions, and winter squash root cellar very well, provided you house them in the right conditions. Some prefer cool conditions, and some like it warmer. Some want their environment really wet, and others want just a touch of moisture.

Vegetables with thin skins such as beets, carrots, turnips, radishes, kohlrabi, parsnips, and cucumbers need storage conditions that are cold and moist. Leave enough of a stem on these vegetables to keep moisture from seeping out. Store each variety separately. See specific directions a little later in the chapter.

Potato sacks, wooden crates, and cardboard boxes are good containers for these vegetables. If you're using cardboard boxes, line them with plastic garbage bags and cut some ventilation holes. You can alternate a layer of moist sawdust or sand with a layer of vegetables. Don't stack vegetables too high in boxes or bins, however, or you'll upset your neat arrangement as you dig through the container searching for your produce. The sand or sawdust doesn't need to be sopping, just damp. Check it every week or so and add some water if it appears to be drying out. Sand and sawdust are available at hardware stores, garden outlets, building supply stores, or even at the sawmill, if you live close to one.

Potatoes

Potatoes need high moisture. They share moisture by huddling together in sacks or bins. You don't need to add any cushioning material, such as sawdust or sand, to potatoes.

Whether you've grown your own potatoes or stocked up on grocery store specials, you'll need to be aware of the difference between new potatoes and potatoes that have set their skins.

All potatoes go through the same maturing process. As soon as the plants have finished blossoming, new potatoes can be harvested. New potatoes are not suitable for wintering over in the root cellar. You can tell a new potato because the skin will rub off easily, exposing the white flesh underneath. They're delicious and much prized, but need to be eaten up quickly.

The potatoes that root cellar well are those that have been harvested after the potato plants die off. It's best to allow these potatoes to harden off in the ground for a couple of weeks before digging them. This ensures that the skins have set. You can tell a hardened-off potato because the skins will not easily rub off. You'll need a potato peeler. These potatoes are good candidates for root cellaring.

Safety Check

Don't let potatoes see the light of day! Sunlight causes chemical changes in potatoes, turning them green. This green color indicates the presence of solanine, and it's not good for you. You can cut out a small amount of green, but if the potato is green clear through, toss it.

Potatoes for storing should be firm and without cracks or black spots. You don't have to leave space between them and can store them in cardboard, wooden boxes, or burlap bags. It's easier if you do some sorting for size before you pile them into containers. Keep one box for bakers (big and smooth), another one for medium-size and irregular shapes, and one box for the little ones, which are excellent creamed or added to soups and stews. Check them from time to time and remove any potatoes that are soft or show signs of spoiling.

Beets

Leave tails on, trim any leaves, and leave ½ inch of the crown. Pack in boxes. Lay down a layer of damp sand, then a layer of beets, then more sand, more beets, etc.

Turnips

These veggies have a strong odor that can wreak havoc with other produce. Store them by themselves in layers of moist sand.

Carrots

Select firm carrots without blemishes. Remove the leaves, leaving ½ inch of the crown. Store in layers of moist sand.

Cabbage

Cabbage has a stronger odor than turnips by far and can insinuate itself into other produce if you're not careful, so it needs its own place. Remove the roots and any browned leaves. Store in boxes and cover with moist sand. If you only have a few heads, wrap each head in newspaper and store away from other produce.

Cauliflower

Cauliflower likes it cold and moist. If you're harvesting your own, keep the roots on and nestle them back into the damp sawdust or sand in the root cellar. This will extend its storage life.

Onions

You can braid onions just as you braid garlic, and they will store nicely hanging from a peg in a cool, airy location. Otherwise, they need to be dried first before storing them on racks or in baskets. They prefer dry conditions.

Winter Squash

Winter squash, including pumpkins, stores beautifully. Leave a bit of stem and allow the cut to harden off before bringing inside to store. These don't like it too cold or too moist, so keep their storage temperature between 50°F and 55°F.

Recipes

You can create all manner of hearty meals from the produce you've root cellared. You've got all the ingredients for soups, stews, and casseroles that will warm you throughout the long, cold winter.

Baked Acorn Squash

Nothing says autumn more than this dish. It's a traditional New England recipe, hearty and easy to make. This is a good side dish to accompany baked ham and scalloped potatoes (see the following recipe).

Serves 1 person per half squash
Prep time: 5 minutes
Cook time: 45 minutes

½ **acorn squash for each person**

1 TB. butter for each half squash

1 TB. brown sugar for each half squash

Cut squash into lengthwise halves. Scrape out seeds and discard. Place squash in a baking pan, add butter and brown sugar to each cavity. Cover loosely with aluminum foil. Bake at 350°F about 45 minutes or until squash is fork tender.

Scalloped Potatoes

Originally these were called "escalloped potatoes," a term that refers to fish scales. The potato slices were arranged in over-lapping rows and resembled fish scales. Over time the term was shortened, but we still try to arrange the potatoes in that overlap-ping pattern.

Serves 4
Prep time: 25 minutes
Cook time: 35 to 40 minutes

2 cups milk

2 TB. butter

2 TB. flour

4 white potatoes, scrubbed and peeled

1. To make the white sauce, combine milk, butter, and flour in a medium saucepan. Beat with a whisk until well blended. Cook over low heat, whisking constantly, until mixture begins to thicken. Remove from heat.

2. Thinly slice potatoes. Place in a medium saucepan, cover with water, and bring to a boil. Turn down heat and simmer until fork tender. Remove from heat and drain. Arrange slices in an 8"×10"×2" glass baking dish. Cover with white sauce. Add the next layer of potatoes and cover with white sauce. Bake at 350°F until brown and bubbly.

Glossary

acid foods   Foods containing enough acid to result in a pH of 4.6 or below; thus, they can be processed in a boiling water bath. Includes most fruits (except for figs and Asian pears), most tomatoes, fermented and pickled vegetables, relishes, jams, jellies, and marmalades.

anaerobic   Means "without oxygen." Specifically, it refers to something that can live in the absence of oxygen and to which oxygen can be toxic.

bacteria   A group of microorganisms, including *salmonella*, *clostridium*, and *E. coli*.

blanching   The process of placing raw foods in boiling water for a specific period of time in order to stop deterioration caused by enzymes.

brining   The process of preserving foods by immersing them in a salt-water solution.

cake tester   A piece of wire with a loop at one end. The tester is anywhere from 3 to 6 inches long. You insert your finger into the loop handle and insert the tester into the middle of the cake or other product you're testing. When it comes out clean, the product is done.

canning   A method of preserving food that uses heat and/or pressure to remove air and create a vacuum seal.

cold frame   A wooden box minus the top and bottom. It's set outdoors on the ground, plants are set inside it for shelter, and the top is usually an old window that's attached with a hinge and propped up with a piece of wood during the day and closed down at night. It provides protection from wind and cold.

corning   A means of preserving meat that gets its name from the large salt crystals, or "corns," that were once rubbed into the meat to cure it.

cryptosporidium   A waterborne protozoa—a parasite that can take up residence in the human intestine and cause illness. In the case of individuals with suppressed immune systems, that illness can be fatal. It is found in waters contaminated with sewage and animal waste.

danger zone   Temperatures at which bacteria will grow (40°F to 140°F), with the most rapid rate of growth occurring between 70°F and 100°F.

drumette   The fleshy part of the poultry wing; it is what you'll be served if you order wings at a restaurant. Many people discard the wings, not realizing there's some good meat there.

dry salting   The process of combining salt with the juices from the food being salted to form a concentrated brine.

enzymes   Substances in food that accelerate changes in flavor, color, texture, and nutrition, especially when the food's surface is exposed to air.

fermentation   Changes in food caused by intentional growth of bacteria, yeast, or mold.

frencher   A small device that clamps onto a counter or table top. You feed green beans into a hopper at the top and then turn a small hand crank that feeds the beans from the hopper to internal stainless steel blades that slice the beans lengthwise.

freshening   The process of rinsing and soaking meat in cold water to remove as much salt as possible before cooking.

headspace   Also called "headroom." In a container, this is the space between the food or liquid and the lid. During heat processing, it provides room for food to expand and also creates the vacuum as the jar cools.

hot pack   Heating raw food in boiling water or steam before filling jars.

low-acid foods   Foods with a pH above 4.6 that must be processed in a pressure canner or acidified to a pH of 4.6 or lower if they are to be processed in a boiling water canner.

marbling   The term given to the white flecks of fat in the muscle. Higher grades have more marbling, which increases the tenderness and flavor of the meat.

microorganism   A life form too small to be seen without magnification. Bacteria, mold, and yeast are microorganisms that can be found in food.

mold   A fungus type of microorganism whose growth on food is usually visible. Molds may grow on many foods, including acid foods such as jams, jellies, and canned fruits.

open-kettle method   An older method of processing acid foods. Food is heat-processed in a covered kettle and then packed hot into sterile jars and sealed. The seal may not hold, and food may spoil by this method.

perishable foods   Foods that will spoil rapidly unless preservation or storage methods are used to prolong shelf life.

pH   The measure of acidity or alkalinity as determined on a scale ranging from 0 to 14. A food is neutral when its pH is 7. Lower values are more acidic, and higher values are more alkaline.

pickling   A method of adding enough vinegar or lemon juice to a low-acid food to lower its pH to 4.6 or lower. These foods may then be safely processed in a boiling water canner.

raw pack   Raw food that is packed into containers and then processed.

sanitize   To clean in a manner that reduces the number of bacteria to safe levels and makes a surface safe for contact with food.

shelf life   The recommended length of time that a food is safe to eat or is palatable. Shelf life depends on the initial number of bacteria, storage temperature, and handling practices. Therefore, shelf life is only an estimation.

steam blanching   A method of blanching that takes longer than regular blanching, but if you prefer not to partially cook your vegetables, you may find this a good alternative. You place a single layer of vegetables in a basket and hold the basket in place over boiling water. The steam generated by the boiling water blanches the veggies. This method works for broccoli, pumpkin, sweet potatoes, winter squash, and mushrooms. *See also* blanching.

struck through   The term used to indicate that a fish has been completely salted and will not accept anymore salt.

superfine sugar   Finely granulated sugar that dissolves almost instantly without leaving a granular residue at the bottom of the bowl.

tomatillo   A relative of the tomato. It originates in Central America and has been cultivated in Mexico and Guatemala since pre-Columbian times. It's also referred to as the "husk tomato," "jamberry," or "groundcherry."

toxin   Poison produced by a living organism such as a bacterium or mold. These toxins include *Staphylococcus aureus*, *Clostridium botulinum*, and *Bacillus cereus*.

venting   In canning, the process by which air is expelled from the canner.

Abbreviations and Equivalencies

General Measurements

tsp. = teaspoon	qt. = quart
TB. = tablespoon	gal. = gallon
oz. = ounce	lb. = pound
pt. = pint	fl. = fluid

Equivalencies

3 tsp. = 1 TB.	1 pt. = 2 cups
¼ cup = 4 TB.	1 lb. = 16 oz.
⅓ cup = 5⅓ TB.	1 qt. = 2 pt.
½ cup = 8 TB.	1 gal. = 4 qt.
1 cup = 8 oz.; 16 TB.; 8 fl. oz.	

Syrup Chart

You can use any strength syrup you want. The following chart gives you ingredients for making sugar syrup in a variety of strengths. The less sugar you use, the lighter your syrup will be. It will also be thinner in consistency. Heavy syrup is downright thick. It can also tend to overshadow the flavor of the fruit.

If you aren't sure what strength you want to use, try mixing up a batch of light first. If this is too sweet for your taste, you'll want to use extra light (or even fruit juice or plain water).

You can always add more sugar until you find the right proportions for your taste, but you can't take it out. For example, if you find the light strength not sweet enough, add a cup of sugar to the mixture and bring it to a boil again. Allow to cool and then taste. Now you'll have medium light syrup. If it's still not sweet enough, add another cup of sugar, bring to a boil, allow to cool, and then taste. By this time you will have reached medium heavy, and there's only one more strength to sample.

Percent	Type	Sugar (Cups)	Water (Cups)	Yield (Cups)
20	Extra light	1¼	5½	6
30	Light	2	4	5
40	Medium light	3	4	5½
50	Medium heavy	4¾	4	6½
60	Heavy	7	4	7¾

Measure exact amount of sugar and water and place in a large cooking pot. Bring to a boil. Turn off heat.

For use in freezing, allow syrup to cool before pouring into containers. For use in canning, pour boiling hot syrup into containers, using a funnel and protection for your hands.

Processing Times Reference Charts

For any additional information or questions, refer to the instruction booklet for your pressure canner or contact your local extension office.

Fruits

Minutes in Boiling Water Bath at 212°F
(Pressure at sea level—make adjustments for altitude)

Fruit	Cold Pack		Hot Pack		Pressure Canner at 5 lb. Pressure
	Pints	*Quarts*	*Pints*	*Quarts*	
Apples	25	30	15	20	10
Applesauce	–	–	10	10	5
Apricots	25	30	15	20	10
Berries, soft	10	15	–	–	–
Cherries	20	25	10	15	10
Cranberry sauce	–	5	–	–	–

continues

Fruits (continued)

Minutes in Boiling Water Bath at 212°F
(Pressure at sea level—make adjustments for altitude)

Fruit	Cold Pack		Hot Pack		Pressure Canner at 5 lb. Pressure
	Pints	*Quarts*	*Pints*	*Quarts*	
Figs	–	–	45	50	–
Fruit cocktail	–	20	25	–	–
Fruit juices (10 minutes for half gal.)	–	–	5	5	–
Grapefruits (sections)	10	10	–	–	–
Grapes	15	20	15	20	–
Nectarines	25	30	15	20	10
Oranges (sections)	10	10	–	–	–
Peaches	25	30	15	20	10
Pears	25	30	20	25	10
Pie fillings	–	–	–	20	–
Pineapple	25	30	15	20	10
Plums	25	30	20	25	10
Rhubarb	–	–	10	10	–
Tomatoes (whole or halves)	35	45	10	15	15
Tomatoes, juice	–	40	45	–	–
Tomatoes, sauce	–	35	40	–	–

Vegetables

Minutes in Weighted Gauge Pressure Canner at 10 lb. Pressure
or Dial Gauge Pressure Canner at 11 lb. Pressure

(Pressure at sea level—make adjustments for altitude)

Vegetable	Type of Pack Cold (C)/Hot (H)	Pints	Quarts
Asparagus	C/H	30	40
Beans, green	C/H	20	25
Beans, lima	C/H	40	50
Beets	H	30	35
Carrots	C/H	25	30
Corn, creamed	H	85	–
Corn, whole	C/H	55	85
Greens	H	70	90
Mixed vegetables	H	75	90
Mushrooms	H	45 (pints or half pints)	–
Okra	H	25	40
Peas	C/H	40	40
Peppers	H	35	–
Potatoes, sweet	H	65	90 (11 lb. pressure)
Potatoes, white	H	35	40 (11 lb. pressure)
Pumpkin (cubes)	H	55	90 (11 lb. pressure)
Soups/stews	H	60	75

Meats, Poultry, and Game

Minutes in Weighted Gauge Pressure Canner at 10 lb. Pressure
or Dial Gauge Pressure Canner at 11 lb. Pressure
(Pressure at sea level—make adjustments for altitude)

Food	Type of Pack Cold (C)/Hot (H)	Pints	Quarts
Beef, pork, lamb	C/H	75	90
Chili con carne	H	75	90
Game	C/H		
Ground meats	H	75	90
Hard sausages	C	75	90
Lamb or pork sausage	H	75	90
Meat stock	H	20	25
Poultry (with bones)	C/H	65	75
Poultry (boned)	C/H	75	90
Rabbit or squirrel (with bones)	C/H	65	75
Rabbit or squirrel (boned)	C/H	75	90

Seafood

Minutes in Weighted Gauge Pressure Canner at 10 lb. Pressure or Dial Gauge Pressure Canner at 11 lb. Pressure

(Pressure at sea level—make adjustments for altitude)

Food	Pints	Quarts
Fish, raw	100 (pints or half pints)	–
Fish, smoked	110	110
Clams, minced	60	70
Clams, whole	60	70
Crab	70	80
Oysters	75	75
Shrimp	45	45
Stew or soup with seafood	100	100

Freezer Storage Chart

Properly prepared and packaged frozen foods held at a constant temperature of 0°F will keep indefinitely. The following suggested storage times are relative to quality only.

Item	Storage Time
Bacon and sausage	1 to 2 months
Casseroles	1 to 2 months
Egg whites or egg substitutes	8 to 12 months
Fish, fresh	3 to 6 months
Fish, cooked	1 month
Fish, smoked	4 to 5 weeks
Fruits and vegetables	12 months
Gravy (meat or poultry)	2 to 3 months
Ham, hotdogs, and lunchmeats	1 to 2 months
Ice cream	2 to 3 weeks
Meat, uncooked roasts	9 months
Meat, uncooked steaks or chops	4 to 6 months
Meat, uncooked ground	3 to 4 months
Meat, cooked	2 to 3 months
Pies and pastries	4 to 6 months
Poultry, uncooked whole	12 months
Poultry, uncooked parts	9 months
Poultry, uncooked giblets	3 to 4 months
Poultry, cooked	3 to 4 months
Soups and stews	2 to 3 months
Wild game, uncooked	8 to 12 months

Source: Freezing Food Safety and Inspection Service Consumer Education and Information, www.fsis.usda.gov/OA/pubs/freezing.htm

Best Preserving Methods for Specific Foods

Many foods can be preserved by more than one method, but some methods produce a better product than others. Here are some recommendations.

Vegetables for Freezing

Asparagus

Beans: lima, green, or yellow wax

Bok choi

Broccoli

Brussels sprouts

Carrots

Cauliflower

Corn

Greens: beet, chard, collard, mustard, turnip

Kohlrabi

Okra

Parsnips

Peas

Peppers, green

Pumpkin

Squash, summer

Squash, winter (mashed)

Sweet potatoes (diced or mashed)

Turnips (diced or mashed)

Vegetables for Canning

Beans: green or yellow wax

Beets

Carrots

Corn

Peas

Vegetables for Drying

Beets

Cabbage

Carrots

Celery

Corn

Mushrooms

Onions

Peas

Peppers, green

Potatoes

Turnips

Vegetables for Root Cellaring

Beets

Cabbage

Carrots

Cauliflower

Onions

Parsnips

Potatoes

Squash, winter

Turnips and rutabagas

Fruits for Freezing

Apples (slices)

Apricots

Avocados

Berries

Cherries

Currants

Figs

Grapefruit

Grapes

Melon

Peaches and nectarines

Pears

Pineapple

Plums and prunes

Rhubarb

Strawberries

Fruits for Canning

Apples

Apricots

Cherries

Peaches and nectarines

Pears

Pineapple

Plums

Rhubarb

Tomatoes

Fruits for Drying

Apples

Apricots

Blueberries

Cherries

Cranberries

Figs

Grapes

Huckleberries

Peaches

Pears

Plums

Fruits for Root Cellaring

Apples

Citrus

Pears

Tomatoes

Herbs for Drying

Chervil

Chives

Dill

Mint

Oregano

Rosemary

Sage

Tarragon

Thyme

Appendix G

Resources

Agencies

American Dietetic Association   This is a good resource for recipes developed for people with food allergies. Find more information on their website: www.eatright.org/cps/rde/xchg/ada/hs.xsl/index.html.

Cooperative Extension Service   The essential resource for the home food preserver is the Cooperative Extension Service, an agency of the USDA. The Extension Service certifies Food Safety Advisors/Master Food Preservers and also exists to answer your questions about food preservation and food safety. You'll find your local branch listed in your telephone directory. To access the national center and find information about your local Extension Office, go to their website: www.csrees.usda.gov/Extension/.

The National Center for Home Food Preservation   The Center provides current research-based recommendations for most methods of home food preservation. It was established with funding from the Cooperative State Research, Education and Extension Service, U.S. Department of Agriculture (CSREES-USDA), to address food safety concerns for those who practice and teach home food preservation and processing methods. You can find all kinds of helpful information on their website: www.uga.edu/nchfp/.

USDA The most comprehensive resource for the home food preserver is the United States Department of Agriculture (USDA). Find out more on their website: www.nal. usda.gov.

Books

Ball Blue Book of Preserving. Alltrista Consumer Products Co., 2004.

Bubel, Mike, and Nancy Bubel. *Root Cellaring—Natural Cold Storage of Fruits & Vegetables.* Storey Publishing, 1991. Readable discussion of the joys and challenges of root cellaring, along with specific instructions for building a root cellar.

Complete Guide to Home Canning. USDA Extension Service, 1994, (Agriculture Information Bulletin (AIB) No. 539). This book can be downloaded from the National Center for Home Food Preservation at www.uga.edu/nchfp//publications/ publications_usda.html.

Greene, Janet, Ruth Hertzberg, and Beatrice Vaughan. *Putting Food By, Fourth Edition.* Plume, 1992. One of the most-beloved books on food preservation, the first edition appeared in 1973. It's been updated for modern times.

Kowalchik, Claire, and William H. Hylton, eds. *Rodale's Illustrated Encyclopedia of Herbs.* Rodale Press, 1998.

Bulletins

Canning Fruits (PNW 199). Pacific Northwest Extension Publications, 1999.

Canning Meat, Poultry, and Game (PNW 361). Pacific Northwest Extension Publications, 1999.

Canning Seafood (PNW 194). Pacific Northwest Extension Publications, 2003.

Canning Tomatoes and Tomato Products (PNW 300). Pacific Northwest Extension Publications, 1999.

Canning Vegetables (PNW 172). Pacific Northwest Extension Publications, 1999.

Drying Fruits and Vegetables (PNW 397). Pacific Northwest Extension Publications, 2003.

Fish Pickling for Home Use (PNW 183). Pacific Northwest Extension Publications, 2001.

Freezing Convenience Foods That You've Prepared at Home (PNW 296). Pacific Northwest Extension Publications, 2002.

Freezing Fruits and Vegetables (PNW 214). Pacific Northwest Extension Publications, 2008.

Home Canning Smoked Fish (PNW 450). Pacific Northwest Extension Publications, 2001.

Pickles, Relishes, and Chutneys (HXT-90). University of California Agricultural Extension Service, 1973.

Pickling Vegetables (PNW 355). Pacific Northwest Extension Publications, 2000.

Salsa Recipes for Canning (PNW 395). Pacific Northwest Extension Publications, 2000.

Smoking Fish at Home—Safely (PNW 238). Pacific Northwest Extension Publications, 2003.

Storing Vegetables and Fruits at Home (EB1326). Cooperative Extension, Washington State University, 2001.

Using and Caring for Your Pressure Canner (PNW 421). Pacific Northwest Extension Publications, 1999.

You Can Prevent Foodborne Illness (PNW 250). Pacific Northwest Extension Publications, 2003.

Websites

Build It Solar www.builditsolar.com/Projects/Cooking/cooking.htm. Good resource for information on solar dryers and root cellars.

Georgia Egg Commission www.georgiaeggs.org. Everything you could ever want or need to know about eggs is on this site. From preparation to storage to recipes, it's the go-to place.

Pick Your Own.org www.pickyourown.org. If you want to pick your own produce, this is the website that lists just about every pick-you-own farm in the United States—and in several other countries as well. The site is user-friendly. Just click on your state and prepare to take notes.

Index